PRAISE FOR
Admission Matters: What Students and Parents Need to Know About Getting into College

2nd Edition by Sally P. Springer, Jon Reider, and Marion R. Franck

 "With more than thirty years in the profession, I have read many books on college admissions, but none with the clarity, scope, depth, or breadth of *Admission Matters*. The authors have tackled the morphing landscape by moving beyond the smoke and mirrors and identifying major and minor topics and providing the real navigational tools to students, parents, and professionals. Kudos to the authors for this outstanding book!"

Marybeth Kravets, past president, National Association for College Admission Counseling (NACAC); college counselor, Deerfield High School, Deerfield, Illinois

"Students, parents, and the college guidance community will find lots of sensible advice in this comprehensive work. From start to finish, it seeks to help people navigate the admissions process—by increasing understanding and decreasing stress and confusion."

John F. Latting, dean of undergraduate admissions, Johns Hopkins University

"Cut through the hype—and the fear—about applying to college with this step-by-step guide to the admissions process. Must reading for high school students, their parents, teachers, and counselors."

Bob Schaeffer, public education director, FairTest, the National Center for Fair and Open Testing

"I hate to sound cliché, but this book *really* is one-stop shopping for students and parents. I might consider my job in jeopardy if this word gets out! I am asking my school to make this a required summer reading book for my juniors—and also my tenth graders—and my ninth graders. This book is for all students with college in their futures."

Bob Turba, chairman of school counseling services, Stanton College Preparatory School

"*Admissions Matters* is the how-to book that I recommend to all of our families. Its straightforward approach, the authors' care for each student's well-being, and the wealth of information that it provides on all aspects of the college admissions process from both the student and college perspective make it an indispensable aid during the junior and senior years of high school."

Ilene Abrams, college counselor, Berkeley High School, Berkeley, California

✳ "Because it provides a comprehensive inside glimpse into what can seem like a confounding and stressful undertaking, *Admission Matters* is a must-read for any student or parent approaching the college admission process."

Paul Marthers, dean of admission, Reed College

✳ "*Admission Matters* is the single best resource available to avoid the barbarity of the 'admission marketplace.' It provides students and their families with essential information and tools to make the college admission process sane and maybe even a great voyage of discovery."

Michael Beseda, vice provost for enrollment and vice president for college communications, Saint Mary's College of California

✳ "*Admission Matters* emphasizes that college admissions is a process which, when conducted properly on both sides, benefits both the applicant and the institutions, rather than being a game or an adversarial struggle. Both reassuring and supportive, it is the most thorough, most balanced, most useful book on college admissions that I have seen."

Bob Laird, former director of undergraduate admission at UC Berkeley; author of *The Case for Affirmative Action in University Admissions*

✳ "This book may not be called an instruction manual, but it does give college-bound students and their families all the information they will need to launch an effective college search. Best of all, when the authors make an assertion and you are tempted to say 'prove it,' they do so with numerous examples and stories that demonstrate Springer, Reider, and Franck have the experience to be considered genuine experts on the college admissions process."

Gary L. Ross, vice president and dean of admission, Colgate University

✳ "The authors, highly experienced in the field, provide a complete introduction to the complex world of selective college admission. A must-read for parents and college-bound students who want to master this process."

George Mills, vice president for enrollment, University of Puget Sound

✳ "*Admission Matters* talks with great success to both students and their parents. Common sense dominates every page and will encourage everyone as they do college admissions together."

F. Sheppard Shanley, senior associate director of admission, Northwestern University

ADMISSION MATTERS

ADMISSION MATTERS

What Students and Parents Need to Know About Getting into College

SECOND EDITION

Sally P. Springer, Jon Reider, and Marion R. Franck

JOSSEY-BASS
A Wiley Imprint
www.josseybass.com

Published by Jossey-Bass
A Wiley Imprint
989 Market Street, San Francisco, CA 94103-1741—www.josseybass.com

Jossey-Bass books and products are available through most bookstores. To contact Jossey-Bass directly call our Customer Care Department within the U.S. at 800-956-7739, outside the U.S. at 317-572-3986, or fax 317-572-4002.

Jossey-Bass also publishes its books in a variety of electronic formats. Some content that appears in print may not be available in electronic books.

Library of Congress Cataloging-in-Publication Data
Springer, Sally P., date-
  Admission matters : what students and parents need to know about getting into college / Sally P. Springer, Jon Reider, and Marion R. Franck.—2nd ed.
    p. cm.
  Includes bibliographical references and index.
  ISBN 978-0-470-48121-9 (pbk.)
  1. Universities and colleges—United States—Admission. 2. College choice—United States.
  I. Reider, Jon. II. Franck, Marion R., 1947- III. Title.
  LB2351.2.S67 2009
  378.1'610973—dc22   2009015718

Printed in the United States of America
SECOND EDITION
PB Printing   10 9 8 7 6 5 4 3 2 1

Contents

To our children

Acknowledgments

The second edition of *Admission Matters*, like the first, was born out of a desire to improve the college application process for both parents and students. We are grateful to those who shared our goal and helped us in the writing of this book. Frances Fee deserves special thanks for lending her expertise on financial aid to our effort. Our chapter on financial aid contains the most up-to-date and authoritative information anywhere, thanks to her contributions. We thank as well the many people who contributed, in different ways, to our efforts with the first edition; their imprint clearly remains. They include Bill Caskey, Cindy Clark, Marilyn Geiger, Fred Hargadon, Arlene Jones, Bruce Madewell, Gail Martinez, Dorothy Missler, George Rooks, Mary Ryan, Courtenay Tessler, Jill Theg, Leon Washington, and Fred Wood. We also want to thank Lesley Iura, education editor at Jossey-Bass, for inviting us to prepare a second edition of *Admission Matters*. The mammoth job of formatting the manuscript was capably handled by her exceptional editorial assistant, Amy Reed; Robin Lloyd, production editor, did a fine job of seeing the manuscript into print. We also thank Marion Franck for her support of the second edition.

FROM SALLY . . .

I am grateful to Jon Reider for joining me in writing the second edition of *Admission Matters*. As an anonymous reviewer of the first edition, he brought many insights that greatly improved the book; I was delighted when he agreed to coauthor the second edition. We had an extremely tight schedule at the worst possible time of year for someone advising a whole class of high school seniors, but with much wisdom, good humor, and grace, Jon worked to meet what seemed like an impossible deadline.

My children, Mollie and Erik, were my inspiration for the first edition of *Admission Matters*, and they remain my inspiration for the second. They were both in high school when I began writing the first edition; now they are a college junior and a college graduate with a master's degree, respectively. Although their accomplishments are clearly their own, I hope that the advice in *Admission Matters*, directly or indirectly, helped them along the way. I owe my greatest debt to my wonderful husband, Håkon Hope, for his unwavering love and encouragement throughout the preparation of the second edition as well as the first. He knew the book was important to me, and so it became important to him as well. He was always willing to listen and to advise, and to provide the time and space I needed to write and revise. In many ways he wrote *Admission Matters* alongside me, and truly, there would be no book without him.

FROM JON . . .

I want to thank Sally Springer for identifying me as an "anonymous reviewer" of the first edition of *Admission Matters* and then for offering me this chance to break into print for the first time as her colleague. She has taken on all the business and organization side of the book with great efficiency and generosity and has allowed me to focus on what I like most: to write. I also want to thank Leah for her loyalty and support of my professional work over our many years together, and, more recently, for tolerating many late nights at work. The journeys to college of our children, Rebecca and Abby, both delighted and enlightened me. Our advice to parents in the book has been enriched at every point by what I learned from them. Others—teachers, friends, and colleagues—have believed in me and have encouraged me at various stages of my career to put down what I have to say so others could share in my experience. Finally, my hundreds of students, both at Stanford and at San Francisco University High School, have provided me with a wealth of raw material from their lives that I could draw on. The opportunity to collaborate with Sally has turned out to be an ideal experience, but many hands have contributed to this work beside my own.

May 2009

Sally P. Springer
Davis, California

Jon Reider
Palo Alto, California

Introduction

I n the four years since the publication of the first edition of *Admission Matters*, much has changed, some it anticipated and some of it very surprising. Among the changes we would have predicted is the continued growth in the number of applications flooding a relatively small number of colleges, resulting in admission rates that continue to drop each year. Also predictable is the high level of anxiety and uncertainty that these changes have brought students and their families. Totally unexpected, however, is the dramatically deteriorating economic situation in the United States and indeed the world, which has placed increasing financial pressure both on colleges and on families hoping to send their children to a college that will be a good fit for them, academically, socially, and financially.

In this new edition, we have worked hard to address all these changes and more, predictable or otherwise, so that you, our student or parent reader, will understand what they mean for you. We hope to provide you with the most up-to-date, insightful, useful, and supportive book on college admissions to be found anywhere. That was the goal of the first edition, and it continues to be for the second. We are very pleased that the core advice of *Admission Matters*, whether dealing with choosing colleges, preparing a strong application, or seeking financial aid, remains sound with the passage of time. In this edition, we have refined and extended that core to make it even more helpful. We have also updated everything so you will have the most current information available.

Admission Matters will give students the tools they need to take charge of the college admissions process and submit strong applications to colleges that are a good fit for them. *Admission Matters* will guide parents in appropriately supporting their child all along the way. Unlike other books about college admissions that address primarily just one audience—students or parents—we wrote *Admission Matters* for both. Sometimes "you" refers to the student. Sometimes it is "you," the parent. The context makes it clear which it is at each point, but both students and parents should read it all. We believe that students and parents need to understand the whole process and what their different but complementary roles should be as they move through it.

Families today find themselves endlessly barraged by evidence of "college mania." Newspapers and magazines regularly regale readers with horror tales about the competition involved in gaining admission to selective colleges as application numbers continue to rise and admission rates fall. Classmates, relatives, neighbors, and even virtual strangers are all too eager to share war stories about terrific kids with great stats and extracurricular activities who were rejected by the colleges of their choice.

Businesses that offer costly SAT prep courses bombard students and parents with advertising that promises dramatic increases in scores for those who sign up. Ironically, at the same time that the test prep industry is burgeoning, some influential educators have argued for downplaying the importance of standardized tests, or even eliminating them altogether, claiming that students waste valuable time preparing for a test that adds little to the ability to predict future success in college. And once students do take the SAT or ACT, they are likely to receive a disturbing avalanche of glossy brochures from colleges all over the country encouraging them to apply. Selective liberal arts colleges commonly send out mailers like this to well over fifty thousand students as they seek to fill a freshman class of less than five hundred students. And these are just a few examples of college mania. You can probably make a list of your own.

When you put all of this together, along with the economic challenges facing our country, it is easy to understand how college admission has become an ordeal for many students and their families. Each year more and more students vie for a limited number of freshman spots at many of the best-known colleges. Application numbers for Fall 2009 broke records at some schools. Families are caught up in a high-stakes competition in which they are uncertain about the rules and even more uncertain about the outcome. Parents feel uncomfortable trying to support their children in a process they do not completely understand and are not sure they can afford. Even those who consider themselves knowledgeable may find that much of what they know is out-of-date or based on unverifiable hearsay.

Furthermore, parents can become emotionally invested in the college admissions process, right along with their children, in ways that are understandable but not always helpful. And the college admissions process has implications that go beyond admission to college—it is also about leaving home and making the transition to adulthood. This simple fact adds to the uncertainty and anxiety of many families.

But it does not have to be, and should not be, an ordeal. A clear understanding of the college admissions process can empower students and their families to make good choices for themselves and allow them to retain their balance and sanity at the same time. That has always been our goal.

Admission Matters explains

- How rankings motivated by magazine profits contribute to the application frenzy
- How the admissions process at selective colleges really works, and what can (and cannot) be controlled
- How you can submit strong, competitive applications to colleges that are a good fit for you
- How standardized testing has changed, and what those changes mean for you
- When an "early application" makes sense, when it can be a mistake, and how to tell the difference at a time when early options are rapidly changing
- What you can expect from financial aid, and how you may be able to increase the chances of receiving more
- What you—student and parent—can do to work together in appropriate and respectful ways throughout the admissions process to achieve a happy outcome

And much more.

We have written this book to demystify the college admissions process by explaining how it works and to level the playing field for those without access to extensive assistance from knowledgeable high school counselors. It will also help those who have access to good counseling but who would still like some extra support. It will give you important insights to put college admissions into perspective, both as a process and as part of life, and to keep the "if only I had known earlier" regret to a minimum. We show how families can navigate the college admissions process happily with their relationship intact or even strengthened, and with an array of fine college choices.

In this revised edition of *Admission Matters,* we have emphasized that most of our advice will help all students applying to a four-year college, not just those seeking admission to a selective college (although much of the admissions frenzy surrounds those colleges). Although *Admission Matters* is a comprehensive guide to college admissions, you may want more information on certain topics than space allows us to include. We provide a list of resources, many of them on the Web, that give detailed information on topics such as financial aid and athletic recruiting to supplement our own coverage. To keep *Admission Matters* as up-to-date as possible, we are maintaining a Web site with updates keyed to the pages in this book throughout the lifetime of this edition. You can access it for free at www.admissionmatters.com. We welcome your feedback.

We'd like now to introduce ourselves. The second edition of *Admission Matters* features a new team of writers. Sally Springer has more than thirty-five years of experience as a psychology professor and senior university administrator on both the East and West Coast. She has devoted her entire career to higher education and has essentially not left school since she entered college at age sixteen. Associate chancellor emerita at the University of California, Davis, she received her B.S. degree from Brooklyn College, where she was a commuter student before venturing cross-country to Stanford University for her doctoral and postdoctoral work. She has been a volunteer admissions reader for the Office of Undergraduate Admissions at UC Davis and is a member of the National Association for College Admission Counseling.

Jon Reider is director of college counseling at San Francisco University High School. He was formerly the senior associate director of admission at Stanford University and a lecturer in the humanities for many years. He is a winner of a Marshall Scholarship to the University of Sussex, where he received a master's degree in sociology, and he also holds a bachelor's degree and a Ph.D. from Stanford in history. He was Phi Beta Kappa, a Danforth Graduate Fellow, and a winner of the Walter Gore Teaching Award for Outstanding Undergraduate Teaching. He is a prolific writer and speaker in the national college admissions world.

Marion Franck writes about family life and local and national issues in a weekly column in the *Davis Enterprise*. She was the founding writer of the "parents page" of the UC Davis alumni magazine and penned feature articles for the campus's Web-based newsletter for parents from 2002 to 2007. Previously, she worked at UC Davis as an adviser to new college teachers, as a lecturer in rhetoric and English, and as a counselor in student judicial affairs. She is a magna cum laude graduate of Brown University and has served as an alumna interviewer for over fifteen years. She holds a master's degree in comparative literature from the University of Wisconsin. Although Marion did not actively participate in the preparation of the second edition, her mini-columns offering her personal perspective on key issues remain part of the book, and her insights and wisdom remain integral to it as well.

We hope *Admission Matters* will become a trusted road map to help you through the college admissions journey.

CHAPTER 1

Why Has College Admissions Become So Competitive?

Applying to college was a simple process for the Baby Boom generation, born between 1946 and 1964. Those bound for a four-year college usually planned to go to a school in their home state or one close by; many considered a college three hundred miles from home to be far away. Few students felt the need to apply to more than two or three colleges, and many applied to just one. College choices were most often based on location, program offerings, cost, and difficulty of admission, with a parental alma mater sometimes thrown in for good measure. For the most part, the whole process was fairly low-key. If students did their homework carefully before deciding where to apply, the outcome was usually predictable. Of course there were surprises—some pleasant and some disappointing—but nothing that would raise the issue of college admissions to the level of a national obsession.

IT USED TO BE SIMPLE . . . BUT NOT ANYMORE

Fast forward to the first part of the twenty-first century. Media headlines tell a story very different for students applying to college now. "Colleges send record number of rejections; competition for admission soaring,"[1] "Student agony grows along with top colleges' wait lists,"[2] "Toward college without a map; lack of counselors leaves students adrift,"[3] "College admissions dance gets longer, more complicated,"[4] "High anxiety of getting into college,"[5] and "Families seek counseling for college stress."[6]

Colleges themselves make announcements that are equally jarring. In spring 2003, Harvard announced that for the first time it had accepted just under 10 percent of the students who applied for freshman admission for the class of 2007, or about 2,000 out of 21,000 applicants. By the spring of 2008, the admissions rate had fallen to 7.1 percent out of an applicant pool of over 27,000 for the class of 2012. On the other coast, UCLA, a public university, reported that it had extended offers of admission to just under 23 percent of the 55,000 students who applied for freshman admission to the class of 2012, the lowest admission rate in its history. The same year, UCLA's northern California neighbor, Stanford University, also reported an admission rate lower than ever before—9.5 percent, down from 12 percent five years earlier. These were just a few of the many colleges reporting record-breaking numbers of applications and record low rates of admission, continuing a trend that began a decade earlier. What has happened to change the college admissions picture so dramatically?

The Echo Boom

The simple explanation for why it is harder to get into four-year colleges now than ever before seems to be supply and demand: more high school graduates than ever are competing for seats in the freshman class. After declining somewhat in the late 1980s and early 1990s, the number of students graduating from high school in the United States has risen steadily each year since. In 1997 there were 2.6 million graduates; in 2003, there were 3 million; by 2009, the number of high school graduates had grown to 3.3 million. Although the numbers will decline slightly from the 2009 peak, they are projected to stay at or above 3.2 million at least until 2022.[7]

> I don't think anyone is complacent about getting a high-quality applicant pool.
> HARVARD UNIVERSITY
> ADMISSIONS OFFICER

Part of the increase is the result of immigration, especially from Asia and Latin America, but most of the growth is due to the children of the Baby Boom generation that created the great demand for higher education in the decades after World War II. Known as the "echo boomers" or the Millennials, these children are part of the largest group of high school graduates ever.

Social Changes

But the problem is not just demographics. Application numbers have grown much faster than the age cohort. Important social changes have taken place as well. Not only are more students graduating from high school each year, proportionally more of them want to go to college. A college education is increasingly seen as key to economic success in our society, just as a high school diploma was once the minimum requirement. Studies confirm the value of a college diploma in terms of lifelong earnings, and many desirable careers require education beyond the bachelor's degree. As a result, more students are seeking to attend four-year colleges, including students from underrepresented minority groups whose college participation rate used to be low.

At the same time, colleges themselves have increased their efforts to attract large, diverse pools of applicants. Many have mounted aggressive programs to spread the word about their offerings nationally and internationally. Through colorful "viewbooks" mailed directly to students, visits to high schools by admissions officers, college nights at local hotels, and information booths at college fairs, colleges reach out to prospective freshmen with unprecedented energy and at great expense.

Started in earnest in the 1980s when the number of college-age students dropped temporarily, these marketing efforts have continued and expanded even as the number of students applying has soared. Sophisticated marketing techniques are used not only by colleges that anticipate problems filling their freshman class but also by colleges with an overabundance of qualified applicants. Colleges want to attract academically qualified, talented, and diverse groups of applicants from which to select their freshman class, and they often go to great lengths to do it. And it works! One result of all these efforts is that more and more college-bound students have become aware of, and are willing to seriously consider, colleges in parts of the country far from their homes.

The Role of the Internet

The Internet also now plays a major role in how students approach college admissions. Although printed material and in-person presentations are still important ways for students to learn about different colleges, the Web is the top source of information for students who have grown up online. Students can visit campuses through sophisticated online tours and webcams and can get many of their questions answered by "frequently asked question" (FAQ) lists posted on the Web, or by tracking college-sponsored blogs. Colleges have invested heavily in technology to help showcase themselves.

Finally, the Internet has made it easier than ever to apply to college. Students no longer have to send for application forms, wait for them to arrive in the mail, and then fill them out by hand. Forms can be downloaded from almost all college sites or, better yet, completed and submitted directly online, saving some of the time and effort, and even postage, that a traditional paper application requires. Some schools—St. Olaf College and Lewis and Clark College are examples—even waive their application fee (most fees are in the $45–$75 range) for those who submit their forms over the Internet. Simplifying things even more, more than 350 colleges now accept the Common Application, a standardized form that can be filled out once (often along with a school-specific supplement) and submitted electronically or by mail to as many participating colleges as a student wishes. With admission harder to predict, students are now submitting more applications than ever. Sending eight to ten applications is now the norm at many private schools and high-performing public high schools—twelve to fifteen or more applications are not uncommon. The Common Application system, coupled with technology in general, has made it easier for students to apply to an ever-larger number of colleges.

> As word spreads about the competition for college admission, students respond by applying to even more colleges to increase their chances of acceptance. In so doing, they end up unwittingly contributing to the very problem they are trying to solve for themselves.
>
> HIGH SCHOOL COUNSELOR CONCERNED ABOUT THE TREND OF STUDENTS APPLYING TO MORE AND MORE SCHOOLS

All these factors taken together—growth in the population of eighteen-year-olds, greater interest in college, sophisticated marketing efforts, and ease of access to information and the ability to apply made possible by the Internet—help explain why it is harder to get into college now than ever before.

But this is not the whole answer.

Where the Real Crunch Lies

Most people are surprised to learn that with relatively few exceptions, four-year colleges in the United States still accept most of their applicants. In fact, each year many fully accredited four-year colleges have vacancies well into the summer for the freshman class that begins in the fall. Despite all the social and demographic changes, ample spots for prospective freshmen still remain in four-year colleges. How can this fact be reconciled with the newspaper headlines (not to mention firsthand reports from students and parents) reporting a crisis in college admissions?

The real crunch in admissions—the crunch that drives the newspaper headlines and the anxiety that afflicts many families at college application time—is limited to about one hundred colleges that attract applicants from all over the country and the world and that are the most selective in their admissions process. Bill Mayher, a private college counselor and author of *The College Admissions Mystique,* summarizes the problem succinctly: "It's hard for kids to get into colleges because they only want to get into colleges that are hard to get into."[8]

WHICH COLLEGES ARE THE MOST SELECTIVE?

The percentage of students offered admission to a college is a major factor in determining its selectivity. As the number of applications to a college increases, the admission rate decreases. Another key factor affecting selectivity at a given college is the academic strength of the applicant pool, since applicants tend to self-select when applying to certain colleges, especially some smaller ones, known for their academic rigor. Such schools may accept a higher percentage of those who apply because their applicant pools tend to be smaller and more uniformly strong. Both factors—admission rate and strength of the applicant pool—help determine the difficulty of gaining admission to a particular school.

To simplify the discussion here, however, we define selectivity only in terms of admission rate, and define a *selective college* as one that has an admission rate of 50 percent or less. We further divide selective colleges into three categories—super-selective colleges (those admitting less than 20 percent of applicants), highly selective colleges (those admitting less than 35 percent of applicants), and very selective colleges (those that admit less than 50 percent of applicants). These are artificial boundaries, of course, and they don't take into account the self-selection factor, but they give a sense of the relative difficulty of gaining admission. Even though more than two thousand four-year institutions of higher education in the United States admit 50 percent or more of those who apply (and most admit more than 80 percent), many students focus their attention on the hundred colleges that fall into one of the three groups defined as selective.

The students applying to selective colleges are the ones experiencing the crisis in college admissions. The crisis does not affect those applying to community colleges or those seeking admission to the many colleges that accept most or all of their applicants. Nevertheless, it is very real to those who are applying to selective colleges now or expect to apply in the next few years. If you are reading this book, you (or your child) may be one of them. Keep reading. Our book is designed to help you build a college list that is right for you and to help you submit strong applications. If you'll be applying to less selective schools, please keep reading as well. Most of what we have to share in this book will help you too. All students face the challenges of identifying colleges that will be a good fit and then submitting well-crafted applications.

WHY SO MUCH INTEREST IN SUCH A SMALL GROUP OF COLLEGES?

What is behind such intense interest in this small group of colleges and universities? Why, in particular, does such a mystique surround the colleges included in the Ivy League, as well as a few others accorded similar status? What benefits do these elite colleges bestow (or do people believe they bestow) on their graduates?

Prestige, of course, is one obvious answer. By definition, the more selective a college, the more difficult it is to get into and the greater the prestige associated with being admitted. The student enjoys the prestige directly (after all, the student is the one who was admitted!), but parents enjoy prestige by association. Parents are often the primary drivers of the push toward prestige, but students also report similar pressures from peers in high school. Just in the last generation, going to a highly ranked college has become a status symbol of greater value than almost any other consumer good, in part because it cannot simply be purchased if you have enough money.

Although some people openly acknowledge considering prestige in college choice, many more will cite the assumed quality of the educational experience as the basis for their interest in an elite college. But this rationale often depends on the unstated, and often untested, assumption that a good indicator of the quality of something is how much others seek it. This means that selective colleges are

Colleges by Admission Rate for the Class of 2011

**Super-Selective
(less than 20 percent
of applicants admitted)**
Amherst College
Bowdoin College
Brown University
Cal Tech
Claremont McKenna
  College
Columbia University
Dartmouth College
Harvard University
MIT
University of Pennsylvania
Pomona College
Princeton University
Stanford University
Swarthmore College
Williams College
Yale University

**Highly Selective
(less than 35 percent
of applicants admitted)**
Bard College
Barnard College
UC Berkeley
Boston College
Brandeis University
Bucknell University
Carleton College
Carnegie Mellon University
University of Chicago
Colby College
Colgate University
Colorado College
Connecticut College
Cornell University
Davidson College
Duke University
Emory University

Georgetown University
Hamilton College
Harvey Mudd College
Haverford College
College of the Holy Cross
Johns Hopkins University
Kenyon College
Lafayette College
Lehigh University
UCLA
Middlebury College
University of North Carolina
Northwestern University
University of Notre Dame
Oberlin College
Pepperdine University
Pitzer College
Reed College
Rice University
University of Southern
  California
Spelman College
Trinity College
  (Connecticut)
Tufts University
Vanderbilt University
Vassar College
Washington and Jefferson
  College
Washington and Lee
  University
Wesleyan University
College of William and Mary

**Very Selective
(less than 50 percent of
applicants admitted)**
Agnes Scott College
Baylor University
Berea College
Binghamton University

Bryn Mawr College
University of Connecticut
Cornell College (Iowa)
University of Delaware
Denison University
Dickinson College
University of Florida
Fordham University
Franklin and Marshall
  College
George Washington
  University
Gettysburg College
Grinnell College
Macalester College
University of Maryland
University of Miami
University of Missouri
Northeastern University
Occidental College
Rensselaer Polytechnic
  Institute
University of Richmond
University of Rochester
Rutgers University
UC San Diego
Sarah Lawrence College
Scripps College
Skidmore College
St. Lawrence University
Stony Brook University
Texas Christian University
Tulane University
Union College
University of Virginia
Wabash College
Wake Forest University
Wellesley College
Wheaton College
  (Massachusetts)
Whitman College

presumed to offer a better education; the more selective, the higher the quality. But is this really true?

Take the eight colleges of the Ivy League, for example—Harvard University, Yale University, Princeton University, Brown University, Dartmouth College, the University of Pennsylvania, Cornell University, and Columbia University. One counselor we know, whose children attended two of these institutions, refers to the group as the "Climbing Vine Schools" to take away a little of the allure of the name. The Ivy League originally referred only to a football league. (Only seven colleges belonged at first. Brown University eventually joined as the eighth member, although several other colleges were considered possibilities at the time.) Over time, though, Ivy League colleges have become known among the general public primarily for academics rather than athletics and are accorded high prestige. The admission rate of each Ivy places it in the super-selective or highly selective

I was happy and proud when my son was accepted at Stanford. I quickly became embarrassed, though, by the gushing responses I received when friends asked where he was going. He had just been accepted to college, after all—he had not won the Nobel Prize. Things have gotten rather warped.

PARENT OF STANFORD FRESHMAN

Lots of times it's kids, I think, trying to define themselves by their school choice, not so much choosing the school that's right for them as trying to look good through it. I'm not sure if they get it from parents or from other kids or from teachers. But they get it from somewhere.

VOLUNTEER IN COUNSELING OFFICE AT PRIVATE HIGH SCHOOL

Harvard is perhaps the most overrated institution of higher learning in America. This is not to imply that Harvard isn't a good school—on the contrary, Harvard is an excellent school. But its reputation creates an unattainable standard; no school could ever be as good as most people think Harvard is.

COMMENT BY HARVARD STUDENT

Some kids want that acceptance letter to Harvard, Yale, or Princeton so desperately, but they really do not know why except to impress family, friends, whomever. It is one thing to include prestige as a factor in your list of schools. It is a problem when it becomes the only factor, and I am seeing this more and more.

PRIVATE COUNSELOR CONCERNED ABOUT THE EMPHASIS ON PRESTIGE

category, and each has renowned faculty as well as fine students. Everyone agrees that they are excellent schools, but do the Ivies automatically offer undergraduates an educational experience better than that at many other institutions? The answer, well known in academic circles but surprising to many others, is assuredly no.

THE IMPORTANCE OF FIT

This book doesn't try to dissuade you if prestige is important to you in selecting a college—you have lots of company. What it does do, however, is discuss many other important dimensions to consider in selecting colleges. We think that the college admissions process should be about fit—the fit between a student and a college. Finding a good fit does not mean that there is just one perfect school for a student—it means exploring an array of factors that can enhance a student's academic and personal success. Many factors besides prestige go into determining fit—we discuss them at length in Chapter Four and encourage you to think carefully about them. You may find, in the end, that you are making the same choices as you would have before, but your choices

> I am extremely skeptical that the quality of a university—any more than the quality of a magazine—can be measured statistically. However, even if it can, the producers of the *U.S. News* rankings remain far from discovering the method.[9]
>
> GERHARD CASPER, FORMER PRESIDENT OF STANFORD UNIVERSITY

will be more informed. You may even find yourself seriously considering other options of which you had been unaware. Either outcome is fine—we simply want to help you understand as much as possible about yourself, the college admissions process, and colleges themselves, so that you can make the best choices for you.

THE RANKINGS GAME

A major contributor to the mystique of selective colleges has been the annual rankings of colleges published by *U.S. News & World Report*. The magazine's first rankings, published in 1983, were based solely on surveys of college administrators. Over time, the rankings became so popular that they outgrew the magazine itself. Each August *U.S. News & World Report* publishes a separate guidebook, "America's Best Colleges," that features college rankings based on a mix

Not Totally Cured, But Still Trying

What I have long viewed as my toughest job as a parent came into play, perhaps more powerfully than ever, during the college application process.

I had to fight the part of me that wants to use my children to feel good about myself. Put more baldly, I had to fight the part of me that wants to show off.

Let me explain.

Many years ago, when my children were toddlers, I confessed to a counselor that I looked forward to the day when their pictures would appear in the newspaper. Our small local newspaper runs frequent photographs of students holding artwork, playing soccer, or receiving awards. I wanted to see my children's smiling faces on those pages. I knew it would feel good, and I couldn't wait.

When I finished telling this to my counselor, she responded very seriously. "What I am about to say is important. Don't live through your children's accomplishments. If you want to be in the newspaper, do it yourself."

I followed her advice to the best of my ability. All through my children's primary school years, I worked hard not to bask in their accomplishments. When their pictures did appear in the newspaper, usually for musical events, I smiled, but I didn't go ape.

When other people's children appeared in the newspaper holding huge, shiny trophies, when I felt a shimmer of jealousy in spite of myself, I remembered the words of my counselor.

When my children applied to college, my internal struggle bubbled up again. I fought it. I worked hard not to pressure my children to apply to big-name schools. I talked about the value of finding a place that felt good, fancy name or not. I really meant it. I gave (and still give) the same advice to friends and family.

Now that my children have graduated, I notice that somewhere along the way I developed a "show off meter," an internal monitor that tells me when I go too far.

An acquaintance will ask, "How are the kids?" and if I finish my answer feeling a little warm, as if I just walked into a stuffy room, I know I've said something that crossed the line. I'm proud of my children, no question, but who they are as people is far more important than where they have gone to school or what they have done. I am grateful to that wise counselor for helping me see what was so clearly before my eyes.

M. F.

of reputation and statistical data about the colleges, as well as information and advice about applying to college. The yearly rankings, though, are what drive the sales of "America's Best Colleges" and generate great attention among readers and great controversy among those, including us, who believe the ranking process is fundamentally flawed. One critic, Lloyd Thacker, a prominent voice for reform of the college admissions process, refers to the ranking business as the "ranksters."

While president of Stanford University, Gerhard Casper expressed his concern about the rankings to the editor of *U.S. News & World Report* as follows: "As the president of a university that is among the top-ranked universities, I hope I have the standing to persuade you that much about these rankings—particularly their specious formulas and spurious precision—is utterly misleading."[10]

What Goes into the Rankings

Twenty-five percent of a college's ranking in the *U.S. News* survey is based on reputational ratings it receives in the poll of college presidents, provosts, and admissions deans that the magazine conducts each year. These administrators are simply asked to rate the academic quality of undergraduate programs at schools with the same mission as their own (for example, liberal arts colleges or research universities) on a 1–5 scale from "marginal" to "distinguished," with an option to respond "don't know." Many of those who receive the questionnaire acknowledge that they lack the detailed knowledge of other colleges that they would need to respond meaningfully. A number of college presidents, mostly in a set of liberal arts colleges known as the Annapolis Group, have signed a statement refusing to participate in the survey either by rating other colleges or, in some cases, by refusing to submit their data in the format the magazine desires.

> I am delighted to announce that, for the third year in a row, [our college] has been placed in the top tier of its category by *U.S. News & World Report*. While we continue to be suspicious of the rankings, this is still a very promising position for the College.[11]
>
> LETTER POSTED BY COLLEGE PRESIDENT ON CAMPUS WEB SITE FOLLOWING RELEASE OF THE *U.S. NEWS* RANKINGS

The remaining 75 percent of a college's ranking in the *U.S. News* survey is based on data collected in five different categories, each weighted in the final calculation as follows: retention and graduation rate (20 percent), faculty resources (20 percent), student selectivity (15 percent), financial resources (10 percent), alumni giving (5 percent), and graduation rate performance (5 percent).[12]

Each of these five categories, in turn, contains several submeasures. For example, *U.S. News* has derived student selectivity from several kinds of data for the freshman class—admission rate, the 25th and 75th percentile of SAT or ACT scores, and the percentage of students in the top 10 percent of their high school class.

The *U.S. News* Formula

All the measures we have just described are collected annually for each college and put into a formula that weights the different kinds of data and then computes an overall "ranking." To avoid comparing apples with oranges, *U.S. News* ranks campuses with those with the same mission, so that research universities and liberal arts colleges, for example, are ranked separately. (We discuss the differences between these two kinds of institutions in Chapter Four, among the factors to consider in choosing colleges.) Only the first hundred colleges in each group are ranked individually; after that, the schools are grouped alphabetically by "tiers." Each year the magazine slightly modifies its formula, ostensibly to improve its utility for assessing educational quality but also to sell the rankings as "new and improved."

> Now more than ever, people believe that the ranking—or the presumed hierarchy of "quality" or "prestige"—of the college or university one attends matters, and matters enormously. More than ever before, education is being viewed as a commodity. ... The large and fundamental problem is that we are at risk of it all seeming and becoming increasingly a game. What matters is less the education and more the brand.[13]
>
> LEE BOLLINGER, PRESIDENT OF COLUMBIA UNIVERSITY

As a consequence of these changes, a college's ranking can shift fairly dramatically from one year to the next simply as a result of changes in the formula used to compute the ratings. The school itself may not have changed at all. Does its quality relative to its peers really change significantly in one year? Of course not. Critics of the rankings argue that meaningful changes in college quality cannot be measured in the short term, and that *U.S. News* changes the formula primarily to sustain interest in the rankings and sell more magazines.

CONCERNS ABOUT RANKINGS

The *U.S. News* rankings are very popular with the general public, particularly parents, and are a source of joy or frustration for colleges themselves, depending on a college's ranking in a given year. The most important criticism of the rankings is that they are not based on any direct measures of educational quality, such as good teaching or student satisfaction. Educators readily acknowledge that educational quality and student satisfaction can be hard to assess and tricky to put into numbers, but there are ways to measure them directly.

For the last several years, the National Survey of Student Engagement (NSSE) based at Indiana University has attempted to measure quality and satisfaction by asking students direct questions about their educational experiences and how they spend their time. *U.S. News* now reports some NSSE data in its "America's Best Colleges" issue, although they are not counted in the calculation of the rankings. Unfortunately, many highly regarded colleges do not participate in NSSE, including most selective ones as we have defined them. And some colleges that do participate do not make the results public. Even though NSSE data are not used or reported as broadly as they might be, we think you should know about them, since they suggest important ways to assess educational quality. You can learn more about NSSE and see which colleges participate in it at www.nsse.iub.edu. We applaud the questions that NSSE asks, and recommend that you ask them on your own when you research and visit colleges. (We talk more about college visits in Chapter Five.)

Critics have pointed out that while the *U.S. News* variables can contribute indirectly to educational quality (perhaps higher salaries lead to better faculty and smaller classes mean more personal attention), educators do not agree on how those variables can be used to measure the quality of a college. To make things worse, some of the factors in the *U.S. News* formula can be manipulated. As much as colleges disparage the ranking process, the *U.S. News* rankings are too high-profile and too influential among the general public for colleges to ignore them. Alumni, boards of trustees, and even bond-rating agencies on Wall Street pay close attention to the rankings and expect to see "improvement." Under pressure, some colleges have actively worked to do better in ways that have little to do with educational quality and much to do with enhancing the school's ranking.

Representative Questions from the National Survey of Student Engagement 2008

1. To what extent has your experience at this institution contributed to your knowledge, skills, and personal development in the following areas (rated from "very much" to "very little" along a four-point scale):

   a. Acquiring a broad general education

   b. Writing clearly and effectively

   c. Thinking critically and analytically

   d. Learning effectively on your own

   e. Understanding people of other racial and ethnic backgrounds

2. Overall, how would you evaluate the quality of academic advising you have received at your institution?

3. In your experience at your institution during the current school year, about how often have you done each of the following (rated from "very often" to "never" along a four-point scale):

   a. Asked questions in class or contributed to class discussion

   b. Worked on a paper or project that required integrating ideas or information from various sources

   c. Discussed ideas about your readings or classes with faculty members outside of class

4. If you could start over again, would you go to the same institution you are now attending? (rated from "definitely yes" to "definitely no" along a four-point scale)

USED WITH PERMISSION FROM INDIANA UNIVERSITY

One common but harmless approach is the production of elegant full-color booklets that typically highlight a college's new programs and facilities, as well as its ambitious plans for the future. In addition to distributing them to support fundraising and recruitment, some college presidents send them to their colleagues at other campuses in the hope that the booklets will raise awareness of their college. That greater awareness may lead the reader to offer a more favorable rating when the *U.S. News* questionnaire arrives the following year. It's impossible to know if this actually works, but the colleges think it does.

Another tactic involves the reporting of data. Colleges have always had some leeway in how they report their statistics, and they sometimes present themselves in the most favorable light for the ratings. In the past, for example, some colleges excluded the scores of recruited athletes in the SAT scores they reported for freshmen. Recruited athletes as a group usually have lower SAT scores than other freshmen and would lower the average score, and hence the college's ranking, if they were included. *U.S. News* says they have stopped this practice, but it is hard to know for sure.

The Common Data Set

The reporting of data has recently become more systematic through the development of the Common Data Set. In this collaborative project among colleges and a number of publishers, the colleges agree to provide standardized statistical data each year, including detailed information about the composition of the freshman class along with admission and wait-list numbers. The participating publishers, including *U.S. News,* then make the data public in various forms, and some of the colleges choose to post the report itself. (You can usually find the report, if available, by checking the college's "institutional research office" Web page or by entering "Common Data Set" as a search term on the campus Web site.) This attempt at standardization has made it easier for different groups to access the same information. It has not, however, eliminated the flexibility that colleges have to report some numbers in a fashion they deem advantageous. As long as the public assumes that rankings measure educational quality, some colleges will feel pressured to provide what they think the market wants.

Admission Rate and Yield

Although it plays only a small role in the *U.S. News* formula, a college's admission rate or selectivity is the one figure that captures the public's attention and the most headlines. A decline from the preceding year in the percentage of students who are accepted is often interpreted as reflecting increased interest in the college, and hence its inherent desirability. Aggressive outreach to students to encourage them to apply, despite knowing that only a fraction of those applying will be admitted, is the easiest way for a college to become more selective. While most colleges engage in outreach with more noble goals, the result is the same. Rachel Toor, a former Duke admissions officer, vividly describes her own experience: "I travel around the country whipping kids (and their parents) into a frenzy so that they will apply. I tell them how great a school Duke is academically and how much fun they will have socially. Then, come April, we reject most of them."[14]

Colleges can also lower their final admission rate by limiting offers to those students who are most likely to enroll. A college's *yield*—the percentage of students offered admission who actually decide to enroll—can affect its admission rate. A college with a high yield can admit fewer students and still fill its classes. If it has a low yield, it has to admit more. Taken to an extreme, this means admitting as large a percentage of the incoming class by "early decision" as possible. Early decision is an admissions option available at many colleges in which students submit a completed application by November 1 or November 15, rather than the traditional January 1, in exchange for a decision by mid-December rather than in the spring. The catch is that early decision applications are binding on the student, meaning that the student is obligated to attend if admitted, subject to the availability of adequate financial aid. A student admitted by early decision is a sure thing for a college, since its staff know that the student will attend.

We talk more about early decision and its cousin, early action, in Chapter Seven, but we mention it now because it allows colleges to increase their yield and thereby reduce their admission rate. Some colleges currently admit from a third to half of their incoming freshman class via early decision, leaving fewer seats available for the much larger number of students applying in the regular admissions round. For the class of 2012, for example, Wesleyan University admitted 38 percent of its freshman class via early decision, while the University of Pennsylvania admitted 47 percent via its early decision program. Some colleges are reducing these percentages, however, for reasons that we explain in Chapter Seven.

> I overheard a conversation at a reception for the parents of newly admitted students at [Elite U]. A mom was chatting with a young admissions officer who was mingling with parents on the lawn of the president's house. "I have a question I'd like to ask you," she said. "Since [Elite U] takes less than 15 percent of those who apply, why does the university work so hard to encourage more applications?" The admissions officer was silent for a moment. "I'm afraid you'll have to ask the dean of admissions that question," she said.
>
> PARENT OF PROSPECTIVE FRESHMAN

A college can also increase its yield and lower its admission rate by rejecting, or more likely wait-listing, students considered "overqualified" because the college believes they won't accept the offer of admission and will go elsewhere. The dean of admissions at one such college defended the practice at his institution. "We know our place in the food chain of higher education," he said. "We're not a community college. And we're not Harvard."[15] This practice is not common, but it is not rare, either.

Showing That You Are Interested

Some colleges try to identify who is seriously interested in them by tracking how much contact a student has had with the college—such as requesting an interview, chatting with a representative at a college fair, e-mailing a question to an admissions officer, visiting campus—and using that information when making the final decision. A student who has initiated a good deal of contact with a college is seen as more likely to enroll than a student whose first contact with the college is the arrival of the application over the Internet, and hence is a better bet for admission. Given hard choices among candidates with similar credentials, "demonstrated interest" can make the difference between an offer of acceptance and placement on the wait-list at some colleges.

Emory University openly lets students know that level of contact matters. Its application form states, "We carefully note demonstrated interest during the admissions process and expect candidates to have done their homework on us. Have you met us at a college fair, ordered the Emory video visit, attended an information session, or perhaps visited campus? . . . We are honest in the fact that demonstrated interest can be a tip factor when we make admission decisions." Not all colleges are this refreshingly candid, however, and not all consider demonstrated interest in the admissions process. In general, this counts less at the super-selective colleges that already have the highest yields. They have little to gain by showing preference to those who try to demonstrate interest.

> To think that when my older son applied we refrained from contacting colleges because we thought we were doing admissions offices a favor by not cluttering up their e-mail or phone lines. We won't pester them, but we won't have the same worry when our younger son applies.
>
> Parent of a college sophomore and another child in the admissions pipeline

WHY ARE RANKINGS SO POPULAR?

It is not surprising that students and parents will turn to rankings like those in *U.S. News* when they are thinking about colleges. Deciding where to apply isn't easy, and having supposed experts do the evaluating is an attractive alternative to figuring things out on your own, especially if you have no experience. As a society, we are obsessed with rating consumer goods in the quest for the best. We accept ratings that assess washing machines, restaurants, football teams, hospitals, and movies, so why not include colleges as well?

> Students may have a better sense of their potential ability than college admissions committees. To cite one prominent example, Steven Spielberg was rejected by the University of Southern California and UCLA film schools.[16]
>
> STACEY DALE AND ALAN KRUEGER, RESEARCHERS WHO STUDIED THE LONG-TERM EFFECTS OF ATTENDING DIFFERENT TYPES OF COLLEGES

College rankings, though, are very different. The rankings simply don't measure what they are supposed to assess—the educational experience for an individual student. Doing that requires a personalized look at a college through the eyes of the student who might potentially enroll. Although you no doubt have much in common with your friends and classmates, you also differ in important ways. There is simply no easy substitute for investing the time and effort to determine which colleges will be a good fit for you. Merely knowing which ones are the most selective or enjoy the highest reputations among college presidents (which, in large measure, is what the *U.S. News* rankings are telling you) doesn't get you very far toward finding a good match for you, a place where you will be happy and learn what you want to know.

Another Myth: "I'll Make More Money If I Graduate from an Elite College"

But let's return now to the basic question of why there is so much interest in the group of the most selective hundred or so colleges. OK, you say, you now see that name recognition and rankings do not necessarily indicate educational quality. But maybe that is irrelevant. Isn't the real value of an elite college education the contacts you make while there? Everyone knows that the rich, the famous, and the well-connected attend these colleges. Wouldn't attending one of them increase your chances of making the right contacts, getting into a prestigious graduate school, or getting an important career-enhancing break—all eventually leading to fortune if not fame?

Several studies have actually been interpreted as supporting this conclusion. Years after graduation, graduates of elite institutions have a higher income than that of graduates of less well-known colleges, just as the income of college graduates is higher than that of those with a high school education. The simple interpretation is that the experience of going to a selective college is responsible for the income difference. But researchers Stacy Dale and Alan Krueger considered another possibility.[17] Perhaps, they hypothesized, the students who applied to and were accepted by elite colleges had personal qualities to begin with that led in some way to the income differences later in life. Maybe the kind of college which students attended wasn't as important as who they were as people.

To test their hypothesis, Dale and Krueger compared income figures for individuals who were accepted by elite colleges and actually attended those colleges with the income of people who were accepted by elite colleges but who chose to attend less selective ones. The results showed no difference in income between the two groups! (The only exception was that low-income students who attended an elite college had higher incomes later in life.) The data even suggested that simply having applied to an elite college, regardless of whether a student was accepted, was the critical factor in predicting later income. Students with the self-confidence and motivation to envision themselves competitive at a selective college showed the enhanced economic benefit normally associated with having actually attended such a college.

> We didn't find any evidence that suggested that the selectivity of a student's undergraduate college was related to the quality of the graduate school they attended.[18]
>
> STACY DALE

> Do not choose a college by the numbers. Most of those numbers are about resources and reputation and not actual quality or performance. Base your choice on your own needs and aspirations and which colleges can best meet them. As Albert Einstein reminded us, "Not everything that counts can be counted, and not everything that can be counted counts."[19]
>
> DAVID DAVENPORT, FORMER PRESIDENT OF PEPPERDINE UNIVERSITY

Getting into Graduate School

What about admission to graduate school? Does attending a selective college affect your chances of getting into a highly regarded law, business, or medical school or other graduate program? Anecdotal evidence and a small amount of published data indicate that, yes, a disproportional number of graduates of selective colleges attend prestigious graduate and professional schools. But here, too, it may be that students admitted to selective colleges bring qualities with them that are responsible for their subsequent success in gaining admission to these schools after graduation. Perhaps those same students would have done just as well if they had gone to a less selective college.

Unfortunately, Dale and Krueger did not have enough data in their study to rigorously test this hypothesis—they could draw firm conclusions only about income. They did, however, have sufficient data to show that people who went to a selective college were no more likely to obtain an advanced degree than those who were admitted to a selective college but chose to attend a less selective school. In addition, preliminary analysis of their admittedly limited data supported the interpretation that it was the qualities of the students themselves, and not anything associated with the college they attended, that were correlated with their graduate schools. Students who were admitted to a selective college but chose to attend a less selective one seemed to fare just as well when it came to graduate or professional school admission as those who actually attended the more selective college.

LOOKING AHEAD

We believe that the college selection process should be about fit—finding colleges that are a good fit for you. A number of factors contribute to fit—academic, extracurricular, social, and geographic, among others—and the determination of fit will be different for different people. Assessing fit takes time and effort and is much harder to do than simply choosing colleges by looking at a list of rankings. But higher education is not like a shoe, something that you slip on once and decide if it fits well. Stephen Lewis, former president of Carleton College, stated it well: "The question should not be, what are the best colleges? The real question should be, best for whom?"[20]

CHAPTER 2

What Do Selective Colleges Look for in an Applicant?

I t is often said that college admissions outcomes are just not predictable. Everyone knows that it is harder to get into selective colleges than ever before, but in addition the criteria for admission seem to be getting murkier and murkier.

Take the student who is admitted to a super-selective college but winds up placed on the wait-list at a less selective one. Or the student admitted to three colleges but denied by three others, all about the same in selectivity. Why aren't decisions more consistent? Even more puzzling can be the result when students from the same high school apply to the same college. One student may have a significantly stronger academic record than the other, yet be denied by a selective college while the classmate receives a fat admissions packet at notification time. Why wasn't the student with the stronger record accepted also? And although many colleges claim they use exactly the same criteria in the admissions process for early decision applications as they use for regular decision applications, anecdotal as well as statistical evidence strongly argues that early applicants sometimes have an edge in the admissions process. Why should when you apply make any difference at all?

This chapter will help you understand the many factors colleges consider in their review of applications. Knowing what colleges look for as they sort through thousands of applications can help you understand the admissions process and help you approach it with confidence. We have no magic bullet or formula to guarantee you acceptance to a selective college—there is no such thing. But the more you know about how colleges select their freshman class, the wiser you will be in approaching the tasks before you—from choosing colleges to preparing your applications to dealing with the successes and, yes, even the disappointments that may occur at the end of it all.

HOW COLLEGE ADMISSIONS HAS CHANGED

Before we begin, we'd like to share a little history that dramatically illustrates how college admissions has changed over the years. Seventy-odd years ago, colleges that are now considered among the most selective filled their classes in ways that reflected the time. Yale University, for example, filled its class of 1936 from a total of 1,330 applicants. Of that group, 959, or 72 percent, were accepted, and 884 of them subsequently enrolled. Almost 30 percent were the sons of Yale University alumni, known as "legacies." Many of those admitted were students from "feeder schools"—elite prep schools with headmasters whose close relationships with college admissions officers virtually assured the admission of their graduates to the school of their choice. Less than 20 percent of the freshman class graduated from a public high school.[1] Women were not eligible to apply to Yale University; they had separate elite colleges, known as the Seven Sisters, with similar admissions standards. Also excluded were young men who, no matter how bright and accomplished, did not fit the mold of privilege and wealth. But few of the latter even considered applying; the criteria for admission, social class included, were well understood by everyone.

Another example, this one from just fifty years ago, makes a similar point. The following description comes from a book on the history of college admissions:

> Until the 1950s admissions staffs typically consisted of one professional and possibly a secretary to take care of clerical work. Often, a dean would split responsibilities between admissions and some other aspect of administration or teaching. Colleges could function effectively with such a simple admissions structure because students tended to apply only to their first choice college, and they were usually accepted. A close collaboration between admissions officers and guidance counselors also facilitated such modest staffing. Admissions officers visited selected high schools, interviewed candidates for admission, and then usually offered admission to students on the spot. Philip Smith, [former] dean of admissions at Williams College, recounted a visit as an admissions officer in the late 1950s. After he interviewed students, Smith sat down with eight

teachers; he was given a pat on the back and a Scotch, and was expected to offer admission to all the candidates right then.[2]

Today, of course, institutions like Yale University and Williams College pride themselves on the diversity of their student body and actively recruit high-achieving men and women from all backgrounds. The 1,952 men and women invited to join the Yale University class of 2012 were selected from an applicant pool of almost 23,000; of the 1,320 enrolling, just 13 percent were legacies. Fifty-five percent of the class came from public high schools. This example is typical of the current admissions picture at other selective colleges as well. Those who in a prior era would have been assured of admission by virtue of birth or circumstance no longer are. Some of the rules have changed.

CHANGING TIMES AT YALE UNIVERSITY

	Class of 1936	Class of 2012
Number of applicants	1,330	22,817
Accepted (%)	72	8.6
Size of freshman class	884	1,320
From public high schools (%)	< 20	55
Legacies (%)	30	13

WHAT MATTERS NOW

The Web pages of most selective colleges provide information about the characteristics they are seeking in their prospective freshmen. The posted information may even include details about how the college weights grades, test scores, or extracurricular activities in the final admissions decision. But information on the Web page is just the public version of the admissions story. The private version is what actually goes on behind closed doors as admissions officers read through many thousands of applications to select a freshman class that may have just a few hundred places. The information on the Web page is not fabricated or intended to mislead. However, it is just part of the story. In this chapter, we talk about the criteria that selective colleges generally take into account in their evaluation. In Chapter Three, we consider the review process itself.

Students and parents are often surprised when they learn about the full range of criteria used by admissions officers at selective colleges. Although some criteria are well known and predictable, others are not. The level of competition for admission to the most selective colleges can also come as a big surprise to those without recent firsthand experience with college admissions.

THE ACADEMIC RECORD

The heart of a college application is the student's academic record—the courses taken and the grades achieved in those courses. Selective colleges uniformly state that they are looking for students who show convincing evidence of being able to do well in a demanding academic program and that they place the greatest weight in admissions decisions on that record.

 What Do Admissions Committees Look At?

Academic Record
- Grades
- Class rank
- Rigor of curriculum

Standardized Test Scores
- SAT
- ACT
- SAT Subject Tests

Engagement Outside the Classroom
- Extracurricular activities
- Community service
- Work experience

Personal Qualities
- Letters of recommendation
- Essays
- Interview report

Hooks and Institutional Priorities
- Legacy connection
- Donation potential
- Underrepresented race or ethnicity
- Recruited athlete status
- Socioeconomic and geographic background
- Exceptional talent

How Challenging Is Your Academic Program?

Many colleges provide students with guidelines about the kinds of preparation they expect successful applicants to have in high school—the number of years of English, mathematics, foreign language, and so forth. Williams College, for example, provides the following guidelines to prospective students:

> Applicants should pursue the strongest program of study offered by their schools. Wherever possible, you should take honors or advanced level courses, especially in fields of great interest to you. A challenging and well-balanced program of study ideally should include: a full four-year sequence in English and mathematics; study of one foreign language for three or, preferably, four years; and three years of study each in the social sciences and laboratory sciences. These are not absolute requirements for admission; rather they are recommendations for developing a strong high school record.

Usually, these are minimum recommendations; additional years of a single foreign language or mathematics, for example, are viewed favorably. Colleges also expect students to take advantage of opportunities their school may offer to challenge themselves academically through honors or Advanced Placement (AP) courses, or by participating in the International Baccalaureate (IB) program. If opportunities for challenging classes are open to you, a selective college will expect you to have taken advantage of them.

AP courses are designed to allow students in high school to take individual college-level classes in subjects of their choosing. The IB is a rigorous two-year curriculum covering a range of subjects, also at the college level. Both are prized among college admissions officers at selective colleges, since they each culminate in rigorous subject matter tests scored by independent graders using calibrated standards. Strong performance in these courses (and particularly on the AP and IB tests themselves) indicates that a student can do college-level work. It has also become fairly common for students, particularly juniors and seniors, to take classes at a local community college or nearby four-year college in subjects where the students have exhausted their high school's offerings. College admissions officers also favorably note these classes.

The bottom line is that a straight A record will not make up for a weak course load if your school offers the option of more advanced coursework. Good grades are important, but the rigor of your course load is even more important. Many high schools reward a student who has taken a challenging course with a weighted grade at the end of the semester. If an A in a regular course is worth four points, for example, an A in an AP class may be worth five points. Grade weighting sometimes extends to the pluses and minuses that a student may receive as well, so that an A+ in an AP course might be assigned a total of 5.25 points, while an A– in such a course might be worth 4.75 points. The weighting of honors, IB, and AP classes can result in some astronomical grade point averages (GPAs) for students who take heavy loads of such courses and do exceptionally well in them.

> If your school offers AP classes, you look bad not taking them. You shouldn't take so many that you get bad grades, but you need to challenge yourself.
>
> COLLEGE FRESHMAN REFLECTING ON THE HIGH SCHOOL EXPERIENCE

It is sometimes disheartening for students to learn that some colleges recompute each applicant's GPA in unweighted form, including only the years (usually tenth, eleventh, and twelfth) and classes (usually academic "solids" such as English, foreign language, math, science, and social studies) they wish to consider. Admissions officers do this to have a common standard for discussion. But despite any recalculation, due consideration will be given to the nature of the courses you are taking, within the context of the opportunities you have had. A high GPA in a weak curriculum will definitely be less well received by a selective college than a somewhat more mixed record in a challenging one. In addition, two students may have similar GPAs in comparable courses, although one has shown improvement over time while the other has grades that have been declining. The evaluation of these two students' academic records will be very different; improvement over time will be viewed much more favorably by admissions staff. This is another example of how the evaluation process considers an applicant's record in context.

Putting the GPA in Context

While colleges place great emphasis on grades and courses, they recognize that grades can be hard to evaluate in isolation. Everyone, including college admissions officers, knows that some high schools (and some teachers) are generous with top marks, while others have more rigorous standards. Grade inflation has become a serious problem at many high schools, both public and private. According to the College Board, 43 percent of students in the high school graduating class of 2008 who took the SAT reported GPAs of at least A–. Fifteen years earlier the figure was just 32 percent.

Grade inflation is a major reason selective colleges like to see students do well on AP tests in addition to doing well in the courses themselves. The AP tests you take at the end of the academic year are scored by the College Board according to national norms, so a student who gets a 4 or 5 on an AP exam (scored 1 to 5 with 5 as the highest possible) has demonstrated excellent mastery of the material, independent of local grading standards. Selective colleges invite, but do not require, students to self-report AP test scores, and you are certainly under no obligation to report disappointing scores. But admissions offices will expect to see AP test results from most of the AP courses you have taken through your junior year, or they may question the rigor of the courses themselves.

Some high schools assign a class rank to students on the basis of GPA. Class rank provides information about a student's grades relative to classmates, and colleges have found it makes the task of evaluating grades easier. But fewer and fewer high schools now compute class rank. Private schools in particular are reluctant to rank their students, since they believe it promotes a more competitive environment and magnifies small or insignificant differences in achievement. Class rank also ignores the strength of the student body overall. A student ranked in the lower half of the class at one school might rank in the

> There is simply too much variance between schools, their grading policies, and individual grading by teachers for GPAs to have much meaning by themselves.
>
> HIGH SCHOOL COUNSELOR COMMENTING ON VARIABILITY IN THE GPA

top 10 percent at another. Increasingly, public high schools are recognizing these same drawbacks and have stopped ranking their students as well. The absence of explicit class rank makes the job of the admissions office more challenging, but colleges adapt to it and use the information that is available to get a sense of where students stand in their class, more or less.

The School Profile

High schools generally include a "school profile" with each transcript sent as part of a college application. The profile provides summary information about the school's curriculum and grading policies so that a college can get a general idea of how a student has performed relative to the rest of the class. A profile may show the grade range for each decile of the senior class, as well as the percentage of students who go on to four-year colleges directly from that high school, along with other statistics about the student body such as the SAT distribution, number of students taking and passing AP tests, and so forth. Colleges use this information to supplement data on class rank, or to provide much-needed context when class rank is not provided. Colleges also require students to have a school official, usually a counselor, complete a recommendation form that includes an evaluation of the rigor of a student's academic program relative to the offerings at the high school. This is another way for colleges to calibrate a student's grades while trying to ensure that students from poorer schools that do not offer many advanced classes are not penalized for not having taken a program chock-full of them.

Part of the "college mania" noted in the Introduction is the frequently quoted tidbit that Harvard denies admission to more than 75 percent of the high school valedictorians who apply each year. Several other super-selective and highly selective colleges also deny a majority of the valedictorian applicants. But if you reflect on this for a minute, it is not really surprising. There are more than twenty-seven thousand high schools, both public and private, in the United States. Each of them has someone (or often several students) who achieved the highest grades. Clearly, grades can't be the whole story in college admissions—there are too many students with very high grades, and too much variation in what those grades really mean—for grades alone to determine who is admitted to a selective college.

STANDARDIZED TESTS

Most selective colleges require standardized tests such as the SAT or the ACT. The question students ask most often is how much the tests count in admissions decisions. David Erdmann, dean of admissions at Rollins College, has perhaps given the most candid answer of all: "At most institutions, standardized test scores count less than students think and more than colleges are willing to admit."[3]

How Do Colleges Use the SAT?

Standardized tests seem more objective to colleges because they are independent of the varying grading standards of high schools. They also help separate students from each other since grade inflation means that grades alone no longer do that well. But the tests are not without their critics (we talk much more about standardized tests in Chapter Six) and most colleges are wary of relying too heavily on them because of doubts about what they really measure and lingering concerns that they may be biased in some way. Of special concern is the growth of the test prep industry, which often claims to guarantee significant score improvements for students who take special courses that can cost $1,000 or more. Clearly, usually only those who can afford to pay for those classes can take them.

In response to these concerns, some selective liberal arts colleges have made standardized tests optional—the decision whether to submit scores is left to the student. We discuss test-optional schools and how to find them in Chapter Six. New schools are going test-optional with some frequency.

Despite calls to eliminate standardized tests entirely from the college admissions process, it is likely that the tests will continue to be used by most selective colleges for the foreseeable future. With grades difficult to interpret, most colleges are unwilling to lose the additional information, however imperfect, that a test like the SAT provides.

The College Board, the organization that owns and administers the SAT, encourages colleges to report the SAT scores of the middle 50 percent of their freshman class rather than average SAT scores when providing information to prospective students. It is more useful to know the 25–75 percent midrange of scores (each part of the test is graded on a scale from 200 to 800) than a single average score, since the range gives you some information about how scores are actually distributed. Knowing that the midrange for the freshman class was 570 to 730 on the math section, for example, is more useful than simply knowing that the average score was 650.

> I don't think the SATs are a fair indication of someone's potential for college. The math is insanely tricky. And they're so long. Four hours. By the end, you just can't think. You start making silly mistakes.
>
> HIGH SCHOOL SENIOR WHO WONDERS WHAT THE SAT REALLY MEASURES

Evaluating Your Score

In general, if your test scores fall roughly in the middle 50 percent range of a selective college's freshman class SAT distribution, they won't hurt or help your chances of admission much, but the greater they diverge from the middle, up or down, the more they will help or hurt your chances accordingly. In the example just discussed, a math score of 740 or greater would fall in the top 25 percent of the freshman class and be likely to help make your case for admission. Just how much a higher score will help depends on the actual score, the weight the college places on it, and the rest of your record. Scores falling in the lowest 25 percent of the freshman class for a selective college (560 or less in this example) would usually need to be offset by one or more compelling factors (for example, an outstanding academic record or, as discussed later in this chapter, a special *hook*) for you to be a viable candidate at that college, especially if the college's admission rate is relatively low; that is, it is selective.

SAT scores have also experienced inflation. In the mid-1990s, the College Board "recentered" the test to offset the fact that the average score on each part of the test had been declining over time. As a result of recentering, SAT scores appeared to dramatically improve by as much as 120 points out of a possible total of 1600. In reality, only the numbers and not the actual performance had changed. SAT recentering is the main reason why Baby Boomer parents who took the SAT themselves as teenagers often find that their children's scores are more impressive than their own.

ENGAGEMENT BEYOND THE CLASSROOM: THE EXTRACURRICULAR RECORD

Selective colleges expect students not only to be strong academically but also to be interesting, contributing members of the campus community and the community at large. Colleges used to talk about the importance of being well-rounded and showing evidence of leadership in extracurricular activities. Now admissions officers talk about having a well-rounded class composed of students who each have exceptional talent or commitment in one or two areas. The shift reflects the reality that there are just so many hours in the day and that achieving excellence in a given area can take up most of those hours. Or as David Gould, former dean of admissions at Brandeis, has said, "The embodiment at age seventeen of a Renaissance person is difficult to find. We realized we could accomplish the same thing [for our freshman class] with lots of different people."[4] Colleges look to see whether a student has made a sustained commitment to an activity over a number of years; involvement in one long-term activity can be more impressive than involvement in several short-term ones. Sometimes admissions officers speak about students having "passions." We think "commitment" is a better term, and it is the one we choose to use.

Extracurricular Activities

But just what does exceptional talent or commitment mean? In general, the more selective the college, the higher the bar for evaluating extracurricular activities and leadership. Involvement in debate, for example, can range from participating on a team to winning occasional local tournaments to having a winning record at the regional, state, or national level. The more selective the college, the higher the level of achievement it takes to impress admissions officers. Being a dedicated member of the school orchestra is good, but being first violinist and student concertmaster is better. Better still is winning regional, state, national, or even international competitions as a soloist. We address the special case of athletic talent later in this chapter, under the topic of hooks.

Colleges like to see evidence of leadership in an applicant as well. Being president of an active high school club, serving as a student body officer, or editing the high school newspaper or yearbook are all examples of high school leadership activities commonly seen on applications to selective colleges. In general, the more selective the college, the greater the expectation that applicants will hold leadership positions and that they will be at the highest levels, possibly extending beyond the high school to local, regional, and state organizations. Colleges differ, however, in the emphasis they place on leadership. Fred Hargadon, long-time dean of admission at Princeton, was well known for preferring to see

> Have you seen *Gilmore Girls,* the TV show? There's a character on there who really wants to go to Harvard. She is frantically calling soup kitchens right before Thanksgiving because she won't get into Harvard if she doesn't work at a soup kitchen over Thanksgiving and she's going crazy because she has to work at a soup kitchen. I think that's insane.
>
> HIGH SCHOOL SENIOR WITH FOCUSED INTERESTS

evidence of perseverance in applicants rather than leadership itself. Complicating matters is that leadership can be difficult to assess meaningfully, since the same position can vary greatly in importance and responsibility from high school to high school.

Community Service

Many colleges also like to see that a student has been willing to contribute time and effort to help others through community service. There are lots of ways to do this, and in fact some high schools require a certain number of hours of community service for graduation. Just as in extracurricular activities, sustained involvement over time is a plus, and a major time commitment will have more impact on your application than one that is less extensive. Generally, a leadership role in a community service activity, in addition to a major time commitment to it, will have the most impact of all since it reflects the student's energy level and ability to work effectively with others.

Work Experience

Most college applications give students an opportunity to list their work experience. Depending on its nature, paid work can nicely complement a student's special interests (for example, designing Web pages or working with developmentally disabled children). Work can also demonstrate leadership ability, if the student has a job that involves supervising others. Finally, an extensive work commitment can reflect the student's socioeconomic background and indicate that the income is important to supporting the student and even the family. Admissions officers realize that work responsibilities of this type can limit how much time a student can devote to other activities.

> Students who do activities out of their own interests and passions and who create activities for themselves stand out—even if the activities were done down the street and not in an exotic locale. Students who do activities because their parents pay for them and they need résumé dressing are a dime a dozen and blend into the overall pool.
>
> PARENT WITH EXPERIENCE IN THE ADMISSIONS PROCESS

Follow Your Commitments

In Chapter Nine, we discuss how you can share information about your extracurricular, community service, and work experiences as part of your application. Students interested in applying to selective colleges sometimes try to get involved in specific activities, such as community service, that they think will look good to college admissions officers. In reality, admissions officers prefer a student who has had sustained involvement in one or more activities and grown from them—it doesn't much matter what those activities are.

Second-guessing what colleges want is usually futile—and not much fun. Do what you love. It makes much more sense to get involved in what really interests you than to try to fit your interests to some preconceived (and probably inaccurate) idea about what colleges want to see.

PERSONAL QUALITIES: THE PERSON BEHIND THE PAPER

You know that your written record—test scores, GPA, and even your list of extracurricular activities—doesn't tell the whole story of who you are right now and what kind of person you might become. For that reason, colleges request subjective information as well: letters from people who know you, essays, and in some cases, an interview.

Letters

As we discuss in Chapter Nine, almost all selective colleges require a letter of recommendation from a student's high school counselor and one or two letters from teachers. (The University of California system and some other public universities are notable exceptions.) Most private colleges ask for two letters from teachers, but a few (Georgetown University, the University of Southern California, and St. Olaf College, for example) ask for only one. Admissions officers look at letters for evidence that a student has, for want of a better word, "sparkle." They are looking for someone who is smart, intellectually curious, good-hearted, talented, and energetic.

Letters of recommendation can vary widely, however, in their usefulness. Sheila McMillen taught English at the University of Virginia and was drafted one year to serve as a reader in the undergraduate admissions office. This is how she described her experience reading letters: "I had to take into account that the harried guidance counselors at the large urban school, writing hundreds of recommendations, often did not know the applicant well—this letter would be short and vague. The applicants attending private schools, where the rate of college acceptances is an important recruiting tool, received four-page tomes from their counselors. . . . Fairness demanded that I factor in the inequity, but invariably I was told more—though in hyperbolic terms—about the private school student than I ever learned about the public school one."[5]

Although four-page letters are very rare from any counselor, private or public, the lesson here is clear. Regardless of where you go to high school, try to get to know your counselor, even if your opportunities are limited. Some students go to schools with low student-to-counselor ratios and can get to know a counselor easily. Others have to work harder at it. It's not always easy, and it isn't fair, but it can be done.

It is also to your advantage to get to know several teachers well since you will have to ask one or two of them to write on your behalf. Being memorable (in a positive way) and being an active participant in your classes are the best ways to ensure that your teachers will be willing to write and will have something helpful to say. Hold on to your best papers and projects from your classes. At letter-writing time you may want to remind the teachers you ask for references about the work you did in their classes. A few colleges (for example, Reed College, Sarah Lawrence College, Bard College, and Mount Holyoke College) even ask applicants to submit a graded school paper, so you may have additional uses for work that you have saved.

The Essay

Perhaps no other part of the application process besides the SAT or ACT is as dreaded as the essay. The essay seems to ask students to expose themselves to a stranger who will be judging their person, not just their grades and scores. It is also something students have not done much of before; they know colleges want high grades and scores, but what exactly does a college want in an essay? Just what does it mean to "be yourself" in an essay? It is important to remember that these essays are an opportunity to show how you write, but more important, how you think and how you have been able to learn from your experiences. Some colleges require one long essay

> Save for the few instances in which candidates write essays so completely lacking in taste as to make us marvel at the fact that they even bothered to apply, in my experience no one is ever admitted solely on the basis of a great essay and no one was ever denied admission solely on the basis of a poor essay.[6]
>
> FRED HARGADON, FORMER DEAN OF ADMISSION AT PRINCETON UNIVERSITY

of about five hundred words, some require two. Short paragraph-length answers to specific questions are also often required.

College admissions officers see the essay as one more way to gain insight into who the student is. With so many applicants who look similar in terms of grades, GPAs, and activities, the essay becomes a way for you to convey your own individuality. So it is good to look at the essay as an opportunity to be thoughtful about yourself, not as something to be dreaded. An effective essay leaves readers feeling that they have gotten to know the student, and that they like what they see.

How much do essays count in admissions decisions? A recent survey attempting to answer this question found that students and parents rated the essay as more important than admissions officers said it was. But the results confirmed that the essay can still make a difference in the admissions decision.[7]

A good essay can strengthen an application to a selective school, particularly if your qualifications are already strong. Not surprisingly, a boring, poorly written, arrogant, or silly essay can hurt your chances, especially if your qualifications are borderline. But even if your record is very strong, a weak essay can spoil your chances at a college that has many strong candidates to choose from. An essay that falls in the middle—neither strong nor weak but simply undistinguished—does little to reduce the reader's uncertainty about accepting you based on the rest of your file. A wise student tries to have as many factors in the "plus" column as possible—including the essay, which need not be dreaded if you start early. We talk more about writing your essays in Chapter Eight.

Interviews

Interviews are perhaps the most misunderstood part of the college admissions process. Some colleges find them helpful in the overall evaluation of candidates, while others see them as a way for students to get more information about a college. Some feel they add little value to the admissions process for either the student or the college and don't offer any interviews at all.

In a small percentage of cases, new information becomes available through an interview—either exceptionally positive or exceptionally negative. A student who acts boorish or immature could have an application jeopardized by an interview, but short of such exceptional behavior, an interview is unlikely to affect the outcome of an admissions decision negatively. Most of the time, an interview confirms, more or less, what is already clear from the application. A great interview, however, may serve as a small tip factor in favor of admission.

Since it is hard to predict whether, and by how much, an interview will count, it is best to approach it as a serious yet friendly conversation that will give you a chance to personalize your candidacy, especially if you are applying to a smaller college. If nothing else, participating in an interview indicates your interest in a college. As noted in Chapter One, "demonstrated interest" may be part of the decision-making process at some colleges, especially in close cases. Chapter Nine talks more about the different kinds of interviews, what you can expect, and how you can make a good impression.

HOOKS

In admissions parlance, a *hook* is a special characteristic a college deems desirable, over and above the qualities it is generally seeking in its students. Hooks are institutional priorities that don't appear explicitly on any of the admissions forms but that can be powerful factors, tipping the outcome in favor of the applicant. A good understanding of the different kinds of hooks and their role in admissions decisions can help you appreciate the many considerations beyond the traditional academic and extracurricular record that can lead to an "admissions tip."

> Most applicants compete not with the whole applicant pool but within specific categories, where the applicant-to-available space ratio may be more, or less, favorable than in the pool at large. . . . Students in the selected categories, which vary from institution to institution, have a "hook" because they help meet institutional needs.[8]
>
> PAUL MARTHERS, DEAN OF ADMISSION AT REED COLLEGE, REFLECTING ON ADMISSIONS PRACTICES AT SELECTIVE INSTITUTIONS

Legacy Status

A *legacy* is a child of someone who received an undergraduate degree from the school (and the alum doesn't even have to be famous). Some colleges, like MIT and the University of Pennsylvania, also count grandchildren of alumni as legacies, and a few, like Stanford University, consider children to be legacies if a parent received an undergraduate or graduate degree there. Colleges are usually eager to recruit legacy children, since they believe that legacies are likely to have a strong commitment to their parent's college, accept an offer of admission, and become enthusiastic, contributing students. Parents, in turn, like the idea of having a child follow in their footsteps and are more likely to support their alma mater financially and in other ways if their child enrolls there.

Another reason for the legacy practice is the image of the college as a humane, caring community. Legacy status is sometimes regarded as akin to giving preference to a member of one's own family. But the bottom line plays a major role as well. Giving special admissions preference to legacies can be a wise financial decision for colleges that depend heavily on contributions to support their programs. Colleges and universities throughout the country regularly solicit alumni for donations. Tuition pays only part of the cost of educating a student at private institutions, so fundraising and other forms of external support are critical for colleges to operate successfully. Many public research universities also receive considerably less than half of their funding from state sources and tuition. While legacy status may be a factor in admissions at some public institutions, it plays an important role in admissions at most private ones. Some private colleges, in fact, have special information sessions for legacy applicants, special legacy-only interviews, and staff assigned to deal specifically with legacy concerns.

How Big Is the Legacy Advantage?

At many selective private colleges, legacies tend to be admitted at up to twice the overall rate of admission or more. At Dartmouth College, for example, where about 30 percent of legacy applicants were offered admission to the class of 2012, less than 13 percent of applicants overall were admitted. At Middlebury College, about 48 percent of legacy applicants for the class of 2012 were accepted compared to the general acceptance rate of 18 percent.

> We take a look at the level of loyalty— contributions, alumni interviewing, etc. that graduates have maintained over the years. If alumni have been engaged in the community since they left, supporting them in return just makes sense.[9]
>
> CHARLES DEACON, DEAN OF UNDERGRADUATE ADMISSIONS AT GEORGETOWN UNIVERSITY

> If it weren't for the generosity of alumni, we would not be able to provide the education we do. So yes, we do give preference.[10]
>
> THOMAS PARKER, DEAN OF ADMISSIONS AND FINANCIAL AID AT AMHERST COLLEGE

The Legacy of Being a Legacy

My daughter was a legacy candidate at the Ivy League college I attended back in the 1960s. She liked the school, too, and applied early action, which guaranteed a response on December 15.

She jumped for joy when the coveted big envelope arrived. We hugged and danced around the house. She grabbed the telephone.

After a few calls, however, she returned to the living room looking suddenly weary. More than weary, she looked distressed.

"How do I know they really want me?" she asked. "Maybe I just got in because of you."

I reassured her that her SAT scores and her GPA were all mid-range for the college. I got ready to pull out the *Fiske Guide* to prove it. But this wasn't about numbers. Like me, my daughter knew that the tiniest tweak can sometimes make the difference between acceptance and denial. It was perfectly natural for her to worry that being a legacy, rather than her own accomplishments, had given her an edge.

Meanwhile, I—the proud mother—thought about all the factors that legitimately make her special. Any one of them could have led to her success: playing the oboe, reading every book Jane Austen ever wrote, publishing a humorous essay in the local newspaper. Maybe she hadn't slid in on a legacy but marched in on diligence and skill.

We would never know, of course, although years later, when I started working on this book, my husband said, "Maybe you could have access to her file now. Find out why she got in."

I shrugged him off because it doesn't matter anymore.

My daughter tells me that the feeling of not being worthy did persist well into her time at college. It hurt whenever she heard the word *legacy*. Then her grades started accumulating, and she realized that she was not only up to the rigors of an Ivy League school, she excelled.

Finally, she felt that she deserved to be there.

M. F.

Admission rates differ partly because the legacy pool overall is usually somewhat stronger than the general applicant pool. Also, many legacies choose to apply early action or early decision, which, by itself, can boost the chances of admission. But clearly a separate, distinct boost comes with legacy status at many institutions. Being a legacy by no means ensures admission, however, since selective colleges have low admission rates to begin with.

The practice of legacy admissions comes under fire from time to time as inconsistent with the values of equal opportunity. Critics claim that because most alumni of selective colleges are well-off Caucasians, the use of legacy status as an admissions factor amounts to affirmative action for well-to-do white students. Colleges, however, claim that the legacy preference is small while the benefit to the institution is potentially great. They see alumni as a major source of donations, some of which support need-based financial aid programs that help diversify the student body. Alumni whose children are admitted, the colleges argue, are more likely to make the contributions that make institutionally based financial aid possible for those who need it, and it keeps the family of the college together for another generation. For now, legacy status continues to be a hook, and an important one, at most private colleges, selective by our definition or not.

Development Admits

Many selective colleges have a small number of so-called development admits each year—students who would be unlikely to be admitted were it not for their potential to bring significant donations to the college. Some alumni are major donors to a college. Their children get a double hook when they apply—as legacies as well as development cases. In addition, the nonlegacy children of wealthy donors who have contributed significant sums of money to a college (or are about to do so) are also hooked.

There are typically ten or fewer major development cases each year. There is a rigorous standard to be treated as a development case. Significant donations over a period of years such as donating a building or something. Schools with big endowments don't really give that much advantage because their applicant pools are so large and well qualified and because they have so much money.[11]

KARL FURSTENBERG, FORMER DEAN OF ADMISSIONS AND FINANCIAL AID AT DARTMOUTH COLLEGE

How big a donation does it have to be? This varies from college to college, and not surprisingly, colleges do not advertise what those amounts might be. Colleges justify development admits because of the institution's need for additional funding to support the school in various ways. The development office is probably not actively involved in recruiting such students. But once they enter the applicant pool, development admits are usually flagged for special admissions consideration. In these cases, admissions staff determine whether such students can do the work that will allow them to graduate from the institution. The ability to graduate from the college, not an easy thing to define, is usually what is meant when an institution says that a student is "qualified" to attend.

Development admits don't significantly affect the admission of other students because there aren't very many of them. Nevertheless, the practice is kept low profile to avoid publicity that would call attention to it. This changed, at least for a while, with the publication of *The Price of Admission* by Daniel Golden, a former *Wall Street Journal* reporter who threw new light on these often-controversial practices.[12] The colleges were generally not pleased with the publicity, but none of them argued with his facts.

Underrepresented Students

Being a member of a traditionally underrepresented group (African American, Native American, or Hispanic) can also be a hook at colleges eager to diversify their student bodies. Asian Americans are occasionally included in this group, especially at colleges in parts of the country with low Asian American populations, but most often are not. Most colleges believe that a diverse student body is an essential part of a high-quality educational experience for all students, and many applicants agree.

The diversity hook in college admissions is formally known as race-sensitive admissions or, more commonly, as affirmative action. Race-sensitive admissions policies were challenged on the constitutional level in a case heard by the Supreme Court in 2003. *Gratz v. Bollinger* involved a white student denied admission to the University of Michigan's College of Literature and Science, although she had higher GPA and standardized test scores than some African American, Hispanic, and Native American applicants who were admitted. (Lee Bollinger, now president of Columbia University, was president of the University of Michigan when the lawsuit was first filed; hence the case bears his name.)

The Court ruled 6–3 against Michigan's policy of awarding an additional twenty points, out of a possible 150, to students who fell into one of these three racial categories (100 points were sufficient to earn admission to the university). The majority of the Court believed that a system that automatically awarded a substantial bonus to those belonging to particular groups placed too much emphasis on race. At the same time, however, a majority of the Court upheld racial and ethnic diversity as a "compelling state interest" and reaffirmed the importance of giving colleges and universities some leeway in how they make decisions. Although a simple point system can no longer be used to achieve diversity, the Court's ruling allows colleges to use race as a factor in the decision mix in more subtle ways.

Most colleges that practice race-sensitive admissions have been unaffected by the ruling, since they did not use a point system to begin with. They can continue to consider race in the admissions process as they have in the past to ensure a diverse student body. Campuses using a point system had to revise their processes, however, to continue to consider race in admissions. The ruling does not affect campuses that do not practice race-sensitive admissions. *Gratz v. Bollinger* does not apply to public universities in California and Florida, for example, since state laws there prohibit public universities from using race-sensitive admissions in any form. Ensuring diversity without directly considering race has been a major challenge for those campuses.

Recruited Athletes

Yet another important institutional priority or hook is outstanding athletic ability. Many selective colleges have active athletics programs (Harvard, for example, has forty-one varsity teams) that they see as integral to the college experience. The student body wants the school's teams to win. So does the development office, whose fundraising success may rise and fall along with teams' win-loss record. Most selective colleges allow coaches to identify a limited number of athletes they strongly support for admission. We define a recruited athlete as one who earns a spot on the coach's final list for admissions purposes. The more important the sport at a college, the greater the weight of a coach's recommendations for admission. For basketball and football, the two highest-profile sports on most campuses, the coach's recommendation counts for a lot. Although some recruited athletes have fine academic records that would earn them admission independent of their special talent, some do not.

In *Reclaiming the Game,* William Bowen, former president of Princeton University, and his associate Sarah Levin, examined the role of athletic recruiting in the admissions process at Ivy League universities and selective liberal arts colleges.[13] They present convincing data showing that some recruited athletes are only marginally qualified to attend the college that recruited them and that as a group, recruited athletes tend to underperform in college. *Underperforming* means that students do less well academically than would be predicted by their precollege academic record.

> The kids who get in on sports, they're good enough students to go there and hang in there, but they're not always students who were good enough to have gotten there on academics alone.
>
> HIGH SCHOOL SENIOR WHO UNDERSTANDS THE ATHLETIC HOOK

What Is the Admissions Advantage for Athletes?

Bowen and Levin present data showing what they call the "admissions advantage" for athletes at Ivy League colleges—the difference between the average admission probability for a recruited athlete and the average admission probability for any other applicant after controlling for differences in academic records. The difference for male and female athletes was 51 percent and 56 percent, respectively. Since the average probability of admission in the Ivy League was around 15 percent, they reasoned that a boost of 51 percentage points meant that a typical male athletic recruit had an admission probability of 66 percent (the 15 percent base rate for everyone added to the 51 percent athletic advantage). The average male recruited athlete, then, had four times the chance of being admitted to an Ivy League college than a male student with a comparable academic record who was not a recruited athlete and had no other hooks.

The admissions advantage for underrepresented minorities and legacies, calculated in the same manner, turned out to be much smaller. Using the same Ivy League data set, Bowen and Levin report that the admissions advantage for underrepresented men and women was 26 percent and 31 percent, respectively. For male and female legacies, the respective admissions advantages were 26 percent and 28 percent. Although the Bowen and Levin data are now ten years old, experienced counselors believe that their conclusions generally hold today as well. Thus, exceptional athletic ability may be the strongest hook of all at most selective colleges, aside, perhaps, from development, where the data are not public. We talk at greater length about athletes and college admissions in Chapter Nine.

Socioeconomic and Geographic Diversity

Most selective colleges are eager to assemble a freshman class from a wide variety of backgrounds. Colleges are particularly interested in identifying students who are the first in their families to attend college and have succeeded against the odds. These are often called "first-generation" students. High school students from disadvantaged backgrounds who do well in school despite the challenges of low income or poor schools, or both, are likely to be highly motivated, successful college students.

Colleges are becoming increasingly aware of the need to actively seek out and support such students, since they have less access to information about college and may not even apply to selective colleges. In 2004, Harvard University made national headlines by announcing a change in its financial aid policy so that families with annual incomes of $40,000 or less would no longer be expected to contribute to the cost of attendance. "We want to send the strongest possible message that Harvard is open to talented students from all economic backgrounds," said President Lawrence Summers at that time.[14] Since then, Harvard has raised the income ceiling to $60,000, and several other well-endowed colleges, including Dartmouth College, Princeton University, and Stanford University, have made similar changes to their financial aid policies.

Geographical diversity is another variable that many colleges consider in selecting their freshman class, since geographical diversity often correlates with diversity of life experience. Students who come from underrepresented parts of the country can find themselves at an advantage when it comes to admission to a selective college. But the definition of *underrepresented region* is relative; it depends in part on the college in question. Although few students from Nevada may apply to Colby College in Maine, Pitzer College in California is likely to have an ample supply from which to choose. Talented students from sparsely populated Wyoming or rural Mississippi are in short supply everywhere. Major exceptions to the geographic diversity advantage are selective public institutions such as the University of Texas, the University of North Carolina at Chapel Hill, and the University of California, Berkeley. In these cases, students from other states are held to higher standards for admission.

It is interesting that while many private colleges seek geographic diversity in their student body, they may also give a small preference to students from their own local area in an effort to build goodwill with the community. Tufts University, Duke University, and Northeastern University are among those that acknowledge this kind of preference.

Special Talents

Still other hooks include exceptional talent—in music, dance, or ice skating; as a visual artist or published writer; or as a scientist, among others—that a college would like to have represented in its student body. An Olympic ice skater, someone who has appeared in commercial films, the author of a published novel, and the winner of a major Intel science award—all of these applicants have hooks based on exceptional talent that will catch the attention of admissions committees. A diverse class with a wide range of exceptional talents is an interesting class. Some of these talents, for example, the science award winner or the published author, may add to the educational mission of the school. Others may just add some glamour. Although the majority of students admitted even to the most selective colleges do not have a special talent at this level, some do. If you are fortunate enough to fall into this category, it will be a definite plus in your evaluation. In Chapter Nine, we talk about how a student with a special talent can bring this to the attention of admissions officers.

Are hooks fair? This is a tough question. If you have one, you are likely to be glad of it; in the highly competitive world of admissions these days, few students are willing to give up an advantage, real or imagined. If you don't have a hook, and most applicants don't, you may feel that the system is structured against you in some way. Unfortunately, this contributes to the widely held idea that admissions is a game and you have to know the fine points of the rules to win. If you find yourself feeling this way, remember that a majority of students admitted to every college do not have one of these hooks, and that most students are admitted on the basis of the normal mixture of criteria: grades, test scores, activities, essays, and recommendations.

FITTING IT ALL TOGETHER

We hope this chapter has given you a good sense of the many factors that play a role in selective college admissions. Another important consideration—the timing of a student's application—is covered in Chapter Seven, which deals with early acceptance programs. There is no single answer to how college admissions offices weight these factors and what process they use to make their decisions. Each college is free to shape its own admissions policies and practices based on college priorities, tradition, and sometimes the previous experience of a newly hired admissions dean. In the next chapter, we consider how selective colleges generally go about the actual process of reviewing applications to reach their decision about whom they will admit.

CHAPTER 3

How Do Colleges Make Their Decisions?

For most students and their parents, the college admissions process is shrouded in mystery. Hundreds of thousands of applications are submitted every year to selective colleges. Each one distills the academic and personal accomplishments of a teenager hoping for admission. In return, after a period ranging from a few weeks to several months, the college's verdict arrives: the student is accepted, denied, wait-listed, or (in the case of some early applicants) deferred until a later round of decision making. This chapter focuses on what goes on behind the scenes between the time a student submits an application and the time the mail carrier (or, more often these days, the computer) delivers the college's response.

Personal glimpses into the confidential process of college admissions can be found in books written by former admissions officers, as well as in the firsthand reports of journalists who have had the opportunity to observe college admissions deliberations as the proverbial fly on the wall. Although specific details vary from college to college and change with time, most selective colleges go about choosing students in much the same way. This makes it fairly easy to construct a composite picture that captures the essence of the process for all of them.

WHO WORKS IN ADMISSIONS?

The people who work in college admissions have varied backgrounds. Some make college admissions their careers and have many years of related experience, whereas others come to admissions after working outside higher education entirely. Or they can be younger people, spending a few years in admissions before starting graduate school or embarking on other careers. Often the latter are recent graduates of the college where they work who display the energy, maturity, and dedication to do a good job in a very demanding position.

Colleges want an ethnically diverse admissions staff with varied personal interests and backgrounds. In addition to being sensitive to affirmative action, colleges consciously want different life perspectives to be heard at the table at decision time. The regular admissions officers who represent the school play the most important role in the actual decision-making process. The larger schools with many thousands of applications also hire "readers" to help evaluate applicant files. Readers do not usually participate in making the final decisions.

Evaluating applications is only part of an admissions officer's job, however. Admissions officers typically do much more than read applications and make decisions. The most senior officers work with the dean of admissions, who heads the office, to develop the strategy for spreading the word about the college. This includes planning all the brochures, letters, and other mailings that come from the admissions office, as well as the Web site that increasingly has become the major way students and parents receive information about a college. They decide who will get which mailings and when they will get them. Applications and viewbooks, of course, are sent to all students who request them, but special unsolicited mailings from some colleges target selected students as early as their sophomore year. We talk more about these mailings in Chapter Five.

AMBASSADORS *AND* GATEKEEPERS

Because outreach to prospective students involves much more than mailings, admissions officers play a role as ambassadors, personally spreading the word about their college. Each fall, they spend as many as six to eight weeks on the road, visiting high schools to meet with students and counselors. Some colleges assign their officers to different regions of the country (and increasingly to foreign countries), so these visits help officers learn more about the high schools in those areas. Officers also participate in college nights at schools, hotels, or community centers in their assigned region. These events, sometimes hosted by a single college but often by several together, are a way to familiarize parents and students with a college. More of them are being held in the spring to reach juniors as the following year's application cycle begins.

> This morning the U.S. mail delivered thirty tubs full of applications, counselor statements, and teacher recommendations. Two staff members spent all day just opening the envelopes, another fifteen concentrated on logging everything in, and yet our mail room still looks as though a paper bomb went off in it.
>
> ADMISSIONS STAFFER AT A LARGE PUBLIC UNIVERSITY

Admissions officers also conduct group information sessions on their campus for visitors to the college. Each fall brings a steady, continuing stream of high school seniors (and, increasingly, juniors and even sophomores) and their parents to visit colleges. These one-hour information sessions, along with a student-led campus tour, attempt to communicate to visitors what makes the college special.

Once the fruits of the admissions officers' outreach efforts arrive—the large pool of applications from eager, well-prepared high school seniors—the primary focus of their work shifts. Formerly ambassadors, admissions officers now become gatekeepers, determining who is admitted and who is denied.

WHAT HAPPENS TO YOUR FILE?

Thousands upon thousands of pieces of correspondence descend upon college admissions offices right around application deadlines—the applications themselves, letters of recommendation from teachers, and transcripts and counselor recommendations. All of it has to be opened, date stamped, and sorted into applicants' files. The physical task of doing this is staggering and very time-consuming. Despite the definite trend toward online applications and even online review, the process is still paper-intensive. Some colleges that accept online applications still print them out before they are read, so that adds to the deluge of paper as well. But once a file is complete, with all parts accounted for, it is ready for review.

At a typical college, especially a selective one, an application file may be read twice, and sometimes more than that, depending on the file itself. Of the two people who review a file, one is frequently the admissions officer assigned to the part of the country where an applicant attends school. This same officer may have visited an applicant's high school early in the fall to meet students and the school counselor and may also have conducted a formal regional presentation for parents and students at a hotel in a nearby city. The other evaluator is often randomly selected from among the remaining admissions officers or readers. Sometimes both evaluators are randomly selected. Many colleges also have an admissions officer assigned the task of recruiting applicants from one or more minority groups. The appropriate officer may read the file of students of color as a third reader. A few colleges (for example, Cal Tech and the University of Michigan) actively involve faculty members in the routine review of files, but many more use faculty as occasional evaluators of special talents—mathematical, musical, and so forth—where a professional assessment is needed.

Reading

Each of the two people assigned to a given file reads it thoroughly. The first person to read a file is usually responsible for extracting key information and entering it into an electronic file or on a summary card. Grades, class rank, SAT or ACT scores, notations about curriculum, codes for extracurricular activities—all get entered for an at-a-glance view of the file in objective terms. Other factors are noted as well—any special interest in the applicant by coaches or the development office, minority background, exceptional talents, and so forth.

Both readers then write summary comments about the candidate's essay (or essays), letters of recommendation, and personal qualities that convey a sense of the student beyond a list of grades and activities. The first reader, whether an admissions officer or part-time reader, will usually make more detailed notes than the second. Those notes are then generally read out loud if the file finds its way to committee discussion. A simple application might take only ten to fifteen minutes to read and work up. A complex file could take thirty minutes to digest fully. Admissions staff typically have to read twenty-five to thirty files a day during peak reading season, which normally runs from early January through mid-March. Long days and weeks are the norm for admissions staff once reading begins. On many campuses an admissions officer may read a thousand files or more over the application cycle.

Rating

Usually each evaluator assigns a rating along at least two dimensions—academic qualifications and personal qualifications—as well as an overall rating that combines the two in some way. The scale used by colleges can vary—from 1 to 5 at one, from 1 to 9 at another. But the idea is the same: to rate applicants along those dimensions as a rough basis for further consideration. Evaluators may have a list of specific qualities to rate as a key to guide them in assigning ratings on the broader dimensions. At Wesleyan University, for example, the academic rating is a rough average of the ratings, from 1 to 9 with 9 the highest possible, in three academic categories: academic achievement, intellectual curiosity, and commitment.[1] SAT or ACT scores get factored into the overall academic rating as well. And where applicant pools are strong, and many students have top grades and strong academic programs, the test scores can play an important role in separating students out on a linear scale.

At Wesleyan, a rating of 4 in academic achievement is used for those with "fair to good recommendations" with "some weaknesses apparent in application." A rating of 5 is reserved for students with a "solid academic" load, while a rating of 6 or 7 is used for "an excellent academic record in a demanding curriculum." The top ratings of 8 or 9 go to those with a "flawless academic record in the most demanding curriculum." A rating of 5 in intellectual curiosity would go to a student described as "conscientious," while "strong interest and activity" in "research, independent projects, competitions, etc." would receive a rating of 6 or 7. A student with a "sophisticated grasp of world events and technical information" and "passionate interest in numerous disciplines" would be rated 8 or 9 on the intellectual curiosity dimension. Other colleges use similar rating systems but don't try to average the ratings; instead, they simply total the ratings to get an overall score. Personal qualities are rated in a similar manner, with each reader assigning an overall "personal" rating or score based on different aspects of the record, such as evidence of unusual commitment to community service, leadership, or engagement in activities.

Rating systems such as the one at Wesleyan are based on your overall record through high school. Although you will never know the ratings assigned to you by various schools, we describe it to show you how three-plus years of high school can be sifted and analyzed so that very different applicants can be compared to each other on a numerical scale.

TENTATIVE DECISIONS

Once a reader or an admissions officer completes the ratings and notes for a given applicant, it is decision-time to declare the applicant's status: admit, deny, wait-list, or perhaps something less definitive such as admit-minus or deny-plus. On some campuses, the decision can be the equivalent of admit, deny, or further review. (Stanford calls this latter group "swims," as if they are treading water before a final review.) This call can be a very difficult, subjective one. In reality, most applicants to selective colleges can succeed—that is, do well enough to be able to graduate within four years. Who, then, should be given that opportunity?

At this point, the full range of a college's priorities plays out, along with the personal preferences and inclinations of the readers. Colleges are complex academic communities that seek to create a rich, stimulating environment academically, culturally, athletically, and socially. This means crafting a class that includes not only academic superstars but winning athletes, talented performers and musicians, students from all parts of the country and a diverse array of ethnic and socioeconomic backgrounds, the children of alumni, as well as some whose parents are willing and able to make exceptionally generous donations. These categories are not necessarily mutually exclusive, but realistically, few, if any, students can excel in everything. Thus decisions are made about individual students so that the class as a whole embodies the priorities of the campus. Here the hooks described in Chapter Two come into play. With lots of applicants to choose from with similar grades and test scores, schools have a lot of leeway in exactly which students to accept. Institutional priorities can play a big role in the outcome.

Clear-Cut?

Sometimes, though, the decision is clear-cut. Some applicants are so outstanding in dimensions important to the college that the decision is obvious to both reviewers of a file: admit. Sometimes a file may be so outstanding that it is sent right to the dean with a recommendation to admit after being read by only one experienced admissions officer. Colleges that compute a rating total may automatically admit students who score at or above a very high threshold without further review.

Similarly, at the other end of the continuum, files are prescreened to identify applicants who fall far short of a college's standards. Identifying these before they are thoroughly read can help readers save their time for the stronger files that require careful consideration. These decisions can be made on the basis of grades, test scores, or some other easily detected major weakness, relative to the rest of the pool, that cannot be offset by other factors. It may sound harsh to learn that some files get a decision after only five minutes of evaluation, but that can be the case. The number of applications is usually too large for every file to receive the same level of analysis.

> The *New York Times* ran an article yesterday about a Web site that provides kids with the probability of being accepted at eighty elite colleges for a $79.95 fee. I want the admissions staffs at those eighty elite colleges to be aware that there are computer programs out there that know just how and what you think. Before you start your discussions, you may want to make sure the room is not bugged in a clandestine effort to further enhance the prediction software.
>
> SKEPTICAL HIGH SCHOOL COUNSELOR

Sometimes a file is forwarded for review, and after careful consideration both readers independently recommend denial. At highly competitive colleges with many more applicants than spots in the freshman class, this is often the fate of applicants who do not distinguish themselves in some way, even if their grades and scores are competitive. Here, too, this can be the end of the decision process or, depending on the college, the dean may review the file briefly to confirm the decision made by others. Colleges using ratings totals may also establish a threshold at the low end—students who score below the threshold will be denied without further review.

The Gray Zone

The most difficult decisions, of course, have to be made for those in the middle of the pack—the deny-plus or admit-minus applicants, those whose ratings total falls between the deny and admit thresholds, or the ones referred for additional review. A good number of applicants fall into this gray zone. These applicants have a lot that makes them attractive to the two reviewers, but so do many other applicants. Here the decisions get tougher—more personal and more human—and as a consequence, more unpredictable and, to some extent, arbitrary, at least as seen from the outside.

MAKING THE FINAL DECISION

The final round is often review by committee. Consisting of all or a subset of the senior admissions officers (or subcommittee chairs), and occasionally including a small number

> Years ago, Dartmouth College let me sit in on its process. I was struck by some of the vagaries. For example, the time—if your application came up at nine-thirty in the morning when everybody was full of energy, that made a difference, as opposed to coming up at five in the afternoon when people are thinking, "I'd rather be somewhere else."[2]
>
> JOHN MERROW, THE MERROW REPORT

of faculty and students, the committee typically hears an oral overview of each applicant who is referred to it. That overview is usually provided by the admissions officer from the applicant's geographic region, who serves as the applicant's advocate in arguing for admission. One young admissions officer, when asked by a high school counselor what he had learned in his first year that he could apply in his second, replied, "I learned who it was worth bringing to committee. You can't bring them all." Questions go back and forth, thoughts are exchanged and debated, and then a final, usually decisive, vote is taken: admit, deny, or wait-list (or defer, in the case of early action or early decision). At some colleges, the committee may review and act on all decisions, even the easiest ones, while other colleges do not use committees at all, even in difficult cases.

Regardless of how the process unfolds, clearly many of the final decisions are difficult—decisions that, on another day and with another set of reviewers, might have turned out differently. The qualitative nature of admissions reviews, along with all the dimensions that a college may consider in crafting its class, creates a lot of uncertainty. Two equally wonderful students apply to a college, and one is admitted, but one is not. Why? Unfortunately, there may not be a clear answer, or the answer may be one that makes you uncomfortable. As Shawn Abbott, now director of undergraduate admissions at Stanford University, has stated, "Most of the highly selective institutions in the country could easily fill their classes twice over with candidates possessing similar academic credentials."[3] The decisions are not always easy to explain or defend, and colleges almost never explain their decisions to applicants, and only rarely even to guidance counselors. It is easier for them to talk about the "tremendous quality and size of the applicant pool" and "what a tough year it was."

I don't know what colleges want. My daughter has the GPA and the curriculum (full International Baccalaureate with two extra certificates), extracurriculars (two state championships), high class rank and SATs, and still got deferred from [Elite U]. She is one of those amazing kids who parents and teachers think is so unique that of course they would want her. I guess we should have had her practice walking on water at birth.

FRUSTRATED PARENT WHO DIDN'T UNDERSTAND HOW COMPETITIVE THE APPLICANT POOL ACTUALLY WAS

BUILDING THE FRESHMAN CLASS

It should be clear by now that admissions officers consider many factors—not just academic record and extracurricular activities—in their final decisions. Nan Keohane, former president of Duke University, offered the following candid explanation of the role that alumni and development concerns play in admissions decisions. Responding to a *Wall Street Journal* reporter on this topic, she wrote:

Every year, highly selective institutions like Duke admit many students who are less "qualified" than some of those we do not admit. Hundreds of high school valedictorians and students with perfect SAT scores have to be disappointed, in order for us to take other factors besides academic talent in the narrow sense into account. This may seem unfair to those who are turned down, but unfortunately a place like Duke has room only to accept a small fraction of the wonderfully talented students who would like to be here. . . . Every student must be able to succeed at Duke, in the judgment of the Admissions Office, but above that threshold—a demanding threshold, to be sure—many different factors come into play. We are committed to ethnic, racial, cultural, socioeconomic, and geographic diversity, to becoming more international, giving particular support to students from North and South Carolina (by reason of our founding indenture and our commitment to our region), admitting students with a range of probable academic commitments, succeeding in athletics, making sure that our drama and music and arts programs have students who will continue and enjoy their traditions, and more. Alumni and development concerns are just one part of this mix.[4]

I applied early to Yale and was rejected. I had great grades, high SATs, lots of ECs, blah, blah, blah. Everyone thought I was a shoo-in—my parents, my teachers, my relatives, my friends. Then I was rejected. Just plain rejected. I was bummed out for a few days but got over it. But my mom couldn't understand how this could happen. She sent a nice e-mail to the admissions office asking for reasons. This is what they wrote back:

> Realize the personalities on Yale's committee are distinctive to Yale, as are the personalities on admission committees at other schools. And even within a given school, there are sometimes multiple committees that have different constellations of personalities presiding and voting as they see fit. Also within a single committee, three people may like an essay, recommendation, extracurricular activity, etc., but four or even three others on the committee may feel very differently. Such a divided sensibility would result in an unfavorable outcome. Frequently committee members do not agree, which leads to some tough arguments and split votes. This does not mean that the applicant is not extraordinary; it just means that not enough people voted favorably.

I'm not sure this made her feel any better.

HIGH SCHOOL SENIOR

Having my older sister go ahead of me helped me understand how random college admissions can be. She didn't get into Yale or Princeton. So I'm kind of ready to accept whatever happens.

COLLEGE APPLICANT WHOSE SISTER ATTENDS HARVARD

I went to a college reunion. Some guy got up and said, "You all need to know that 65 percent of you sitting here would not get into this college if you applied today." Parents don't understand that. In our day, if you were a really bright kid, got good grades, did well on your SAT, and could afford it, you could go. Today kids are playing, not just on a different field, but on a different planet. Kids feel that to please their parents they need to get in [to a highly selective college] and it just may not be do-able.

MOM WHO VOLUNTEERS IN THE GUIDANCE OFFICE AT A PRIVATE HIGH SCHOOL

The Outcome Can Be Unpredictable

Parents and students need to realize how complex and fundamentally messy college admissions decisions at selective colleges can be. The purpose of sharing this information is not to discourage you but to help you approach college admissions with the right mind-set and to encourage you to develop a list of good-fit colleges that includes some where your admission is assured.

> It looks to the family that this is a perfect student, but most of the students look like that. We're making hairline decisions.[5]
>
> ANN WRIGHT, FORMER VICE PRESIDENT FOR ENROLLMENT, RICE UNIVERSITY

Almost no one has a record that will guarantee admission to the most selective colleges in the country—there are too many variables in the admissions equation, including institutional priorities that are not under your control, to predict the outcome with any certainty. Knowing this may initially be disillusioning, but it can also be liberating. It can help you understand, in both your head and heart, that the admit-or-deny decision made in the admissions office of a selective college is not an evaluation of your worth as a student and as a person. And equally true, the decision does not measure the success of a parent's child-rearing efforts.

Appreciating what goes on behind the scenes in the college admissions process can help explain some of the puzzling situations cited earlier in this chapter. A student with a terrific record may receive serious consideration at several highly selective schools. But because of the judgments involved, the differing needs of each college, and the qualitative nature of the process of review, some of the schools may offer admission at once, while others may end up wait-listing or even denying admission instead. Same application and similar schools, but different readers, different applicant pools, different institutional priorities, thus different outcomes.

But It Is Not Random

Although the result of an admissions review may be unpredictable, it is not random. A super-selective college may have a 10 percent admission rate, but that does not mean that all applicants to that college have the same one in ten chance of admission. The overall admission rate for a college is just that—an overall rate that does not consider the factors that make an individual applicant more (or less) likely to be accepted.

If a college collected and shared more information about its admissions process, in principle you could know the probability of acceptance for a male legacy with a mid-range (for that school) SAT score and 3.9 unweighted GPA in a demanding curriculum. Maybe the chances of acceptance for a student with that profile are 80 percent, not the 10 percent figure for the overall applicant pool.

But even that would still leave a fair amount of uncertainty about the outcome. An 80 percent chance of admission means that on average, eight out of ten applicants with that profile will be admitted, but two will not. What may seem like a fair outcome to one of the chosen eight may seem capricious to the unlucky two. Although the same chance of admission applies to all ten, the outcome for a given individual can be very different.

> I have seen some kids get into selective schools with unlikely stats and some with very high stats get turned down. As a rule, though, the better the kid's stats, the better the chances. Every applicant does not have the same odds.
>
> EXPERIENCED INDEPENDENT COUNSELOR

THE ROLE OF YOUR HIGH SCHOOL COUNSELOR

We believe you should take full advantage of the counseling services offered at your school. Ideally, your counselor will know you well and have the knowledge and time to help you identify a list of good-fit colleges, as well as provide you with information about and assistance with the application process itself. The more background work you do on your own, researching colleges and learning about the college admissions process, however, the more productive and useful your time with your counselor will be. Your counselor is also responsible for preparing the "secondary school report" that is required by many colleges. The report often serves as both a letter of recommendation and as an evaluation of your academic record relative to that of your classmates.

We realize that at many schools, heavy workloads with hundreds of students simply make it impossible for many counselors, even the most dedicated and hard-working, to do everything they would like to do. There is no getting around the fact that the college admissions process is easier for students who have

> Ironically you want to look unpackaged and raw—someone like me can be behind the scenes and make someone look raw without overpackaging them.[6]
>
> "PLATINUM PACKAGE" INDEPENDENT COUNSELOR WHO SEES ONLY HALF OF THE IRONY

extensive, high-quality assistance from their high school counseling office. If help from your school is limited, the best approach is to take advantage of what is available and to be prepared to fill in the gaps yourself. Rest assured that you are far from the only student to do so. If you are willing to make the effort and continue reading this book carefully, you will do just fine.

A FEW WORDS ABOUT INDEPENDENT COLLEGE COUNSELORS

In many areas of the country, independent, fee-based counselors have become much more popular than they were just a few years ago. Independent counseling services can range from an hour or two of help with college selection to multiyear "platinum packages" that provide extensive guidance, costing as much as $40,000, geared to preparing students starting as young as thirteen or fourteen years of age for admission to selective colleges. The platinum package approach is rare, however, and the vast majority of independent counselors charge much more modest fees for their services.

Who, if anyone, actually needs the services of an independent counselor? In reality, an independent counselor can do nothing for you that you can't do for yourself, albeit with time and effort. Although we strongly believe that no one needs to have an independent counselor, under certain conditions it can be helpful.

When parents and students have limited access to good counseling, an independent counselor can help a student do an honest self-analysis and identify a list of good-fit colleges to consider. A counselor can also act as a gentle buffer between parent and child when it comes to deadlines—the counselor becomes the taskmaster, not the parent. And finally, when school counselors lack the time, independent counselors may help students play to their strengths by suggesting specific activities or interests to highlight in their application essays.

All of this is light-years away from the "platinum package" approach to college counseling, which involves retaining an expensive, multi-year personal trainer who essentially makes admission to an elite college the center of every life decision made by each teenage client. We think that is an unwise and an unnecessary investment of the few remaining years of childhood, and it puts too much emphasis on living only for the sake of getting into the so-called right college. Nor is it good training for college and adulthood, where young people must make their own way in the world.

If you do hire an independent counselor, you should always remember that you still need your high school counselor to know you as well as possible so as to write an effective recommendation for you. You cannot substitute an independent counselor for your high school counselor. Professional independent counselors should be willing to discuss the advice they give you with your school counselor. The National Association for College Admission Counseling has excellent advice about independent counselors on its Web site at www.nacacnet.org. Additional information can be found on the Web site of the Independent Educational Consultants Association, www.iecaonline.com.

> It's not for me, but I understand some people might find the need to pay someone for services like this. I'd feel weird about it and want whatever college that accepts me to want me, not the hyped-up image some stranger tried to create to look like a better version of myself.
>
> High school senior

THE PARENTS' ROLE

Parents, of course, play a role in their child's college admissions process long before an application is even filed. A loving home where education is valued is the most lasting, important gift a parent can give a child. When it comes time to seriously begin thinking about college, however, you can take some specific steps to help your child deal with an unfamiliar and sometimes daunting process.

Teens differ in the kind and amount of help they need and are willing to accept, however, so you will have to see what works for both of you. In the following chapters we provide specific suggestions for ways to support your child. For now, we'd like to offer a word of caution about overinvolvement. Marilee Jones, former dean of admissions at MIT, has vividly described what can happen at the extremes when parents lose perspective:

> More and more, today's parents are getting too involved in their child's college admissions process, and in many cases, their actions and attitudes are getting out of hand. . . . At MIT we've been asked to return an application already in

process so that the parent can double-check his/her child's spelling. We've been sent daily faxes by parents with updates on their child's life. We've been asked by parents whether they should use their official letterhead when writing a letter of recommendation for their own child. Parents write their kids' essays and even attempt to attend their interviews. They make excuses for their child's bad grades and threaten to sue high school personnel who reveal any information perceived to be potentially harmful to their child's chances of admission.[7]

Fortunately, antics like these are still far from typical, but many behaviors that might seem less extreme are still worth avoiding. One counselor gives this advice: "It seems very important at the moment to get everything just right. The temptation to micromanage is strong. You have experience, and you are probably correct. They are young and have no experience. But they will be your children for the rest of your lives. Don't do anything between now and May 1 of the senior year (or even after that) that might hurt your long-term relationship with your child." Wise words—but this same counselor steamed open his daughter's SAT scores when they arrived in the mail so that he could see them while she was away at camp. Sometimes it is hard to take your own advice. Overinvolvement sends a clear signal to both children and colleges that the applicants can't make it on their own. Neither message is a good one.

A lot of parents—this annoys me as a student—do their kids' applications for them. I work at Starbucks, and this dad will come in and say, "I was just doing Allison's applications today." They're really on their kids about what they want them to write and what they want them to do. I think applications are one of those things kids should do because they're also a learning process. I don't think you get as much out of it if your parents are doing it for you. Some people's parents are really too pushy. I was in a "gifted and talented" program in grade school. A lot of those kids are still under the same pressure they were in fourth grade. I know a group of girls from that class; they still hang out, and if you ever talk to them, all they do is talk about college. Just being around them is stressful. Thinking about college all the time, when you should be hanging out with friends, is not fun. I think a lot of this is the parents' influence. My parents were more hands-off.

HIGH SCHOOL SENIOR

CHAPTER 4

How Colleges (and Students) Differ

Finding What Fits

Everyone knows some students who have thought about college since sixth grade and know exactly where they want to go. It may be their parents' Ivy League alma mater or the highly regarded state university the family has been talking about all their life. But scratch the surface and ask those same students why a particular college is their first choice, and you might not get much of an answer. Ask what other colleges they are considering if, heaven forbid, they are not accepted at their top choice, and you may find an unwillingness to consider such an unthinkable outcome.

At the other extreme are students, and we know lots of them, too, who have a hard time even beginning to construct a list of potential colleges. Not only do they not have a first choice, they don't have any well-defined choices at all, nor do they have a clear idea what they should be seeking. Most students, of course, fall in between. They have some ideas about college choices but no good way to determine whether those choices are really the best ones for them. Regardless of where you are at this point in your thinking, reading this chapter and the next will help you build your college list with confidence.

SO MANY CHOICES: HOW DO YOU BEGIN?

For all these students—even those who think they know what they want—the first step in developing a good college list is an honest self-assessment. A little later in this chapter we talk about what should go into a self-assessment. We then consider the many ways that colleges differ. Chapter Five covers how to go about identifying specific campuses for your personal college list. Right now, though, we want to emphasize that as much as the viewbooks and campus tour guides would have you believe otherwise, there is no such thing as a perfect college. The college application process is all about fit—finding colleges that are a good match for you based on your interests, abilities, values, aspirations, and preferences, both social and academic. The more you know about yourself and the more you know about colleges, the better that fit can be. Although no perfect college exists, you can find many where you would be perfectly happy. That itself is a key point to accept. Even if you eventually apply to one college for early decision because you are convinced that it is *the* college for you, it is actually only one of many that you could have chosen and where you would be happy.

> My original criteria for choosing a college were (1) it had to have cute squirrels, (2) it had to be bigger than my high school, and (3) PE should not be required. But my school does have PE; you have to take a whole year. Their squirrels are vicious. And it's about the same size as my high school. So I violated all three of my criteria. I'm sure I could have found my own niche somewhere else, too, but I absolutely love it here.
>
> COLLEGE SOPHOMORE HAPPY WITH HER CHOICE

In deciding where to apply, you are in full control. Based on your research, *you* create the list of colleges to which you will be applying. The colleges do not make the decision for you, even though they are marketing themselves to you like crazy. Make the most of the opportunity and select carefully. Later on in the college admissions process, control will shift from you to the admissions offices, where the colleges decide whom they will accept. At that point, you can only wait patiently for the review process to play out. Finally, at the end of the process, control shifts back to you as you decide which offer of admission to accept, ideally from among two or more fine choices that you like.

But we don't want to get ahead of ourselves. We are still back at the beginning, laying the foundation for building a list of good-fit colleges. Thoughtfully considering your own preferences as well as how colleges differ, and then narrowing the list carefully to the right choices for you, are critical parts of the admissions process. College rankings can't do this for you. And no matter how great your record, how eloquent your essays, and how full of praise your letters of recommendation, a college will never accept you if you don't apply! One admissions officer used to ask campus visitors what they thought all the successful applicants of the previous year had in common. After listening to assorted (wrong) guesses, he'd always say, "They all applied." Doing your homework to identify a group of good-fit colleges is well worth the effort. It is easily half the battle.

SOME QUESTIONS TO ASK YOURSELF

Be honest with yourself as you try to answer each of the questions that follow. Most students find some of these questions easy to answer and others much more difficult. You may have strong preferences or weak ones. Perhaps you have never thought about your preferences before, and maybe you just plain don't know. That's OK. You have lots of company regardless of which description fits you.

- *What are your academic interests?* Do you have a strong interest in a particular field, such as nursing or engineering, and plan to work in that field after college or pursue graduate study in that area? How specialized is that field? Are you undecided about a major and want to explore different options before making a commitment? Are you somewhere in between?

- *What kind of student are you?* Are you strongly self-motivated to achieve, or are you somewhat less ambitious academically (although you may have done very well)? Do you thrive on intellectual engagement with bright and talented peers, or is that less of a priority? Do you need to be at or near the top of your class to feel good about yourself, or is lower down OK if the competition is stiff? Are you willing to actively seek out help or resources if you need them, or do you want them easily available with little effort on your part?

- *How do you learn best?* Does the format of your classes matter to you? Do you prefer large classes with no pressure to participate actively, or small classes where you are expected to contribute to the discussion and always be prepared? Do you want some of both?

- *What activities outside of class matter most to you?* Do you enjoy being involved in a number of different activities at once, or do you prefer to focus on one or two? Are you interested in intercollegiate or intramural athletics? How specialized is your sport, and what is your level of skill? Is your sport relatively unusual (and therefore available only on some campuses)? How involved do you want to be in community service? Do you strive to be a leader in every activity, or is being a contributor OK?

- *How important is prestige to you?* Do you want people to be visibly impressed when they hear where you are going to college? Would you be disappointed if they have never heard of your school or don't know much about it? Even if this is true, just how important is this to you when balanced against other factors?

- *Do you want a diverse college?* Do you want to be on a campus that is highly diverse in gender, race, ethnicity, and sexual and religious preference? Or would you prefer a more homogeneous campus? How important to you are campus programs that openly welcome and celebrate diversity?

- *What kind of social and cultural environment would you like best?* Would you like to join a fraternity or sorority, or do you plan to be an independent? Do you want a campus with a strong sense of community, or would you prefer to "do your own thing"? Do you like the feeling of knowing almost everyone, or are you comfortable with a large campus where you will never know most of the students? Do you prefer an "artsy" environment, a politically active one (liberal or conservative), or something else? Preppy or not? Do you want lots of options on how to spend a Friday night, or will a smaller list of possibilities work for you?

- *Where do you want to live for the next four years?* Do you want or need to stay close to home, or are you interested in experiencing a new part of the country? Do big cities excite you, or do you prefer a small town, suburban, or country setting? Do you want guaranteed on-campus housing for four years, or are you eager to live off campus, maybe as soon as sophomore year? Do you want to be near skiing, surfing, or lots of bookstores? What kind of weather do you like, and what kind can you tolerate?

Try to keep these questions in mind as you research colleges. As your list develops, you may be surprised by your emerging preferences and by just how flexible you really are (or aren't). The self-assessment process is designed to help you identify your preferences so you can begin to consider colleges systematically. You will also need to know how colleges differ from each other so that you can narrow your choices. The rest of this chapter discusses the differences among colleges. At the end is a questionnaire to help you record your preferences for later use in evaluating specific colleges.

Institutional mission—the goals a college sets for itself—is key to understanding how colleges differ. An important distinction is between a liberal arts college and a research university. Most selective institutions as we have defined them fall into one of these two categories. A little later, we discuss other kinds of colleges and universities as well.

LIBERAL ARTS COLLEGES

Undergraduate education is the primary, and often the only, mission of a liberal arts college. Union College, Macalester College, Davidson College, Reed College, and Claremont McKenna College are examples of selective liberal arts colleges. They award most of their degrees in the liberal arts disciplines, which include the social sciences and sciences as well as humanities and arts. This distinguishes them from colleges with programs that lead to more practical outcomes, such as engineering or business—although there are exceptions. Smith College and Swarthmore College, for example, offer engineering in addition to their regular liberal arts subjects. But these programs are small relative to the total number of degrees offered at those schools. Most liberal arts colleges enroll only undergraduates, but some have small graduate programs, primarily at the master's degree level. Almost 90 percent of the 220-plus liberal arts colleges in the United States are private.

Liberal arts colleges provide students with a sound foundation in core disciplines such as English, philosophy, history, psychology, music, physics, and mathematics. They also offer interdisciplinary programs that draw

> I think you build self-confidence at a small college. You get the message you're special.
>
> PARENT OF STUDENT AT A
> SMALL LIBERAL ARTS COLLEGE

from several fields, like women's studies and philosophy of science. Liberal arts programs are not career-focused. They assume that a broad nonvocationally oriented education is excellent preparation for any later career choice. And their graduates bear this out by succeeding in all walks of life.

Enrollment at liberal arts colleges typically ranges from about 1,000 to 2,500 undergraduates. They usually have small classes taught exclusively by faculty members. Small classes generally mean more opportunities to write and to contribute to class discussion. Classes are often seminars rather than lectures, leading to greater student engagement.

Since many liberal arts colleges are located in small towns and in suburbs, student life tends to center on the college and its extracurricular activities. Obviously, a smaller school cannot offer as many courses in any subject as are offered at larger institutions, but undergraduates only take a dozen or so courses in their major anyway, so there are always enough courses to satisfy an eager learner. In addition, students get to know their teachers and classmates well and form close bonds. In turn, this develops the strong sense of community that is the identifying mark of a liberal arts college.

Many liberal arts colleges have athletic programs at the National Collegiate Athletic Association (NCAA) Division III level. The NCAA divides its member teams into three categories, Division I, Division II, and Division III, in descending order of athletic competitiveness. With fewer students and a less intense level of competition than that found at Division I schools, at liberal arts colleges a higher percentage of their students can participate in varsity-level competition.

The same principle applies to other extracurricular activities. With fewer students vying for a newspaper job or a seat in the violin section of the orchestra, a greater percentage of students can get involved. But the scale of the activity may be smaller. The campus newspaper at a liberal arts college may come out just once a week, while a larger school is likely to have a daily (and bigger) paper. There may also be fewer organized activities to choose from at a liberal arts college compared to a larger school, but again, regardless of the absolute number, students always find many options for involvement at a liberal arts college. Students are also encouraged to start new activities if they want to. You'll keep bumping into your friends and acquaintances, even in diverse activities, because the community is small.

RESEARCH UNIVERSITIES

In contrast to liberal arts colleges, research universities have three connected missions: research, public service, and teaching undergraduate and graduate students. Research generates new knowledge, and public service means that knowledge is shared with society at large. All of the Ivy League schools, Duke University, the University of Michigan, and the University of Virginia are examples of selective research universities. An institution is classified as a research university based on the number of doctoral degrees it awards each year across a number of fields. About 260 institutions fall into this category: two-thirds are public, and one-third are private.

> My mother kept talking about the small class size at [Liberal Arts College], but I didn't care about that. I liked the idea of having just about every possible option open to me.
>
> FRESHMAN HAPPY AT A
> LARGE RESEARCH UNIVERSITY

> For our faculty, research intensity is higher, and they are expected to continue research throughout their entire career. It's harder to stay current at a small school.
>
> DEAN AT A LARGE RESEARCH UNIVERSITY

Faculty members at research universities are evaluated on the quality and quantity of their research as well as the quality of their teaching. At the strongest and best-known research universities, faculty members do research at the frontiers of their fields using well-equipped research laboratories and libraries. This does not mean that undergraduates are ignored at these schools, however. You are still important, but you are not the center of the enterprise, as you are in high school or at a liberal arts college. In fact, learning from professors who are active in research is a valuable opportunity for undergraduates, particularly those majoring in the sciences or social sciences where new research can rapidly change a field. It is exciting to learn from teachers who are doing research that will appear in tomorrow's headlines and next year's textbooks, and who can convey, firsthand, what discovery and scholarship are all about. Research universities offer many opportunities for undergraduates, not just graduate students, to become involved in faculty research projects, but you have to be energetic in seeking them out. Liberal arts colleges also offer many research opportunities, but their variety and scope will generally be more modest, particularly in the sciences.

Research universities come in all sizes. They range from quite small (Cal Tech, for example, has fewer than 1,000 undergraduate students and about 1,200 graduate students) to medium (Harvard University has about 6,600 undergraduates and 10,000 graduate students) to very large (University of Texas, Austin, has about 37,000 undergraduates and 11,000 graduate students). Most research universities have 15,000 or more students enrolled, graduate and undergraduate combined.

Classes at research universities, particularly introductory classes, may be quite large, although smaller discussion sections usually accompany large lecture classes. Research university faculty generally teach fewer classes per term because of their other responsibilities, and they may be less accessible to students than faculty at liberal arts colleges because of these additional responsibilities. How you feel about this will depend on how much contact you want with professors, and how active you will be in dealing with the relative anonymity of large classes. Students at research universities will also probably find themselves in discussion sections or perhaps even classes taught by graduate students serving as teaching assistants (TAs). Research universities vary greatly in how much they use TAs for undergraduate instruction. While often enthusiastic and committed teachers, TAs have less teaching experience than faculty, and they may be hard to find when you need letters of recommendation for a job or graduate school.

Research universities often have honors programs or other special opportunities for their most academically motivated and able students. To a degree, they are trying to replicate part of the experience of a small college. Good examples can be found at the University of Michigan, Pennsylvania State University, Arizona State University, and UCLA. These programs can be wonderful opportunities for highly qualified students to learn in smaller classes and receive the personal attention of a liberal arts college in a setting that also provides the advantages of a large research university.

WHAT'S IN A NAME?

Don't let the name of an institution mislead you. Bucknell University, for example, is a liberal arts college, while Dartmouth College is a medium-sized research university. You'll need to look deeper than its name to determine a school's mission. It also pays to watch out for similar names that can be easily confused. As examples, Trinity College and Wesleyan University are both in Connecticut, but Trinity University and Wesleyan College are in Texas and Ohio, respectively. The University of Miami is located in Florida, but Miami University is located in Ohio. We could offer more examples, but you get the idea.

OTHER TYPES OF FOUR-YEAR INSTITUTIONS

Research universities and liberal arts colleges as they have been traditionally defined make up a little less than 25 percent of all four-year colleges and universities. Although these two categories are the ones that are most visible nationally and internationally, other types of colleges offer excellent educational opportunities. Depending on your career goals and other factors, one of these might be right for you.

Master's Universities and General Baccalaureate Colleges

The most common alternatives to liberal arts colleges and research universities are master's universities and general baccalaureate colleges. These terms are not commonly used outside of higher education circles, and the colleges will probably not describe themselves using these labels. Master's universities, both public and private, typically offer bachelor's degrees in a wide range of fields, including business, engineering, education, nursing, and other applied areas, as well as the liberal arts, but they award over half of their degrees to students enrolled in master's degree programs. They usually draw their undergraduate and graduate students from their local geographic region. The more than 600 universities in this category are about evenly divided between public and private control. San Francisco State University, Morehead State University (Kentucky), and Jacksonville State University (Alabama) are examples. Their regional focus contrasts with liberal arts colleges and research universities that typically draw students from across the country and the world.

General baccalaureate colleges primarily emphasize undergraduate education like liberal arts colleges, but they award more than half of their degrees in applied fields such as business, nursing, and education. About 85 percent of the approximately 320 institutions in this category are private. Examples include

Elizabethtown College (Pennsylvania), Asbury College (Kentucky), and Linfield College (Oregon).

Master's universities and general baccalaureate colleges vary greatly in selectivity, but only a small number meet the definition of a selective institution that we are using; that is, one that accepts less than half of its applicants. Although master's universities and general baccalaureate colleges are not the focus of our book, we encourage you to consider them as part of your exploration of colleges. They can be affordable, accessible alternatives to more selective liberal arts colleges or research universities and can balance out a college list. The approach to finding a good fit that we describe later works well for colleges in these categories, too.

Specialized Programs

Yet another kind of college is the highly specialized school like a music conservatory (such as Julliard and the New England Conservatory of Music), art institute (such as the California Institute of the Arts or the Rhode Island School of Design), or undergraduate business (such as Babson College or Bentley College, both in Massachusetts) or engineering school (such as Cooper Union in New York, Rose-Hulman Institute of Technology in Indiana, and Colorado School of Mines). Some, but not all, are quite selective in admissions.

Specialized schools can be appropriate for students with highly focused, well-developed interests and clear career goals. Other students who want to study these same subjects may find that attending a liberal arts college or research university will allow them greater breadth in their education in addition to courses in their special area of interest. It is much easier to explore other fields if the courses are readily available, and, if your interests change, it is certainly easier to switch majors within a given school than it is to switch schools. A lot depends on your level of commitment to the field—you need to be very sure this is what you want to study when you apply to such schools.

Admission Matters is written primarily for students considering colleges that offer a range of programs across many fields of knowledge. The Resources section at the back of the book, however, provides links to help you explore the option of more focused study. We include links to information about U.S. military academies as well.

WHICH KIND OF COLLEGE IS BEST FOR YOU?

What kind of college is best for you? Well, as with most things in life generally and in college admissions, it depends. It depends on your personality, your learning style, and your academic interests. Given the results of your self-assessment, do your preferences seem to fit better with one type of college than another? If so, you have made a major step toward developing your college list. You may also find, though, that you do not have a clear preference. Many students feel comfortable in different kinds of settings, and their final choice depends in the end on where they are admitted as well as the other factors that they discovered as part of their self-assessment. In the next section, we talk more about some characteristics of colleges to think about as you reflect on your own preferences.

> I was really surprised by my son's reaction to certain colleges. The original Birkenstock-wearing California kid, he fell in love with a small liberal arts college in rural Massachusetts (enrollment 2,000) as well as a large research university in New York City (enrollment 23,000). Go figure.
>
> OBSERVATION BY SURPRISED PARENT

> At UC Santa Cruz, I thought, "This is so neat," but my son said, "This is the boonies." At UCLA, I thought, "He'll get lost in a place like this," but he came back beaming.
>
> CALIFORNIA PARENT

Location, Location, Location

When you close your eyes and try to imagine yourself in your ideal college environment, what do you see? A bustling city, with all the excitement, anonymity, and diversity that accompany it? Or a more bucolic setting, perhaps near a small town, with expansive lawns and a slower pace? Or something in between? Perhaps you have no clear preference, and you would be at home in any of these.

Despite the trend for students to think nationally rather than locally when considering colleges, the majority of students still go to college in the same part of the country in which they live—those in the South go to southern schools; westerners tend to stay west of the Rockies; those in the Northeast usually choose a school in that area, and so forth. Some students, however, see college as an opportunity to explore a different part of the country and factor this into their college search plans accordingly. Each area of the country has its own weather and elements of its own culture. Try to keep your mind and options open, and don't automatically rule out a part of the country without carefully considering why. Be aware, though, that a campus in rural Maine or the Upper Midwest that is gorgeous when you visit in the fall could be less appealing in winter if you don't care for snow. Cultural differences can also pose a challenge for some. We know a young woman from the East who was determined to go to the most prestigious college that accepted her, no matter what. She chose to attend a super-selective college on the West Coast for that reason and ended up miserable because she thought it rained too much and that everyone was too laid-back. Few people would describe Stanford University that way, but she did. The fit, for her, was a poor one.

If you find yourself drawn to colleges in other parts of the country, be sure to do your homework to determine what life would actually be like if you were to spend four years there. Be aware of possible differences in food, politics, weather, and lifestyle in general. In addition, it can sometimes be hard to get home from colleges in remote locations. Living in a different part of the country can be a wonderful experience if you are prepared to be flexible, or it can be a long four years.

Size

Academic institutions vary greatly in size. Some have fewer than 1,000 students total, and a handful have 45,000 or more, with the rest somewhere in between. As a general rule, liberal arts colleges tend to be among the smallest, but even they range from Pitzer College with about 1,000 students to Bucknell University with about 3,600, while the largest campuses are research universities, usually public. Size can play a major role in how a campus feels to you. Michael Tamada, director of institutional research at Occidental College, has reflected on the differences. "A small college is like a small town; simply walking through the quad, you will pass by faces that are familiar and likely to be people whom you know. A large university is more like a city; as you walk through the quad or hallways, you'll mainly see faces of strangers, with an occasional encounter with someone who you know. These experiences can be comforting, stifling, liberating, or alienating depending on your personality."[1]

> My son grew up in a town with a big university, and that's what he's used to. When we toured small schools, he would say, "This is their union? This is their athletic facility?"
>
> MOTHER OF COLLEGE FRESHMAN
> HAPPY AT A LARGE UNIVERSITY

Size affects not only the ambience of a campus but often the educational experience as well. For one thing, a larger campus will usually have a broader choice of programs and courses. But the downside is that the larger the campus, the larger the classes, at least at the introductory level. Exceptions to this, as we mentioned earlier, are the honors programs within a college or university. If you care about class size, you'll want to find out about the size of specific classes you are likely to take. They will probably be smaller in philosophy or anthropology than in economics or biology. The student-faculty ratios that colleges often cite tell you very little about the size of actual classes, since all faculty are counted, even those who do little or no undergraduate teaching.

Size has no right or wrong. Fit will vary from person to person. Some students find it helpful to visit colleges near home, even if they are not interested in attending them, just to see what schools of different sizes are like.

CURRICULUM AND REQUIREMENTS

Some students enter college with a clearly defined plan of study, while others are completely undecided. How should this play into your consideration of colleges? If you are interested in special programs (for example, engineering, dance, or business), it is important to determine who offers these subjects. It makes no sense to apply to a college that does not have the program you want. However, you also need to remember that the average student switches majors at least once before graduation. Ideally, you want to look for colleges that offer the kinds of programs that fit your interests, as well as the flexibility of being able to switch fields if your interests change.

Some schools offer special "dual degree" programs that allow students to obtain a bachelor's degree and a graduate degree in less time than it would take if the two were pursued separately. These programs can be attractive to students with focused career objectives. In dual B.A.-M.D. programs, for example, a student receives both degrees at the end of seven years, dual B.A.-J.D. programs can be completed in six years, and dual B.A.-M.B.A. programs take just five years. These programs generally save a year of both time and tuition. Similar programs exist for B.A.-M.A. programs in some fields at some schools. Smaller colleges offering these programs usually have cooperative arrangements with a university that offers graduate degrees, while large universities may offer both parts themselves. In either case, being accepted to a dual program means that if you do well, you won't have to endure a second admissions process to achieve your educational goals.

Picking a Major

A student majoring in a particular field must take a certain number of credits in that field and in related fields to help build knowledge and skills in that subject. Some specific courses will usually be required for everyone in that major, while other courses are electives, which means that you can choose which courses to take from a large array. At some schools, you can declare a minor, or a concentration in a different field requiring fewer credits. Double majors (and occasionally triple majors, for the very energetic) are sometimes possible, and some schools allow students to create their own custom majors.

> They're so right about freshmen changing their majors. I've changed from electrical engineering to computer science to pre-dental to political science—and I've only been here a semester.
>
> UNDECIDED FRESHMAN AT A RESEARCH UNIVERSITY

Be aware that some colleges, selective or otherwise, require you to declare your general area of interest when you apply, especially if the major is very popular and the college could not meet the demand if the major were open to everyone. Such colleges may have higher admissions requirements for students interested in some majors than for those interested in others. If you are admitted to that college but not to a specific major, it may be difficult if not impossible to switch later.

The college catalog and admissions materials will help you sort this out. We talk more about the college catalog in Chapter Five. If you still have questions about flexibility in choosing majors and when they must be declared after reading those materials, ask for help. A quick e-mail to the admissions office should get you answers to any remaining questions.

General Education Requirements

Another important aspect of the curriculum is how a college organizes its general education requirements, if it has any at all. General education refers to an effort to ensure that every student, regardless of major, will emerge from college with the background considered necessary to be an educated person. This means exposing the student majoring in the humanities to the social sciences and sciences, and the engineering student to the humanities and social sciences. Most colleges believe this is an important part of an education and build a set of general courses into the requirements for graduation.

General education requirements can vary from a Chinese menu–style approach where a student must take a certain number of courses in the sciences, humanities, and social sciences to more integrated approaches where special courses (such as Introduction to the Humanities, at Stanford) are required of all students. Sometimes the two approaches are combined.

College is often the last chance to be exposed to such a broad range of fields; the benefits of that exposure can be lifelong. When students must take courses to meet general education requirements, however, they may have fewer opportunities to take courses in their major or other areas of special interest. Brown University, Hamilton College, and Amherst College believe that students should have complete freedom to choose their curriculum—these schools have no requirements other than for majors. They hope that their students will not specialize too much and that they will still take a broad range of courses, but of their own free will. At the other end of the spectrum, Columbia University has a highly structured, required core curriculum of four humanities courses over the first two years that receives high praise from students. Most colleges fall somewhere in between. Be sure to find out the approach taken by the colleges you are exploring, so you won't be surprised or disappointed once you enroll. In the end, you are not likely to have to take more than one or two courses more because of general education than you would have anyway, so even a complex set of requirements may seem less onerous once you see you can choose from many courses.

COLLEGES WITH SPECIAL AFFILIATIONS

Some colleges have historical affiliations that appeal to students because of their distinctive environment.

Religious Affiliations

Many fine institutions in the United States have a religious affiliation. Perhaps best known are the Jesuit colleges, such as Georgetown University and Boston College. Davidson College was founded by Presbyterians; Brigham Young University is a formal part of the Mormon Church; and Brandeis University has its roots in Judaism. There are hundreds more. Most colleges with religious origins welcome students of all backgrounds, but a majority of the students at those colleges may be affiliated with the founding religion. These colleges differ widely in the extent to which religion is a visible part of everyday campus life.

Although most campuses offer many optional religious organizations and religious services, some students seek a more central role for religion in their daily lives. You need to decide whether the presence or absence of a religious affiliation is a plus, a minus, or a neutral factor for you in choosing a college.

Historically Black Colleges

Known as "historically black," a number of colleges in the South have traditionally had a student body that is almost exclusively African American. Established when many American universities were not open to African Americans, these colleges continue to provide an important educational option for African American students who would like a college experience in a nurturing African American community. Most, like Howard University, are coeducational, but a few, like Spelman College and Morehouse College, enroll only women or men, respectively. The historically black colleges provide a supportive environment and successfully launch their students on careers of distinction. More information about historically black colleges can be found in the Resources section at the back of this book.

Women's Colleges

For most of the twentieth century, some of the best-known colleges in the United States were single sex. By the mid-1970s, however, much had changed. For practical as well as philosophical reasons, almost all formerly all-male colleges opened their doors to women, and colleges that had once been women-only became coed. Yale University, Williams College, and Amherst College are all examples of formerly male-only institutions that are now about 50 percent women. Vassar College, Connecticut College, and Sarah Lawrence College, former women's colleges, now welcome men, but still have female majorities in their student bodies.

A number of high-profile women's colleges have elected to remain open to women only, however, and as a group they are an academically strong and attractive option for students who would welcome the kind of supportive environment that a student body comprising only women provides. Women-only colleges include Scripps College, Wellesley College, Mount Holyoke College, Agnes Scott College, Smith College, and a number of others.

A few women's colleges are part of a formal consortium that allows member colleges to share resources and facilities. Scripps College, for example, is part of the Claremont Consortium, permitting Scripps students to register for courses at the other four member colleges of the consortium, and vice versa. Other colleges have arrangements with individual colleges—Barnard College, for example, has a cooperative arrangement with Columbia University. Bryn Mawr College has a similar working relationship with Haverford College and Swarthmore College. Such arrangements provide students with coeducational experiences while still retaining important elements of a women's college. Research has documented that alumnae of women's colleges are more positive about their experiences than alumnae of coed schools. Some major figures in contemporary American life like Hillary Clinton, Diane Sawyer, and Gloria Steinem are graduates of women's colleges.

More information about women's colleges can be found at www.womens colleges.org.

THE INTANGIBLES

Size, location, and curriculum—all of these are readily observable and easily described and compared. More difficult to assess and compare are the many factors that contribute to the feel of a campus—the ambience—both academically and socially. Ambience also has no right or wrong: everyone has a unique set of preferences and needs. What is important is finding a set of colleges that all feel right for you.

Where Do Students Live?

Most colleges with residence halls require or strongly recommend that freshmen live on campus but are more flexible when it comes to sophomores, juniors, and seniors. Where do most students live after freshman year? On or off campus? How far away do students live if they are off campus? Do they seem generally satisfied with their housing options? Campuses where most students live on or near campus tend to feel more like a community than those where many students commute from a distance. Consider your own preferences, including the economic implications of commuting to school but probably saving on food if you live off campus, and factor them into your decision making.

Campus safety can also be an issue. Is the campus well lit at night? Is an escort service available for a student who is working late at night in a library or lab and would prefer not to walk back to the dorm alone? Is access to dorms secure? Unfortunately, no campus is immune from crime, but a campus can take steps to reduce it. Federal law requires every campus to publish an annual Clery Report providing statistics about crime on campus. Entering "Clery Report" on a college's home page will take you to that institution's report.

What Is the Campus Social Life Like?

Do fraternities and sororities play a big role on campus? What percentage of students affiliate with a Greek organization, and how many live in a fraternity or sorority house? Do the answers fit with what you are looking for? Campuses also differ in their ethnic, racial, and geographic diversity. Some are very diverse, others less so, and some quite homogeneous. Colleges readily provide information about the gender and racial mix of their student body, as well as their geographical diversity. These numbers can give you a preliminary sense of the diversity of the student body. Other factors contribute to the social atmosphere as well. How big a role does athletics play on campus? Is there a lot of team spirit, and does campus life tend to revolve around home games? Does this appeal to you? Finally, some campuses are known for their liberal, eclectic student bodies, while others have a reputation for attracting more conservative students. These labels develop and stick because people like to put colleges into categories. The labels may not be real, or they may be out of date, as the campus has changed. Each school probably has more variety inside it than can be seen from the outside. Think about where you would best fit, but don't take the labels at face value any more than the rankings. They may serve someone else's purposes more than your own.

What Is the Intellectual Atmosphere of the Campus?

Campuses differ in their reputations for academic intensity. Although some students work harder than others at any college, some colleges seem to have greater expectations for intellectual engagement among their students. And at some campuses, students seem to place greater demands on themselves. Campuses known for intellectual rigor and the work ethos of the student body can be exciting places in which to live and study. They can be a perfect match for some students—and a poor fit for others. Swarthmore College and the University of Chicago fit this description quite well, but many others do too.

Ultimately, however, academic intensity is subjective. Different people will assess it from their own perspective. We encourage you to do some thoughtful research both about colleges and yourself. High school students who are overtly intellectual are often hesitant to admit this because it rarely makes anyone the most popular kid in their class. But every college is looking for students with what one school calls "intellectual vitality." Your own assessment of a campus is, after all, the only one that really counts in the end.

How Do Students Spend Their Time Outside Class?

A typical full-time student takes three or four courses each term, and classes don't meet every day as they usually do in high school. That leaves lots of time outside of class, even after studying is over. How do students spend their free time? Do students have a wide choice of student groups to belong to? More important, are there groups in your areas of interest? Are the recreational facilities attractive and accessible? Will there be enough for you to do on Saturday night? If you visit a campus, ask your tour guide and other students you meet how they spent last weekend.

Campuses also vary to some extent in their tolerance for alcohol use by underage students. Excessive and abusive use of alcohol among college students is a serious problem at the national level and at all types of colleges, except the most religiously observant. Although no college we know of encourages underage students to drink alcohol, they differ in how strictly they enforce the rules and hence in how much drinking takes place on campus. Do students feel pressured to drink by their classmates, or can you be comfortable in abstaining? Are alcohol- and substance-free residence halls available for those who want them?

How Easily Can You Get Help If You Have a Problem?

Students occasionally get sick or injured and need to go to the campus health center. Some experience psychological difficulties and need counseling or psychiatric care, and some just get lonely or homesick. Others have learning disabilities or may need to bolster their study skills or get extra help in some subjects. And almost all need help in selecting their courses, deciding on a major, and applying for jobs or graduate school. Colleges offer support programs to meet these needs, and you should try to assess their effectiveness and accessibility. How good is the student advising program? What resources are available for students with learning disabilities or physical disabilities? How good is the medical care at the student health center? (Parents worry about this more than students.) Where do students go for help with study skills if they need it? What support services are available in residence halls? Overall, how well does the campus take care of its students? It is well worth asking current students these questions, probing more deeply into the areas that are of special interest to you. In particular, we strongly encourage parents of students with preexisting mental health problems or learning disabilities to contact the appropriate campus offices to discuss the available support services. You want to be sure that appropriate help will be there when it is needed.

WHAT MAKES FOR A QUALITY UNDERGRADUATE EXPERIENCE?

Up to this point, we have been talking about your preferences and interests and how you should identify colleges that match those preferences and interests. But what about quality? How can you assess the quality of the undergraduate education you would receive at a college?

The late Ernest Boyer, president of the Carnegie Foundation for the Advancement of Teaching, identified a number of key characteristics associated with a quality educational experience.[2] We've selected a few that we think are especially important. These criteria have nothing to do with the selectivity of a college, and they can be found at any type of school: a liberal arts college or a research university, a master's university or baccalaureate college, at a small or large campus, in an urban setting or a rural one.

- *Does the college do a good job of helping students make the transition to college?* Is there a program to orient new students to campus life? (These are now universal, but it's good to know what they entail.) Is there a good advising system to help students throughout their college careers? (Complaints about advising are also almost universal. It's hard for colleges to get this right.)

- *Does the college give priority to developing written and oral communication skills, not only in special classes for freshmen but also in all fields?* This is sometimes called "Writing Across the Curriculum." Do students do lots of writing throughout their college careers? Are there ample opportunities for students to give oral presentations? The best way to learn to write and speak effectively and to think critically is to practice those skills; there are no shortcuts.

- *Does the college encourage quality undergraduate teaching through teaching evaluations, programs for faculty to improve teaching, and rewards for good teaching?* Are teaching evaluations obtained at the end of every course and used to provide feedback to the faculty? Do students feel challenged intellectually by their teachers?

- *Does the college encourage students to be active rather than passive learners?* Is independent, self-directed study encouraged? Do students have opportunities to participate in faculty research projects, small breakout sections of large classes, and internships?

- *Does the campus offer a wide range of activities—lectures, concerts, athletic events—that encourage community, support college tradition, and foster social and intellectual exchange?* Do students from varied backgrounds have enough extracurricular activities to choose from? Does everyone feel like a welcomed member of the campus community?

Although we acknowledge that no college is perfect, we suggest that you keep Boyer's criteria in mind as you ask questions about colleges. The more a college meets these quality criteria along with your own personal criteria, the greater your chance of a good experience.

GETTING THE INFORMATION YOU NEED

This chapter has been designed to help you learn more about colleges and more about yourself. While everything is still fresh in your mind, we encourage you to fill out the questionnaire that follows. Your answers will help you identify what to look for in colleges that will be a good fit for you. Chapter Five shows you how to get information about specific colleges that match your priorities.

Determining Your Priorities

This questionnaire will help you identify what is most important to you as you think about choosing colleges. Questions are divided into three categories: Physical Environment, Academic Environment, and Extracurricular and Social Environment. Answer each question as accurately as you can. For each one, note whether your preference is very important (V), somewhat important (S), or not important (N) to you.

		Importance		
Physical Environment	**Your Preference**	V	S	N
1. How far from home would you like to live? Close by? Easy or longer drive? Accessible by plane?				
2. Do you prefer a large city, small city or town, suburb, or country environment?				
3. Does weather matter to you? Is there an area of the country where you do not want to live?				
4. What size college do you prefer: small (< 2,500), medium (< 10,000), large (< 20,000), very large (> 20,000)				
5. Do you want to live on or off campus after freshman year?				
Other:				
Other:				

Academic Environment	Your Preference	Importance		
		V	S	N
1. Do you have a preference between a liberal arts college and research university?				
2. Are there specific majors or courses that you want a college to offer?				
3. Do you prefer small classes, large classes, or a mix?				
4. Are you interested in a specific major?				
5. Are there any special curricular features that you want (core curriculum, honors program, and so forth)?				
6. What kind of intellectual environment do you prefer? Exceptionally rigorous, midrange, less intense?				
7. Do you want a "name brand" or prestigious college?				
8. Do you need special support services (for example, for learning disabilities, health issues)?				
Other:				
Other:				

		Importance		
Extracurricular and Social Environment	**Your Preference**	V	S	N
1. Are there particular extracurricular activities or special facilities that you would like to have available?				
2. Do you want to participate in certain sports at the varsity level? At the club sport or intramural level?				
3. How big a role should athletics play on campus?				
4. Do you want fraternities and sororities to be available and an important part of campus life?				
5. How diverse a campus do you want? What kinds of diversity are you seeking?				
6. Do you want a campus with a special focus such as religious affiliation or women-only? Are you open to considering them even if you are not actively seeking such a focus?				
7. Do you seek a particular kind of atmosphere? Artsy, politically active, cohesive community, other?				
Other:				
Other:				

Miscellaneous	Your Preference	Importance		
		V	S	N
1. Do your parents have any requirements?				
Other:				
Other:				

List the preferences you have identified as very important or somewhat important in the spaces provided below. Then rank them in order of importance to you within each group. This list will guide you in identifying colleges before you apply and will help you in making a final decision once your acceptances are in.

Priorities Summary
The following preferences are Very Important to me:

_____

_____

_____

_____

The following preferences are Somewhat Important to me:

_____

_____

_____

_____

CHAPTER 5

Where Should *You* Apply?

In Chapter Four, you began building your college list by considering how colleges differ and identifying your own personal preferences. But with more than two thousand four-year colleges and universities in the United States, how can you find the ones that fit your criteria?

We recommend starting with a "big book" that provides anecdotal and statistical information about a wide range of colleges. The annual *Fiske Guide to Colleges* is our favorite,[1] although there are other good ones as well. The *Fiske Guide* is updated and published each August and contains data on more than three hundred colleges—size, selectivity, the characteristics of the freshman class, and so forth—as well as descriptive and anecdotal information about the academic and social life on campus. The authors have interviewed students on each campus and include representative comments that give you a feel for the campus beyond the numbers.

We've found that having a copy (parents, this is a cue to you) lying on a table in front of the television or in the kitchen is a good way to get the college selection process going in a low-key way. Another helpful book along similar lines is the *Insider's Guide to the Colleges.*[2] The *Insider's Guide*, published by staff at the Yale student newspaper, is a bit more irreverent than the *Fiske*, but it offers interesting additional anecdotal perspectives about colleges. It is best used as a supplement to the *Fiske Guide*, not as a substitute.

Although it can be fun to browse, the big book is most helpful as a reference when a specific college lands on your radar screen. Otherwise, it is a bit like trying to use a telephone directory to locate a restaurant if you are not searching for a specific one. You can spend a lot of time looking at listings before you find what you want. That's why we recommend a key next step: talking to people who are in a good position to make suggestions. Once you get started, you can branch out using many other sources of information.

START AT YOUR COUNSELING OFFICE

Your high school counseling office is the best place to begin your college search. Your counselor may be able to combine personal knowledge about a wide range of colleges with information about your academic record and preferences to help you generate an initial list of colleges to explore more fully. The more specific your preferences, the easier it will be for your counselor to help you. Counselors will know more about some colleges than others, of course. If you haven't already built a relationship, this is a good time to start. Remember that your counselor will be preparing your secondary school reports, including writing a letter on your behalf to many colleges when you apply in the fall, so helping your counselor get to know you now will serve you well in the future. Wait till after Christmas vacation of your junior year, when your counselor is finished advising the seniors, and make an appointment to introduce yourself if you haven't already been invited to do so. You want to give a face to your name even before you start to actively seek advice about college. Continue this contact as needed throughout the admissions process.

The initial list you'll get from talking with your counselor is just a beginning. You'll also want to talk with your parents, other family members, friends and classmates, and others who know you well and who may have suggestions. Don't worry if your list is long at this point. You'll have plenty of opportunities to narrow it down later.

Online Searches and Other Tools

Computer search tools can also help you identify potential colleges. Some high school guidance offices have software designed specifically to help students make college and career choices. There are also a number of free search programs online. The College Board Web site at www.collegeboard.com has a college search tool that will generate a list of possible colleges after you specify size, location, potential major, your GPA, your standardized test scores, and other factors. You can easily change your criteria and run the search again to get additional options. The U.S. Department of Education has a search tool called College Navigator that serves a similar function. You can find the link in the Resources section at the end of this book. Online searches are easy and fun to do. It's worth trying several to see what schools they generate for you. Pay special attention to colleges that appear more than once—they may be particularly good matches.

Another helpful resource is a book called *The College Finder* by Steven Antonoff, a respected independent college counselor.[3] *The College Finder* is essentially a book of lists that identifies strong programs in more than sixty-five majors—from international relations to business to marine science—across a wide range of colleges. It also contains other lists dealing with such topics as financial aid, sports, and different aspects of student life. Although lists like these are not exhaustive or infallible, they can help you begin to narrow what might otherwise be a bewildering number of possibilities. Some counselors find it a helpful reference themselves and may have a copy you can look at.

College Fairs

Attend a college fair in your junior year, if one is offered near you, and use it to learn about different colleges. Usually held in the fall or spring, college fairs typically have dozens and dozens of colleges that set up individual tables staffed by admissions representatives (or alumni representatives in some cases). A college fair can be a very efficient way to gather information and get some questions answered. You can discover unfamiliar colleges, as well as gather information about colleges already on your list. Sometimes, though, a fair can be a free-for-all with people crowding the tables of the most popular colleges. In this case, the best you can usually hope to do is to pick up some marketing literature and add your name to the mailing list. Less well-known colleges will be much more accessible at the fairs. Go right up, introduce yourself to the rep, and ask anything you want. Be active! They are there to serve you.

In addition to having representatives from many colleges, college fairs usually feature presentations on different aspects of the college admissions process with an opportunity for you to ask questions. They are free and open to the public, and parents are welcome too. Your high school counseling office will have information about dates and locations of fairs in your area. The National Association for College Admission Counseling also posts an up-to-date list of college fairs on its Web site, www.nacacnet.org.

College Representative Visits to Your High School

Try to attend at least a few of the visits that college representatives make to your high school. Between Labor Day and mid-November, admissions staff members travel to selected high schools to speak with interested students. Watch the schedule announced by your counseling office, and try to attend those of greatest interest—if you can take the time from class. It is fine to come even if you are just curious and know nothing previously about the college.

These sessions usually last about thirty to sixty minutes. The college admissions representative makes a short presentation and then answers questions. Representatives will typically do four or five of these over the course of a day, so they cannot spend a lot of time at one school. If you attend, your name will get on a list of students who have shown interest in the college, and you will receive mailings. When the groups are small, the admissions officer may jot down brief notes about the students in attendance for later reference. Participating in a high school visit is an easy way to show interest. More important, it can provide information to help you decide whether the college is a good fit. Prepare some questions in advance based on your interests. The visiting rep will frequently be the first reader of your file if you apply, so making a favorable impression at the visit, or even just showing your face, can be helpful later.

Occasionally, admissions representatives will conduct individual student interviews as part of the school visit, or perhaps on the nearest weekend. If you are already on the school's mailing list, you should be notified of this. Don't hesitate to ask.

The Visiting Road Show

A number of colleges sponsor regional events intended for parents and students in addition to, or in lieu of, high school visits. This allows them to reach more students than they can by just visiting high schools. These events typically include presentations from an admissions officer and young alumni, a slide show, and the opportunity to get printed materials and to ask questions. Students who have previously expressed an interest in the college by requesting material may get a special invitation, but the events are always open to all students, and they notify high schools in advance. They are usually held in the evening or on a weekend afternoon in a large meeting room at a hotel or other public place.

Sometimes colleges combine their efforts and offer a joint session. For example, Harvard University, Duke University, Georgetown University, Stanford University, and the University of Pennsylvania travel together across the country every year and hold a joint program called "Exploring College Options" in more than fifty cities. In this way, they draw more people than any one college would by itself. Some women's colleges, including Wellesley College, Barnard College, and Smith College, have a similar series. Families hear a short presentation on each institution followed by a question-and-answer session. Even if you don't ask questions yourself, you'll benefit from hearing the answers to questions asked by others. Colleges usually put the schedule of their regional trips on the Web. It is worth checking college Web sites to see if colleges that interest you will be sponsoring a program near where you live.

Read Everything They Send You, But Don't Let It Go to Your Head

If you've already taken the PSAT or SAT and checked the box saying you would be willing to participate in the College Search Service of the College Board, you are probably finding your mailbox filling with glossy mailers from colleges. The sponsors of the ACT offer a similar service that sells the names and addresses of students willing to receive materials from colleges. Colleges buy this information about students who meet certain criteria (for example, geography, scores above a certain point, interest in a specific major, or religious affiliation). They use the information to develop a targeted mailing list of students who might be interested in their institution. We suggest that you read the literature you receive and then check out the colleges that seem interesting in your big book. The idea is to cast your net broadly at first—perhaps exploring as many as twenty to thirty colleges—and then narrow the list down based on more information.

Sometimes colleges send personalized letters, rather than brochures, to encourage students to seek more information and then apply. Be wary of reading too much into a personalized search letter from a college, particularly one from a highly selective college. These colleges send out thousands of letters to students who score well on the PSAT, SAT, or ACT, or who have other desirable demographic characteristics. This helps them build a strong pool of candidates, but they know they can only accept a small percentage of them. They justify this on the grounds of greater diversity and making the opportunity to attend their college

My mom got really excited when the letter from [Elite Liberal Arts College] arrived. It was personally signed by the dean of admissions himself and really encouraged me to apply. I did pretty well on the PSAT so that's probably how they got my name. I had visited the college and liked it, and my mom said a personal letter meant they were very interested in me, too. I decided to apply. In May the thin envelope arrived—rejected. This time, the letter wasn't hand signed. A computer inserted the dean's signature. No big deal. I gave the letter to my mom, who files everything. When she was putting it away, she pulled out the original letter from the dean and noticed something strange. Both came from the same person, but the signatures were different. The light bulb went on. The dean hadn't personally signed the first letter. Staff members in his office probably took turns signing his name on thousands of "personal" letters that went out. We read too much into it.

COLLEGE FRESHMAN

more widely known. The problem is that the letters are often so flattering and warm that students and their families can be led to believe that they have an inside track on admission.

The following phrases come from actual search letters:

- "I hope that this is the beginning of a long-term relationship between you and Williams and that you will be interested enough to keep us in mind as you apply to schools in the fall."

- "As you plan your educational future, we hope you will consider carefully the unique opportunities at Harvard."

- "We feel honored that you have expressed an interest in the University of Chicago."

- "I write to extend to you a special invitation to consider your educational future here at Chapel Hill."

In the vast majority of cases, search letters simply mean you *might* be a viable candidate—no more and no less. They are nice to receive, certainly, but keep in mind that your letters are just very sophisticated marketing materials from the colleges.

Reading a Catalog

Prospective students don't read college catalogs, also known as college bulletins, often enough. Designed primarily as a reference for current or newly admitted students, a catalog is usually a no-nonsense document fairly free of marketing efforts and containing a wealth of information. The catalog describes courses and requirements for all the majors, lists the faculty in each department, and may even show who teaches each course. You can tell how many courses the school has, how much variety there is, and whether a department has a special emphasis. It also explains graduation requirements such as general education courses and a senior thesis, information about dual-degree programs and honors programs, the academic calendar, housing policies, and honor code. You can also use the catalog to read about opportunities to study abroad, internship programs, and other features of the campus.

Because of the cost, colleges have mostly stopped providing free paper catalogs on request, but they often post their catalog on their Web site, making it accessible to all. Copies may be available in the admissions office when you visit, and you can always buy one in the campus bookstore or through the mail if you really want one. They also send them to high school counseling offices, so you should check there too. They don't change much from year to year, so a recent one should be as useful as the current year's.

A catalog can also help you figure out how to study a field in which the college does not offer a formal major. For example, you can often find courses on criminology in sociology, psychology, and political science, or courses on architecture offered through art, economics, and urban studies.

College Web Sites

Clicking on "admissions" or "prospective students" from a college home page will lead you to lots of useful information. You'll usually find statistics about the freshman class admitted the previous year, a description of the entrance requirements, and a list of academic programs. Links to academic departments will give you detailed information about faculty and their specializations. Colleges try to make their Web pages attractive and easy to use, since they know that many students and families use the Internet extensively.

Information about application deadlines and testing requirements is prominently featured on most sites, along with the application and detailed instructions. You can also request by e-mail to be added to a college's mailing list. You'll generally receive a viewbook with lots of pictures of the college, a paper application form and instructions, and information about financial aid. Some colleges may send follow-up mailings as well, sometimes lots of them. The admissions Web page is also a good place to learn about visiting the college, including listings of nearby hotels and airport shuttle companies. Increasingly common are admissions chat rooms that allow prospective students to talk to admissions officers and current students. Admissions Web sites post the details of these chat sessions, which anyone can join. Some colleges have admissions blogs, accessible through their Web sites, where admissions officers and others post useful information and comments. You can also read most student newspapers online. It is worth checking them out to get a feel for the hot issues on campus.

Other Sources of Information on the Web

As you can probably tell from our discussion of college rankings in Chapter One, we think rankings are a pretty useless tool for selecting colleges, since they distract you from focusing on fit. That doesn't mean, though, that some of the measures that go into ranking formulas aren't helpful. The best known purveyor of rankings, *U.S. News & World Report,* charges a modest fee for online access to a wealth of factual data about colleges (www.usnews.com). Examples include the percentage of students who graduate within six years of entering and the percentage of classes with enrollment under twenty students. You can usually find this information on your own by using a big book and college Web sites, but the *U.S. News* database makes the job easier by having all the data in one place and allowing you to sort colleges by specific measures.

Another good source of online information is the free College Board Web site at www.collegeboard.com. We've mentioned the site's college search feature, which lets you enter specific criteria to look for colleges that meet your needs. The Web site also offers key information about many colleges in an easy-to-use, uniform format. You can check out majors, application deadlines, admissions criteria, and many other facts about individual colleges simply by entering the name of the college into the "search" feature.

THE COLLEGE VISIT

Once you have learned as much as you can about a preliminary list of colleges from indirect sources, you will find campus visits extremely helpful in narrowing your list further. Some students take a college tour to look at several colleges, usually with parents or with an organized group, during spring break in their junior year. A tour at that time has the advantage of letting you see schools while classes are in session and the campuses are fully alive. A visit usually includes an hour-long group information session led by an admissions officer, sometimes with a student participant as well, and a group tour led by a student tour guide. Both help you get a quick overview of a college and answer some questions you may have.

Don't limit your visit to the formal tour and information session, however. Try to spend some time on your own exploring the campus. The student union and the library are good places to check out. Have lunch in the union and get a feel not only for the food but also for the pace of the campus. Sit down at a table with some students and ask them what they like about the school and what they would like to see improved. Of course, remember that they are a random sample, but most students enjoy talking about their experience, and you will get honest responses. Read the notices posted on the bulletin boards: what is being advertised? What are the upcoming events on campus? Pick up the school paper; better yet, go to the newspaper office and scan several back issues. Walk through the library and see how the students are studying. Are they studying at all, and if so, are they mostly

On paper every college looks more or less the same. But when you go there, you get a totally different feel if you know what to look for. You have to see whether you like the atmosphere. If you can imagine yourself there, then maybe it's for you.

COLLEGE SOPHOMORE WHO WENT
TO SCHOOL FAR FROM HOME

I had a bench test. At the end of every campus visit I found a bench and sat on it. I thought, "Is this the place for me?"

HIGH SCHOOL SENIOR

We went to visit a campus. It was on a hill. It was a great place, but I didn't want to climb a big hill every day. These little things make an impression on you.

COLLEGE STUDENT HAPPILY
ENROLLED ON A FLAT CAMPUS

🌿 Things to Do on a College Visit

(Items marked * must usually be arranged in advance.)

- [ ] Take a campus tour led by a current student.
- [ ] Attend a group information session.
- [ ] Fill out a visitor card at the admissions office and pick up a catalog, viewbook, and application.
- [ ] Have lunch in the student union. While there, scan the postings on the bulletin boards and pick up a copy of the student newspaper.
- [ ] Browse in the bookstore.
- [ ] Walk through the library. Does it look like a comfortable place to study?
- [ ] Check out the recreational facilities that interest you.
- [ ] Sit in on a class.*
- [ ] Stay overnight in a dorm with a current student.*
- [ ] Have a formal interview.*
- [ ] Meet with a coach or faculty member in your area of interest.*
- [ ] Ask students you meet what they like best about the campus and what they would change if they could.
- [ ] Explore the nearest town and transportation options.
- [ ] Sit on a bench and watch students walk by. Can you imagine yourself happily among them?

working alone, or are they interacting in small groups? Is the library well lit with lots of comfortable places to sit?

Most important, look around at the students and try to imagine yourself among them. And don't hesitate to ask questions. A tour guide's job is to answer them, but most students you will meet on your visit will be happy to offer their perspectives as well. Keep your list of questions handy—the ones that are important to you and that are not answered in written materials—and don't be shy about asking them. Almost anyone will share an opinion if you are willing to listen! Remember also to take notes about what you see. If you visit several colleges, you'll need notes to keep everything straight in your mind not only now but also when you have to make a final decision about where to attend. Taking a few photos can also help.

Depending on your particular interests, you may also want to try to speak with a coach in your sport or a professor in your major field of interest as part of your visit. The admissions office can help you arrange such meetings, which should be

> I recall an incident when we visited [Elite U]. A very articulate and personable kid led the tour around campus. Near the end, one parent asked the guide if he could describe the college's negative side. The kid stopped dead in his tracks and said, "Look, what do you take me for? I'm a tour guide. Do you really think they pay me to tell you what's wrong with [Elite U]?"
>
> FATHER WHO ACCOMPANIED HIS DAUGHTER

set up ahead of time. E-mail addresses of faculty and coaches are easily found on college Web sites.

We suggest you check out a wonderful brochure called "A Pocket Guide to Choosing a College: Are You Asking the Right Questions on a College Campus Visit?" Published by the National Survey of Student Engagement at Indiana University, it suggests a series of questions you might consider asking about the level of student engagement at a college: how much contact students have with professors; how good the advising system is; how students can arrange to do research, and the like. You can download it for free at http://nsse.iub.edu/html/pocket_guide_intro.cfm.

Timing Your Visit

We don't recommend visiting colleges before the second half of the junior year. Most students just aren't ready to think seriously about college before that. They haven't had time to do the preliminary thinking about themselves, and all they see are the buildings. In one case we know, a father told his daughter that her upcoming visits in the spring of her senior year would be especially useful because she had seen all those colleges and more the summer before her junior year. She said, "Oh, I don't remember anything from that trip, Dad. That was your trip."

The summer is a popular time to visit campuses, since it fits well with vacations. All colleges offer tours and information sessions in the summer even if classes are not in session. However, things may be awfully quiet without classes or many students around. Visiting in the fall of your senior year may give you the additional option of scheduling an overnight stay in a dorm with a student host through the admissions office. (This is not available at all colleges; usually the bigger or more popular the college, the harder dorm lodging is to arrange. You may have to set this up on your own if you know someone there.) Staying overnight is a great way to get to know current students and to learn what students talk about at 10 P.M. in the dorm. Students who visit during the school year can also often sit in on a class in an area that interests them. This is usually a lecture class where a visitor is not

My first-choice school invited me to a weekend program even before I was formally accepted. I had visited the campus once before, but now I was going to stay overnight. I didn't know what to expect, but I was excited about going. I was put in with this pretty crazy girl, and she and her friends were doing all this drinking and stuff. I was really scared because I wasn't expecting that. I had no experience with alcohol. I think the workshop leaders knew what was going on, but they just said things like, "Be careful at night," and stuff like that. I came home and thought, "I don't really fit in at that campus." Later I learned I was in the part of the campus known for party dorms. I wonder if I had been with a different roommate, if I would have had a different feeling. Anyway, I chose another school, and I like it so much here that I didn't want to come home for Christmas.

College freshman

intruding or even noticed. Although you don't want to draw general conclusions from just one class, notice whether the presentation is well organized and clear, and if students are attentive and engaged (that is, not surfing the Internet on their laptops during the lecture).

Senior year fall visits can be a great way to see a campus after your thinking about colleges has progressed. The disadvantage of a fall visit is that you will probably miss some school back home. If you can schedule fall visits with minimal disruption to your schedule, then consider them; otherwise, plan ahead and do your visiting in the spring of your junior year and over the summer.

Remember, though, that many factors can affect your initial impression of a campus, not the least of which are the personality of the tour guide and the weather during your visit. Colleges know that students relate best to other students, so they hire tour guides who are energetic, enthusiastic students who are eager to present it in the best light. Sometimes, though, a guide may be poorly trained, or just new at it, and less than an ideal ambassador for a campus. So try to keep an eye on the bigger picture. Similarly, a campus seen in beautiful weather has a big leg up on one seen in the pouring rain. Try to keep this in mind as you compare your impressions of different colleges. No matter how long you spend on campus, you are only seeing a tiny slice of its life, good or bad.

How Can Parents Help?

Although some students visit colleges on their own or with groups of other students, most visit colleges with their parents. Whether the trip is part of a vacation or scheduled specifically for the purpose of looking at colleges, the parent perspective can be a very valuable lens through which to view colleges. This can be quality time with your child, but remember that ultimately it is the student who must want to go to the college, regardless of the parents' views. As a parent, you can provide an extra set of eyes and ears on the visit and serve as a sounding board for reactions. Virtually all campuses invite parents to join their children on the formal tours, but wise parents make sure to give their children plenty of freedom to look at what interests them and to ask the questions they want to ask.

> We're just starting the search all over again. If I had known it would be this exhausting, I would have had my children further apart.
>
> MOTHER OF TWO

What If You Can't Visit?

What if scheduling or cost prevents you from seeing a campus firsthand? Fortunately, many resources can help fill that gap, such as viewbooks, catalogs, and the virtual online tours available on many campus Web sites.

Consider e-mailing short questions about campus life (including "What do you like best?" and "What would you most like to change about your campus?") to several current students. Admissions officers can usually provide the names and e-mail addresses of current students (often called "student ambassadors") willing to respond to such queries. Use these opportunities to fill in the gaps in your knowledge. Your guidance counselor also probably knows the names of graduates of your high school who attend different colleges. In our experience, current students are always willing to share their ideas about college. Once you have some names, it is usually easy to find contact information through college online directories.

SELECTIVITY AND YOUR COLLEGE LIST

Wise students distribute their college choices among three categories based on likelihood of admission. The first category, which we call *good-bet* colleges, includes those where you are almost certain to be admitted. The next category, which we call *possible* colleges, involves chances that can range from fairly likely to fifty-fifty to not too likely. It is the broadest of the categories. The final category, which we call *long-shot* colleges, includes those where the college's acceptance rate in conjunction with your own record makes admission unlikely but not impossible. These three categories correspond to popular terminology with which you may be more familiar: *safety, target,* and *reach* colleges. We feel that our terms—*good-bet, possible,* and *long-shot* colleges—more accurately capture the objective reality of admissions, rather than the scale of your hopes. Whatever the language used, the issue is selectivity, not quality. The problem is in confusing the two. Just because a school is a long shot doesn't necessarily mean it is desirable for you. It is just popular and hard to get into.

How Long Should Your College List Be?

In general, it is a good idea to develop a college list with one to three good-bet colleges that you would be happy to attend. This is important: *these have to be schools that you like, not just that you can get into.* If you can't find such schools, it means you are not looking hard enough. It is critical to spend significant time and energy selecting these colleges. Too often students select them as an afterthought, which can prove problematic if, at the end of the admissions process, it's necessary to choose one of them. A good list of good-bet colleges is a crucial cushion in what can otherwise be a very uncertain process. Two to four possible colleges and two to three long-shot colleges can round out the final list.

These guidelines lead to college lists ranging in length from five to ten. But some students apply to fewer than five colleges (and they do just fine if they've chosen well and not picked all long shots), and others to twelve, fifteen, or even more if they are especially eager for acceptance at possible or long-shot colleges, or if they need substantial financial aid. Shorter lists are fine as long as they include at least one or two good bets that a student would be happy to attend. Longer lists add to the expense and time involved in applying, since so many colleges now have their own supplemental questions on the Common Application. So do your research and whittle the list down to a reasonable number.

Some high schools, private as well as public, limit the number of applications a student can file by restricting the number of counselor recommendations they are willing to send in for a single student. By limiting the number of recommendations

> I wish I had applied to more "middle range" schools. I feel like I overshot on most of my schools and then didn't like the others.
>
> HIGH SCHOOL STUDENT IN SPRING OF SENIOR YEAR

> I know girls in my class who have applied to fifteen schools. Even in my sister's year (two years ago) I don't think people applied to as many schools. With my eight or nine I still think, "Oh, my gosh, what if I don't get in anywhere?" You want to do the reaches but you also want your maybes, then you get insecure about your maybes and think maybe you should have more backups and I think that's how people get up to fifteen.
>
> HIGH SCHOOL SENIOR

it will send on a student's behalf, a high school is telling students to research their choices carefully and to make each one count.

In Chapter Seven, we discuss early decision and early action options that involve identifying one college as your top choice and submitting an application to that college by an early deadline in exchange for early review by that college. Under the right circumstances and at some schools you can reap a significant advantage in submitting such an application, but it doesn't eliminate the need to develop your full college list carefully. If you are not admitted early to your first-choice college, you will want to have your carefully researched list of alternatives ready to go.

DETERMINING YOUR CHANCES

How can you tell what your chances of admission are at different colleges? Here it helps to have the most current edition of the big book recommended at the beginning of this chapter. The big book provides data for each college for the most recent year available from the Common Data Set (usually two years earlier than the year listed on the book cover) showing the SAT range (or ACT range) for the middle 50 percent of freshmen, as well as the percentage of freshmen ranking in the top 10, 25, and 50 percent of their high school classes when that can be determined. Interpreting the data can be tricky, though, since students on the low end of a school's distribution are often in specific groups like athletes who are admitted for their potential contributions to the campus. You might say, "Oh, I'm in the third quartile, so I'm at least in the ballpark for test scores." But it is important to remember that your test scores alone never get you in; they just get you taken seriously. Lower-than-average test scores can hurt, however, because a college may have so many applicants with higher ones. So if you are in the lower end of the test range, you may need some other outstanding quality to help you.

My son seemed to narrow down his list very quickly. Columbia, NYU, UCLA. Five other top schools. Just one safety would have been a good idea. I wasn't as engaged as I should have been.

FATHER OF SON DENIED EVERYWHERE WHO IS NOW "COMPLETELY HAPPY" AT A SCHOOL THAT WASN'T ON HIS LIST BUT SHOULD HAVE BEEN

A few years ago I had a student—number 3 in his class—who was bringing in his applications one by one. I saved them up for a while without looking at them, then took them home over the weekend to work on them. As I filled out one after another I thought to myself, "Oh, no, he hasn't applied to seven schools, he applied to the same school seven times."

HIGH SCHOOL COUNSELOR REFERRING TO A STUDENT WHO DID NOT HAVE A RANGE OF COLLEGES ON HIS LIST

The middle 50 percent of SAT scores helps you place your own scores in a better context of what the student body looks like than the average SAT score. The data in the big book also include the percentage of applicants accepted. If you significantly exceed the midrange of SAT scores of incoming freshmen and have a GPA at the high end of the freshman class the prior year, the college can be considered a good bet for you, especially if its overall acceptance rate is at least 50 percent. The higher the acceptance rate, the lower your SAT or GPA can be relative to the midrange of freshmen for the college to be considered a good bet for you.

A possible college takes many forms. It can be one where your grades and GPA scores place you in the middle range of the freshman class and where the admission rate is 50 percent or higher. At another possible college, your scores might significantly exceed the midrange of freshmen, but the admission rate is 35 percent or even somewhat less. The higher your scores relative to the average freshman, the lower the admission rate can be and still have the school be a possible one for you. But the lower the admission rate, the less test scores and other objective data matter in the end.

Finally, long-shot colleges are ones where, given your profile, you have less than a 35 percent chance of admission. For almost all students, even those with terrific stats, all colleges falling in the super-selective category (the ones with admission rates of 20 percent or less) should be considered long shots. The many factors that affect the admissions decision make it difficult to predict a successful outcome at such schools. It is much easier to predict when a student will not be admitted because of lower grades and scores.

Of course, colleges that are highly selective or very selective are long shots for lots of good students as well, depending on their records relative to those of the freshman class. Highly selective colleges that admit 35 percent of applicants or fewer can be possible colleges for those with exceptional academic records that place them well into the top quarter of the freshman class.

SOME CAUTIONS ABOUT DATA

With growing numbers of college applicants and the explosion of test preparation services, GPA and test scores at selective colleges have been increasing every year, along with the number of applications. To be sure you are using current data, buy the most recent edition of the big book or check individual college statistics on their Web sites. As we mentioned before, even the newest editions of the big books may be slightly out of date, since it takes at least a year to collect the data for publication. Web sites such as www.collegeboard.com also have this built-in lag. Schools can take off in just one year, dropping from a 35 percent to a 25 percent admission rate without warning (even to themselves) because the number of applications spikes unexpectedly. At the super-selective end of the spectrum, the admission rate is already so low that increases in the applicant pool do not affect the admissions statistics very much. They are scary enough as they are anyway.

The most up-to-date numbers are found on the Web sites of the colleges themselves. Most colleges put the statistics for their entering class on the Web by the fall. In the spring, most colleges issue press releases, also found on their Web sites, that give data about the students who were just offered admission. These numbers are often more impressive than the numbers for enrolled students that appear in the fall, since many colleges accept top applicants who choose to go somewhere else. Just be sure you know what data are being presented: are they for admitted students (all those who received offers of admission) or enrolled students (freshman who actually accepted offers of admission the preceding spring)?

Scattergrams Can Help

Although big book data can be very helpful to you in assessing your chances of admission to a given college, important additional information on your chances of admission can be obtained from admissions scattergrams from your high school. A scattergram is a graph of the GPA and SAT (or ACT) scores of students who were accepted, denied, or wait-listed at a college over a period of several years. It is an easy, visual way to determine where your own credentials fall in the context of other students at your school who have recently applied to that college. You usually need at least five data points (meaning that at least five students have applied to this college) for the scattergram to be really useful, however, so if your school has not had many students apply to a particular college recently, the information will be of limited value. Some high schools prepare their own scattergrams, but thousands of high schools now use a company called Naviance. Ask if your high school has it and how you can access the data. You can save yourself a lot of heartache if you take the graphs seriously, and you can also find some good bets this way.

Keep in mind, though, that, even with a good scattergram with a lot of data points, your GPA and standardized test scores are only part of your application. The other factors—extracurricular activities, letters of recommendation, essays, and special talents, for example—may be critical to the outcome and help explain why a student with the lowest GPA and test scores in a group was accepted by a

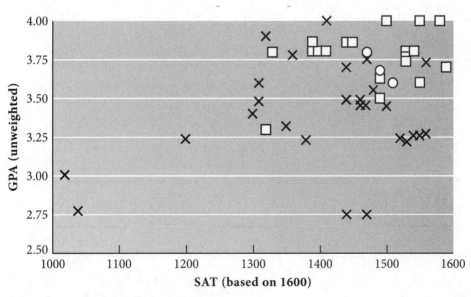

FIGURE 5.1. SAMPLE SCATTERGRAM

particular college while others with higher scores were not. Remember also that institutional priorities play an important role in admissions decisions. The sample scattergram vividly illustrates this point. It is based on real applications from students at a high-performing high school to a selective private university and shows that although admissions offers tended to go to students with the highest GPA and SAT scores, that was not always the case. Other factors, such as legacy status, athletics, or affirmative action, may have played an important role in determining the outcome in some cases.

Some high schools do not actually transform GPA and test data into scattergrams but maintain them in lists that show the GPA and test data for each student who applied to a given college, along with the outcome. In either form, this kind of information is probably the single most important tool you can have to help

SAMPLE COLLEGE APPLICATION OUTCOMES LIST

GPA	SAT (based on 1600)	Early Application?	Outcome
4.00	1580		Accepted
4.00	1490		Accepted
4.00	1420		Denied
3.92	1400	✓	Accepted
3.90	1530		Accepted
3.90	1390		Denied
3.83	1480		Accepted
3.83	1470	✓	Wait-listed
3.68	1510		Wait-listed
3.70	1560		Accepted
3.50	1490		Denied
3.50	1310		Denied
3.20	1200		Denied
3.18	1520		Denied
2.85	1020		Denied

you determine your chances of acceptance to a given college. It allows you to calibrate your own record more accurately than you could if you were using only the summary admissions data from the colleges, since it uses GPA data specific to your high school. The average admitted GPA to a college may mean nothing for you if your high school has tough grading standards, but in the context of your own school, it is much easier to interpret.

Even if your school does not collect this kind of information systematically, your counselor may be able to tell you about the recent admissions experience of students from your high school who applied to specific colleges. Remember that scattergrams and similar data provide ballpark, not definitive, information. But given the complexity of college admissions, it is much better to have something than nothing at all.

> We went to Harvard. I didn't want to apply. I thought, "Harvard's going to be stuck up and it's not going to be very nice."
> But Dad said, "No, you're going to apply just to apply."
>
> STUDENT WHO SAYS, "HARVARD HAD A REALLY NICE REJECTION LETTER."

Have Eight First Choices

The key to developing an appropriate list is to be sure that you could actually see yourself happily attending any of the colleges on it. It is certainly reasonable to want to attend some more than others, but because the outcome of the college admissions process can be so unpredictable, at least one or two of your choices must be in the good-bet category. In fact, Joyce Mitchell, a former admissions officer who became a high school counselor, advises students to have eight first choices—assuming that they are submitting eight applications, of course![4] In other words, aside from a possible early action or early decision option, don't rank your schools by preference too early. Enjoy the idea of any of them.

It also makes good sense, and is common courtesy, to apply only to colleges you would seriously consider attending. Sometimes students get caught up in a prestige game and decide to apply to colleges in which they have no real interest just to see whether they will be admitted. This phenomenon is so common, in fact, that counselors have a name for it: trophy hunting. Parents sometimes directly or indirectly contribute to trophy hunting. Though seemingly harmless except for the waste of time and money, trophy hunting may hurt the chances of other students at your high school.

As discussed in Chapter Two, colleges want to accept students who will actually attend. They also want a diverse student body, so the number of students a given college will accept from one high school may be limited, even though there is no quota or target number. If you apply to a college knowing you would not attend and you are accepted, you may inadvertently cause the denial of another student at your school, perhaps your best friend, who is seriously interested in that college.

SELF-ASSESSMENT AND RESEARCH: THE KEYS TO A GOOD COLLEGE LIST

Developing a college list can be an exciting and demanding process for you and your family. We encourage you to begin with a careful self-assessment using the "Determining Your Priorities" questionnaire at the end of Chapter Four. Make special note of characteristics that are very important or somewhat important to you. Then use the results of your assessment to develop a list of possibilities, narrowing that list as you learn more about the schools themselves and their degree of selectivity in relation to your own record. The "College Research Worksheet" in Appendix A will help you organize your ideas as you do your research. Use photocopies of the worksheet to record key information about the colleges that you are exploring. A good college list comes from thoughtful introspection, as well as thorough research about colleges.

A WORD ABOUT FINANCES

At this point, we would like to introduce another factor in the equation as you consider colleges: finances. Although some students can cover the cost of their education from family resources, many more need financial aid to cover all or part of the cost. A great deal of financial aid is available, with the largest amounts going to those with the lowest incomes and thus the greatest need. Middle-class and upper-middle-class families eligible for aid are often asked to assume loans for part of their college expenses, although some schools with large endowments have eliminated loans in their financial aid packages. How much is your family willing and able to contribute to your education, especially in the current economic climate? How much borrowing is comfortable for you and your family? Finances alone shouldn't dictate your college list, but they can't be ignored, either.

Chapter Ten presents some important information about financing a college education and directs you to online calculators that can estimate how much need-based aid you can expect to receive from colleges. Colleges use complex formulas to determine financial aid in an effort to be fair and equitable. But a college may not be able to give you and your family as much as you feel you need because of the decrease in endowments and the increase in requests for financial aid. In case financial aid does not work out as well as you had hoped, it is a good idea to include on your list at least one college you know you can afford and where you are very likely to be admitted; in other words, a good bet that is also low cost. We call this a "financial good bet." You want your admissions experience to end happily regardless of the admission or financial aid decision you receive from a given college.

CHAPTER 6

The Big Tests

f you are interested in applying to some of the hundred most selective liberal arts colleges and research universities in the United States, you already know—or soon will find out—that most require applicants to submit scores from one or more standardized tests. Less selective colleges generally require them as well. You probably also know that these tests—what they actually measure and the role they play in your getting accepted to college—are at the heart of the most anxiety-provoking part of the college admissions process.

In this chapter we help you understand what the SAT, the best-known and most controversial of these tests, is all about and why so much controversy surrounds it. We discuss how the SAT has changed over time and how colleges weight SAT scores in the admissions process. We suggest how you can prepare for the test. Understanding all this will help you put the SAT in perspective and approach it more confidently. This chapter also considers the ACT Assessment, or ACT for short, which is an alternative test widely accepted in place of the SAT. The ACT is best known in the Midwest and South, although its popularity has grown rapidly in other parts of the country.

THE SAT

Where Did the SAT Come From?

Your parents may remember when the SAT was called the Scholastic Aptitude Test. First developed in the mid-1920s as an adaptation of the Army Alpha test used to assign duties to recruits during World War I, the Scholastic Aptitude Test became widely used as an important tool in college admissions after World War II. Colleges facing unprecedented numbers of applications from returning veterans needed an efficient way to evaluate them. The idea of testing "aptitude" for college as part of the admissions process became popular as the number of applications soared.

Almost sixty-five years later, a version of the Scholastic Aptitude Test is still widely used in the admissions process at most selective institutions, although with considerably more caution. The Scholastic Aptitude Test, originally designed to measure just what its name suggested, morphed into the SAT Reasoning Test, or SAT for short. According to the College Board, the organization that owns and administers the SAT, the SAT now measures "what you have learned in school and how well you can apply that knowledge. It assesses how well you analyze and solve problems."[1]

Concerns About the SAT

The SAT has been challenged as culturally biased and unreliable in predicting success in college. Critics point to the substantial disparities in average scores of African Americans and Hispanics compared to white or Asian students, as well as strong correlations between socioeconomic status and performance on the SAT. Critics also cite data showing that high school GPA is a better predictor of first-year college grades than the SAT.

For those who appreciate history, it is more than a little ironic that the current arguments against the SAT are basically the same ones offered in favor of the Scholastic Aptitude Test by those who promoted its use after World War II. Educators at that time knew that economically disadvantaged students rarely had access to classes and instruction of the caliber offered at prep schools. Thus, they argued,

The SAT has become a symbol of all the anxieties, concerns, fears, and frustrations in the college admissions system.[2]

LEE BOLLINGER, PRESIDENT OF COLUMBIA UNIVERSITY

On the one hand, [standardized tests] are portrayed as an evil that should be purged from our society; on the other, they're viewed as a trustworthy measure of the academic standing of students, schools, and communities—perhaps even the quality of American education.[3]

REBECCA ZWICK, PROFESSOR OF EDUCATION AT THE UNIVERSITY OF CALIFORNIA, SANTA BARBARA, AND FORMER EDUCATIONAL TESTING SERVICE RESEARCHER these students would be at a disadvantage on the subject matter tests that had traditionally been part of the college admissions process. Tests of more abstract reasoning ability like the Scholastic Aptitude Test, however, would presumably be less closely tied to high school quality, thus allowing good students to shine regardless of where they went to school. Additional support for the test came from statistical studies at that time showing "that general verbal and mathematical ability tests predicted college grades better than did achievement tests in particular subjects."[4] New research now leads to the opposite conclusion.

Recent Changes in the SAT

In response to concerns about the SAT, the College Board announced a major revamping of the SAT that took effect in March 2005. The changes included new types of questions, elimination of some existing question types, and an entirely new section on writing. The old SAT had been divided into two parts, verbal and math, each of which was scored from 200 to 800, for a maximum possible score of 1600. The test now has three parts, each still scaled from 200 to 800, so the maximum score is now 2400. The SAT is now about three hours and forty-five minutes of actual test time, roughly forty-five minutes longer than the old version.

The verbal section was renamed "critical reading" and the word analogies that were part of the old SAT verbal section were dropped as a result of criticism that they were unrelated to anything ever taught in the high school curriculum. The analogies were replaced with short reading passages that are included along with the longer reading passages that were already part of the test. The math section was expanded to cover additional math concepts; the questions now assume that a student has studied Algebra II and Geometry in addition to Algebra I. The newest section, writing, requires students to write a short essay in response to a prompt as well as to answer multiple-choice grammar questions. The prompt consists of either a pair of quotations or a short paragraph from a real text. The essay assignment asks the student to write an argument in response to the prompt. You have to take a position one way or the other and support it with examples taken from your reading or personal experience. An example of such a prompt is whether memories hinder or help people in their effort to learn from the past and succeed in the present. You can answer this either way; you are graded on the structure of your argument, not on which side you support.

These changes, the College Board has argued, more closely align the new SAT with the standard American high school curriculum and allow students to demonstrate what they have learned to a greater extent than they could on the earlier version of the test. But not everyone is happy with the changes. The new writing section is of particular concern to nonnative speakers of English, who believe that it puts them at a disadvantage. In addition, even those who support a test of writing skill question the predictive validity of an unedited essay on a previously unknown topic written from start to finish in twenty-five minutes and graded in two minutes (or less). This is a task that you rarely, if ever, face in high school or college, so its relevance is dubious. Furthermore, factual accuracy is irrelevant—you could claim that Picasso discovered America and still get a perfect score. One researcher found a strong correlation between the length of the essay and its score: the more the student wrote, the higher the score tended to be.[5]

The essays are handwritten in pencil but later scanned into a computer and scored on a scale from 1 to 6 by two independent readers. Essays that do not respond to the prompt receive a zero, no matter how well written. The scores from the two readers are then added together to obtain the student's essay score ranging from 2 to 12. The essay score counts about a third of the overall writing score after it is combined with the score on the multiple choice portion of the writing section to produce a scaled score between 200 and 800. Colleges can read the actual essay itself if they wish along with the regular score report, but few take the time, unless something unusual prompts them to do so. In fact, many colleges have been wary about the value of the writing test and continue to focus on scores on the other two parts of the test, although this is gradually changing. In a recent survey, 32 percent of colleges that require or consider test scores said the writing test had "no influence" on their evaluation process, while only 17 percent said it had "great influence."[6]

Is the SAT Coachable?

For most of its existence as the Scholastic Aptitude Test, the test was promoted as a test of a student's supposedly native or innate ability to think and reason critically, which could not be coached (hence the term *aptitude*). Students registering for the SAT received a booklet describing the test along with some sample questions, but no more. Test questions were guarded jealously, both before and after a test. Until 1957, in fact, students did not even receive their scores directly. Results went first to high school counselors who then used the information to guide students toward appropriate colleges.

But some believed that the SAT was coachable. While still in high school in Brooklyn in the 1940s, a young man named Stanley H. Kaplan began tutoring friends to prepare them for the test. Word of his effectiveness spread, and he eventually built a thriving business in the 1960s and 1970s doing what the College Board insisted wasn't possible. Years later, he sold that business to the Washington Post–Newsweek group for $50 million. It still operates under Kaplan's name.

A turning point came in 1987 when New York State passed a truth-in-testing law that required the College Board to make available old exam questions with answers. Up to that time, coaching businesses like Kaplan's relied on exams that mimicked the SAT. With the new law, they gained access to the real thing. Soon after, the College Board itself began to refer to the test as "teachable" and to sell test preparation materials itself. This is now a sizable source of income for the organization, and the whole test prep industry is a billion-dollar enterprise.

How Much Does the SAT Count?

"OK," you say. "This little bit of history is interesting, but what does it mean for me? Just how important is the SAT, and how should I approach it?" As David Erdmann says, "At most institutions, standardized test scores count less than students think and more than colleges are willing to admit." We quoted this in Chapter Two, but it's worth the repetition, as it's a reasonably accurate summary of current practice. At many selective colleges, SAT scores count significantly in the evaluation of a student's academic strengths—but less than GPA, class rank (if available, which is increasingly rare), and the rigor of the student's coursework. Admissions officers also know that demographic and economic factors affect a student's SAT scores, and they try to evaluate scores relative to a student's opportunities and life circumstances. For example, parental education and income correlate strongly with scores (more education and higher income are associated with higher scores), so admissions officers expect to see higher scores from the prep school—educated child of two professionals than from the inner city—educated child of working-class immigrants.

Colleges now usually report scores for the middle 50 percent of their class rather than as averages. This is how you will see them in the "big books" like *Fiske* and in the *U.S. News* rankings. In general, the more selective a college, the higher the scores of students falling in the middle 50 percent of the freshman class. College A, for example, may report that the middle 50 percent had SAT math scores ranging from 550 to 650. This means that 25 percent of freshmen had a math SAT score below 550, 25 percent had a score of 660 or above, and the remaining 50 percent had scores in between. College B may report that the middle 50 percent of its freshman class had SAT math scores of 660 to 760. Comparing the two sets of numbers, 75 percent of the freshmen at College B had a math score of 660 or above, while only 25 percent of the students at College A reached that level. A 550 would place you right at the 25th percentile for College A, but at a much lower percentile at College B.

Of course, many factors other than SAT scores influence admission to the most selective colleges. Scores are just one part of your complex profile. Scores in the bottom 25 percent of a school's freshman class will not by themselves automatically disqualify you. By definition, 25 percent of the students in the class must have scores that fell at or below the 25th percentile. But realistically, scores in the lower end of a college's freshman class will reduce your chances of being admitted. Many of the students in the lower quartile probably had a special admissions hook, such as athletics, that offset their scores.

High scores, of course, can help an application. How high is high depends on the college and its SAT distribution. Using the current example, a score of 660 on the math portion of the SAT would be considered relatively high at College

What Does the SAT Midrange Mean?

College A—Math Midrange of 550 to 650

25% OF STUDENTS SCORED	50% OF STUDENTS	25% OF STUDENTS
less than 550	scored 550 to 650	scored 660 or more

College B—Math Midrange of 660 to 760

25% OF STUDENTS SCORED	50% OF STUDENTS	25% OF STUDENTS
less than 660	scored 660 to 760	scored 770 or more

A, but relatively low for College B. In general, scores falling in the top 25 percent of the range at a college can reasonably be considered high for that college, but it would be a mistake to consider yourself a sure thing, because this does not take the admission rate at that college into account.

As an applicant to a selective college that requires or recommends the SAT, you have no way of knowing how much of a role your SAT scores will play in the decision. The smart approach, then, is obvious: try to obtain the highest scores you can with reasonable preparation.

How Does the PSAT Fit into the Picture?

Each October, the College Board offers an abbreviated version of the SAT called the PSAT. Though rarely spelled out, this stands for Preliminary SAT. The PSAT is basically a shorter version of the SAT with three parts: verbal, math, and writing. The writing section consists only of multiple choice grammar questions; no essay is required. Scored on a scale of 20 to 80 for each section, the test has a maximum score of 240. The reading and math questions are based on the same subject matter and have the same format as the SAT. Students register for the PSAT through their school rather than through the College Board directly. They take the test in mid-October and receive their scores, along with their test booklet and an analysis of their correct and incorrect answers, in mid-December.

The College Board reports that the results of the PSAT correlate highly with what a student's SAT score would be if the student took the SAT at that time. The typical score on the SAT taken a few months later is usually higher, even without test prep. The rationale behind the PSAT is to give students an idea of their potential strengths and weaknesses on the SAT early in their junior year so that they can prepare appropriately for the real thing.

The PSAT also serves as the screening mechanism for the National Merit Scholarship Program, a large nonprofit scholarship and recognition program. The full name of the test is PSAT/NMSQT, reflecting its dual role. In addition, it is used to identify students for the National Achievement Scholarship program (for African Americans) and the National Hispanic Recognition program. Each spring, the National Merit Scholarship Corporation contacts the 50,000 high school juniors who score in the top 2 percent of those taking the PSAT nationwide the preceding October, and invites them to identify two colleges they would like to be notified of their honor. The cutoff score for notification is usually around 200 out of 240 and is the same for all states in a given year. This is helpful to the colleges that get your name and may count as demonstrated interest, but only at those places that normally put weight on that in the admissions process. Colleges do not receive your actual PSAT scores.

In September of their senior year, about 16,000 of the 50,000 students notified the previous spring are informed that they have been selected as National Merit Scholarship semifinalists. Eligibility for semifinalist status varies from year to year and is determined on a state-by-state basis, with the cutoff score based on the top 1 percent of scores in each state. For 2008–09, the cutoff score ranged from a low of 201 in Wyoming and Mississippi to a high of 222 in Massachusetts and the District of Columbia. It was 217 in California, 215 in Texas, and 216 in New York. The cutoffs for different states may vary slightly from year to year and are not widely publicized. However, you can call the National Merit Scholarship Corporation's offices at 847–866–5100 to get the most recent cutoff score for your state if you are curious. The remaining 34,000 students who are not named semifinalists are named "commended students" and receive a small certificate.

Semifinalists are invited to submit an essay, transcript, SAT scores, and a school recommendation to be considered for finalist status. About 90 percent of semifinalists become finalists, and about half of those subsequently receive some monetary award either directly from the National Merit Corporation itself, from a participating company that one of their parents works for, or from one of about two hundred participating colleges eager to enroll National Merit Finalists. A National Merit Finalist who receives a scholarship of any kind is known as a National Merit Scholar. Too many students are named finalists for such an honor to carry much weight at the most selective colleges, however, and some of them, including the entire Ivy League, MIT, the University of California, Stanford University, and many others, award no money of their own through the National Merit Scholarship Program. Some schools have become concerned about using the PSAT as a screening test for the program. The program has great prestige, yet the criterion of "merit" for semifinalist status is performance on one two-hour multiple choice test taken in the junior year. This is a rather thin definition of merit. Additional details about the program (minus the concerns) can be found at www.nationalmerit.org.

For many years, the National Merit Corporation administered its own selection test independent of the PSAT. Now that the PSAT serves as the qualifying test for the National Merit program, some high schools no longer see the PSAT purely as the practice test for juniors that it was originally intended to be. Private schools and high-performing public high schools usually offer the PSAT to sophomores and occasionally even to freshmen. The idea is to give them practice on the so-called practice test they will take as juniors. This is a good example of a decent idea being taken to extremes, with students enrolling in formal PSAT prep courses in response to the current anxiety surrounding testing. Do you really need to practice for a practice test? The mistake is in thinking that the tests, especially the PSAT, are more significant than they really are.

When Should You Take the SAT?

The SAT is offered seven times during the school year: October, November, December, January, March, May, and June. It is generally a good idea for a student to take it for the first time in the second half of the junior year; January, March, and May are good dates. You can register for it very easily online at www.collegeboard.com by using a credit card for a fee of $45. Fee waivers are available through high school counseling offices for low-income students who cannot afford the cost. The test is offered at many sites, mostly at large public and parochial schools, but the sites vary on different dates. Details are available online on the College Board Web site and in the printed registration booklet. Some test sites fill up quickly, so it is good to plan ahead and register early to get the site of your choice, without having to drive a long distance to take the test.

Scores are mailed about three weeks after the test date, or are available by phone or online two weeks after the test. Online scores are available free; a fee is charged for scores by phone. The same Web site where you register for the test will have your scores—password-protected, of course. You can also pay for an answer grid showing your pattern of correct and incorrect answers as a function of question type and difficulty level. For some test dates, but not all, you can even purchase a copy of the actual test you took.

How Often Should You Take the Test?

Once you get your first set of SAT scores, you can decide whether to retake the test later in the spring of your junior year or in the fall of your senior year. The College Board keeps track of your scores and reports them only to colleges you specify. For students who took the SAT in March 2009 or later, the College Board now

I definitely wanted to do well on the SAT, but my parents were totally supportive of me and told me that they would be proud of whatever score I got, so I wasn't too scared. What I know now is—having gotten a good score but wishing I got a great score—I wish I had studied my behind off. I bet I could have gotten an amazingly outstanding score if I had pushed myself that much harder. I improved my math and verbal scores by taking it a second time; my overall score went up 90 points, so I wonder . . . if I had taken it a third time, especially with studying, how would I have done?

On the other hand, taking the test was not a defining moment in my life. I'm at the college where I wanted to be, so the test didn't hurt me or change my plans for the worse or anything. It was a pretty unremarkable event. But I still want to go back and take it again, to kill my old score and get a better one. That darn number just stays with you.

College sophomore

offers Score Choice—an option that lets students decide which test scores they wish to submit to a college if they have taken the SAT more than once. All three parts of a given test administration are reported, but students can now choose which test dates they want to report, even if they wish to report scores from a test taken before March 2009. Previously, the College Board sent all scores from every test administration. They will continue to send all scores unless the student specifically elects Score Choice at the time scores are sent. There is no extra charge for Score Choice.

Score Choice, while welcomed by many, is proving controversial. Critics say that it favors students who can afford to take the test multiple times and disadvantages those who cannot. But Score Choice is unlikely to change anything—either for students or for colleges—since most colleges, especially including private ones, typically count only the highest critical reading, math, and writing scores you have received, regardless of whether they come from the same test date or different dates. And a few selective colleges, including Stanford University, Yale University, the University of Southern California, and the University of Pennsylvania, now ask students to submit all scores, although they say that they, too, count only the highest scores on critical reading, math, and writing regardless of test date. Some other schools (all campuses of the University of California, for example) don't mix and match scores across test dates, but simply use the highest total score from a single test date, regardless of how often a student takes the test.

You can take the SAT as many times as you want, but actually only a small percentage of students take it even twice, and an even smaller percentage three times or more. Three times is a reasonable practical maximum—taking it more than that is probably not the best use of your time. And at $45 a test, the costs can add up. You can take as many practice tests as you want on your own, of course. The College Board publishes *The Official SAT Study Guide for the New SAT*, which contains eight practice tests and is ideal for this purpose. It costs about $20. Commercial publishers and test preparation companies publish similar self-help guides with common inside tips on how to do well. If you have the self-discipline to coach yourself in this way or from a computer program, this can be a low-cost and highly effective form of test prep.

Obviously, the idea of repeating the SAT is to do better—we don't know of anyone who has ever claimed to do it for fun. How can you maximize your chances of doing well on the SAT, regardless of how many times you take it? The fact is that for most students, preparation will help. And for some, it will help a lot.

How Should You Prepare?

Test developers know that the score on a given test is based on three factors. First, how much do you know about the subject matter being tested? If a question requires a certain kind of calculation, you won't get it right if you don't know how to do it. The second factor deals with test-taking skills—how comfortable are you taking such tests in general, and how familiar are you with the construction of the test? And finally, and most disconcerting, each test score has a random component—the luck of the draw—on the day of the test. No exam can exhaustively test your knowledge. It can only sample it at a certain moment. The specific questions on a given test may or may not reflect your broader knowledge well. And you might not be feeling your best that day. There is no box to check if you have the flu, though you can cancel your scores within a few days of taking the test.

If you look at a SAT score report, it shows a score for each part, as well as a "score range." A math score of 650, for example, has a score range from 620 to 680. By reporting a score range, the College Board is suggesting that if you took different editions of the test within a short period of time, your performance might vary a bit but would probably fall within this 60-point spread. This variation would occur independent of any attempts to improve your score through studying or familiarizing yourself with the format of the test. Colleges ignore the score range and count the score itself, just as students do.

Good preparation for the SAT should focus on both subject matter and test-taking skills. You need to be motivated. You also need enough time to absorb the lessons, and you need to study relatively close to the date of the test. It doesn't pay to study over Christmas and take the test in March. The shorter the prep program, the greater its emphasis on test-taking skills, since subject matter preparation generally takes longer. Both approaches can be helpful, however. If you don't have a rich vocabulary, for example, it can be hard to answer questions that require knowing the meaning of unfamiliar words. Building a vocabulary is an important part of SAT preparation, although the English language has far too many words to learn them all. Preparation programs try to ensure that students master the words that most commonly appear on the tests. The Kaplan approach, for example, has always taught the Latin and Greek roots of many English words.

Similarly, knowing simple mathematical formulas may be critical to solving some of the math problems. SAT preparation courses focus on the basic math concepts that test takers are assumed to have mastered. This can be especially helpful for students without recent experience with them. With the introduction of the writing section, practice on writing and grammar is also included.

But for many good students with strong verbal, math, and writing skills, the most valuable part of SAT preparation deals with test-taking skills. Practicing tests under timed conditions can be important, as is learning how to approach various questions. Questions tend to fall into predictable categories and are arranged in increasing level of difficulty. In addition, the test developers also know the kinds of answers that carelessness produces. You can be sure to find some easy wrong answers among the multiple choice options. Identifying these repeated, careless errors can raise scores significantly just by itself.

What Kind of Test Preparation Works Best?

Test preparation comes in many forms. Successful preparation can be done with a $20 book or software program (Kaplan and Princeton Review, the two largest companies offering classroom-based SAT preparation, both publish books they claim contain much of the same material covered in their courses) or a $1,000 course meeting twelve times for three hours each, all the way to an individual one-on-one tutor, who will typically charge $100 an hour or more. Still other options include online courses for those wanting the structure of a course but greater flexibility in timing. At elite private schools and high-performing public schools on the East Coast, almost all students do significant test preparation, often with private tutors. Many of those schools also arrange for a test prep company to offer a course at the school. The test prep companies are, of course, eager to help.

Companies offering prep courses sometimes guarantee that a student's score will increase by a certain number of points. But they only rarely offer a refund. A student who does not improve by the guaranteed amount can simply take the course again for free—not exactly what anyone is really eager to do.

Which approach is most effective? No one knows for sure. The kind of large-scale, carefully controlled research that would be needed to compare the effectiveness of different preparation approaches to each other and to no preparation at all hasn't been done. There are a few studies, but the conclusions that can be drawn from them are very limited. Common sense suggests that as long as similar content is being taught, the particular method of preparation shouldn't matter as long as

I was on this incredible emotional teeter-totter about the SAT. On one hand, I wanted to do well. On the other, I felt that my SAT score did not make or break who I am. It was a strenuous time because I tried to have a balance of a good social and academic life. Should I go watch a movie with my friends and have fun, or stay home and study for the SAT two more hours? Most of the time I chose the academic path. However, I do remember being at a school dance (I had to work at the dance since I was in student government) the night before the SAT. I was sitting in the coat room with a fat SAT book, and my friends kept coming up to me saying, "You're studying at a dance? Oh, come on!" Needless to say, they convinced me to put the book down, and I never regretted it.

It's simple: if you don't know the material already, you're not going to learn it in a few hours, so there's no use cramming. For this same reason, my band teacher never let us play the day of a concert. If you don't know it by now, you're not going to.

COLLEGE JUNIOR

the student is willing to commit the time and effort needed to work through the material and take the practice exams that appear to be critical in improving scores.

Here, once again, you need to assess yourself honestly. If you have the self-discipline and motivation to work from a book or software program consistently and diligently in a timely manner, you can save yourself and your parents hundreds or even thousands of dollars and get results similar to those you would have obtained from an in-person course or tutor. But the key is applying yourself. A course or tutor has the advantage of providing structure for you and, in the case of the tutor, personalized structure and instruction.

Remember, also, that the outcome will be hard to predict. Your scores may go up very little (or even decline a bit, because of the random error that is inherent in any test), or they may go up a lot (but this won't happen if your scores were already very high, since there isn't much room for them to go up). As a result, we believe the best approach to test preparation is a reasonable one that doesn't disrupt your schoolwork and extracurricular activities. Preparation is unreasonable if it takes over your life.

CONSIDERING THE *ACT*

The ACT is the other standardized college admissions exam. It is more widely used in the Midwest and South than the SAT, and is actually required of all high school students in Illinois and Colorado. Unlike the SAT, which began as the work of a Princeton psychologist in the mid-1920s, the American College Testing Program began in 1959 through the efforts of a University of Iowa statistician who had worked on a statewide testing program for Iowa high school students. The ACT used a different philosophy—it was closely tied to specific instructional goals, while the SAT was more abstract and contained only verbal and mathematical sections. Virtually all colleges in the United States that require a student to take a standardized admission test now accept either the SAT or the ACT, although historically the SAT has been the most widely used test on the East and West coasts and at selective colleges everywhere. You should know how the tests differ, so you can judge whether to take one or the other, or maybe even both. High school sophomores at many schools can take a preliminary version of the ACT known as PLAN.

The ACT has traditionally been known as more content-oriented than the SAT. The ACT claims that its questions are tied more to what a student has learned in

SAT–ACT Score Comparisons

SAT Score (Critical Reading + Math)	ACT Composite Score
1600	36
1540–1590	35
1490–1530	34
1440–1480	33
1400–1430	32
1360–1390	31
1330–1350	30
1290–1320	29
1250–1280	28
1210–1240	27
1170–1200	26
1130–1160	25
1090–1120	24
1050–1080	23
1020–1040	22
980–1010	21
940–970	20
900–930	19
860–890	18
820–850	17
770–810	16
720–760	15
670–710	14
620–660	13
560–610	12
510–550	11

Source: SAT/ACT Concordance Table, 2009, from College Board: http://professionals.collegeboard.com/profdownload/act-sat-concordance-tables.pdf.

school in Grades 7 through 12 than to critical thinking and problem solving in general. This is true to an extent, especially in the math section, where you need to know some trigonometry, but it can also be overstated. The ACT focuses on four areas—English, math, reading, and science reasoning. This last section, for example, requires no knowledge of science itself, only a sense of how a scientist reasons inductively from data to general conclusions.

The ACT consists of four sections corresponding to these four areas. Actual testing time is about three hours (with breaks it takes about three and a half hours), and all questions are multiple choice. Results are reported as a composite score as well as scores on each of the four sections, with each part, as well as the composite, scored on a scale from 1 to 36. The ACT also has an optional essay that is similar to that found on the SAT. Scored separately from the ACT itself, the essay is administered at the end of the ACT test and adds an additional thirty minutes of testing time. The more selective colleges tend to require it, but not all do, so you don't have to do it unless one of your colleges requires it. The national average composite score for the ACT is around 21, just as the average SAT score (old version) is about 1000.

WHICH TEST SHOULD YOU TAKE?

One big advantage of the ACT is that some colleges requiring SAT Subject Tests (discussed later in this chapter) will accept the ACT in lieu of both the SAT and the SAT Subject Tests.

Another popular feature of the ACT compared to the SAT is that it doesn't penalize the student for wrong answers, as the SAT does. This encourages guessing, but, contrary to popular understanding, it doesn't make the test any easier because every student gets the same benefit, and the scores are scaled relative to each other, not on an absolute scale. The ACT is also designed to be harder to finish in the allotted time.

Some people think that the ACT is more student-friendly, down to earth, or just easier than the SAT. These beliefs have led to the growing popularity of the ACT and its acceptance by colleges. But in the end, they are both just tests, and most students who take both tests do about the same on each of them. There is no good research that shows that a certain kind of student (by gender, academic interests, or socioeconomic background) tends to do better on one. Of course, some actually do score better on one than the other, but you can't know in advance if you will be among them. Our advice is to take whichever test appeals to you more, see how you do, and if you don't do as well as you think you should, consider taking the other to see if something in the style of the test is holding you back. Of course, you do not have to actually take the tests to compare them—practice tests can serve the same purpose. If you decide to take the ACT, check to see if your schools require the ACT writing test as well. You need to register for that at the same time—it is not included automatically, as is the essay with the SAT. Overall, though, we counsel keeping all of this in perspective and not putting more emphasis on the whole testing enterprise than is called for.

Information about the ACT, as well as online registration, is available on the ACT Web site, www.act.org, and test prep books and online courses are widely available. The test is administered six times a year—in September, October, December, February, April, and June—and students can register online using a credit card just as they can for the SAT. The test currently costs $31, or $46 with the writing test. As with the SAT, fee waivers for the ACT are available through high school counseling offices.

TEST-OPTIONAL SCHOOLS

Since the early 1980s, a small but gradually growing number of selective colleges no longer require any standardized tests, either the SAT or the ACT. Bates College was the first, followed by Bowdoin College, and now there are about forty of them, mostly small liberal arts colleges in the Northeast with strong academic reputations. These now include Smith College, Mount Holyoke College, College of the Holy Cross, Lawrence University, and Bard College. Recently, the first major research university, Wake Forest University, joined them. At all of these colleges, you can choose to submit test scores or not. You can submit your scores to some of them, but not others, if you prefer. It is still in your interest to do so if you have scores higher than the average for these schools, but the schools promise not to discriminate against you if you don't, and they say they will not assume you have low test scores if you don't submit.

Bates College has the longest history of being test-optional. Only minor differences in academic performance were found in a study Bates conducted after

STANDARDIZED TESTS AT A GLANCE

	New SAT	ACT
Sections	Math Critical Reading Writing (includes essay)	Math Reading English Science Reasoning Optional Essay
Scoring	Each section 200–800 Maximum total 2400 Essay scored 2–12	Each section 1–36 Maximum composite 36 Optional essay scored 2–12
Test Length	Approximately 3 hours and 45 minutes including essays	Approximately 3 hours without essay; 3 hours and 45 minutes including essay
Essay Details	Required part of test Essay written at the start of test 25 minutes total	Optional part of test Essay written at the end of test 30 minutes total
Format	Multiple choice and completion (for some math questions only)	Multiple choice only
Question Order	Questions presented in order of difficulty within each section	Questions randomly ordered within each section
Scoring Basis	Random guessing penalized	No penalty for random guessing
Online Information and Test Registration	www.collegeboard.com	www.act.org

twenty years. They saw no reason to change their policy. One college, Sarah Lawrence College, refuses to look at test scores at all. You cannot submit them even if you want to.

Unless you are philosophically opposed to taking standardized tests or know that you are just a poor test taker, it is unlikely that you will apply only to test-optional colleges, though there are now enough such colleges that it is a feasible strategy. So you will probably end up taking tests like everyone else, waiting to see what your scores are, and then deciding where to submit them. A list of test-optional colleges can be found at www.fairtest.org. Be sure to check individual college Web sites to confirm specific details and to check for updates. This is an area where changes happen quickly.

THE SPECIAL CASE OF SPECIAL ACCOMMODATIONS

The organizations that administer the SAT and ACT know that some students require special accommodations to overcome challenges that would otherwise impair their performance. Blind or visually impaired students are the most obvious example, but also included are students with other kinds of physical impairments that make it difficult or impossible to complete the test in the standard way. With appropriate documentation submitted in advance by the student's school, special arrangements can be made to address the student's needs.

Physical impairments represent just a small percentage of cases seeking such accommodations, however. Most special accommodation requests are for extra time to compensate for learning disabilities that would otherwise make it difficult to perform up to ability. Here, too, documentation of the learning disability satisfactory to the testing agency must be submitted in advance of the test. Accommodations can range from time and a half (the most common) to untimed testing, depending on the severity of the learning disability. Just as an exam in larger typeface may be provided to a student with visual problems, extra time accommodations for learning disabilities are an attempt to level the playing field for otherwise able students.

Traditionally, the College Board noted the use of special accommodations on the student's score report. "Score flagging," as it was called, was dropped in 2002 in response to a federal lawsuit filed by a disabled test taker seeking to have the flag removed from another standardized test. At the same time it dropped flagging, however, the College Board began requiring more detailed evidence of a disability before an accommodation was granted so that only those with well-documented disabilities would receive extra time. For years, concern about possible abuse of the system was growing because requests for extra time were coming disproportionately from high schools in wealthy areas, in some cases with questionable documentation.

If your child has a disability that would require special accommodations on the SAT or ACT, you should contact the school's guidance counselor as early in the student's high school career as possible to begin documenting the disability following the new guidelines. Unfortunately, a small percentage of families who tried to manipulate the college admissions process to their advantage have made it more difficult for those who truly need accommodations. Planning ahead is crucial in dealing with the more stringent documentation requirements now in effect.

THE SAT SUBJECT TESTS

As noted earlier in this chapter, the College Board offers one-hour subject matter tests in addition to the SAT in subjects ranging from biology to Hebrew. Like each of the three parts of the new SAT, the SAT Subject Tests are scored from 200 to 800, though the average scores vary widely and are usually much higher than the 500 average for the SAT sections. About 150 colleges require or recommend that students submit scores from one or more of these tests, including most of the colleges defined as selective by our criterion. Some colleges allow students to submit ACT scores in lieu of both the SAT and the SAT Subject Tests in recognition of the content-based nature of the ACT. Almost all colleges requiring or recommending Subject Tests ask students to submit scores from two different tests; only Harvard, Princeton, and Georgetown currently ask for three.

In contrast to its position on SAT coaching, the College Board has always encouraged preparation for the Subject Tests. As content-based tests, they are designed to measure a student's mastery of a specific subject. Studying and reviewing can result in big improvements. The major test preparation companies offer courses to prepare students for some of the Subject Tests and, of course, private tutors do this as well. Many test prep books and software programs are also available. The latter two can work just as well as more expensive alternatives, if a student is willing to put in the time and effort to use them. Also, of course, just studying the material in school can be enough preparation to do well.

On most test dates, students can take either the SAT by itself or up to three Subject Tests. You cannot take the SAT and Subject Tests on the same day. When you do register for Subject Tests, you don't have to specify in advance which test or tests you are going to take. The SAT is offered on all test administration dates, but Subject Tests are not offered on the March date, and some specific tests are offered on certain dates only. It pays to check the College Board Web site at www.college board.com to find out for sure. The basic registration fee for the Subject Tests is $20, plus $9 for each individual test; fee waivers are also available for these tests.

Students should choose their Subject Tests carefully and plan to take appropriate tests when subjects are freshest in their minds. Most students take the Subject Tests at the end of their junior year. However, depending on which ones you plan to take, you may want to take one or more a year earlier if you have the right preparation. For example, if you take chemistry as a sophomore and feel you have mastered the subject, it makes sense to take the SAT Chemistry test at the end of your sophomore year rather than wait until you are a junior. As a result of the recent policy change, as described earlier, the College Board allows students who have taken the SAT in March 2009 or later to choose which test scores, including Subject Test scores, they want a college to see. You can get a booklet about the Subject Tests from your guidance office; the same information is posted on the College Board Web site. Read it carefully and decide which tests make the most sense for you, keeping in mind the requirements of specific colleges that interest you.

As a final note, you can certainly take three Subject Tests on the same day, but that can make for a tough morning. You can spread out your testing if you plan far enough in advance. If you take more than two Subject Tests, the colleges that require only two say that they will consider only the two highest scores, though they will see all of them, unless you use Score Choice.

A SPECIAL WORD TO PARENTS ABOUT STANDARDIZED TESTS

The SAT and ACT generate a lot of anxiety. High school students sometimes feel that their future and their self-esteem depend on the outcome of one test taken in less than four hours on a Saturday morning. This is not healthy for them, nor is it true. Please help your children understand that the SAT and ACT are just tests, and flawed ones at that. Encourage them to prepare thoroughly but reasonably for

The SAT

If someone had told me when my children were applying to college that "the SAT exam is a teaching tool" I would have said, "What are you talking about? It's a big, nasty test that favors some kids over others, and I don't like it."

I might still say that, but it turns out that both things are true: it is a big test, but students do learn from it.

When I interviewed young people about the SAT, most mentioned stress, and many expressed disappointment in themselves for not studying more. But they also learned things, not just multi-syllabic vocabulary words but how privilege works and what they value in themselves and others.

One said, "Students who come from affluent families have free time and the resources to take test prep courses. Other students might work or care for siblings. In my opinion, there is more truth in personal statements and recommendations than on any answer sheet or test booklet."

Another commented, "A test prep class improved my scores, but I didn't become more intelligent. I just learned how to capitalize on some key test-taking concepts."

"I didn't feel the SAT measured intelligence but rather one's ability to take a test," wrote one student. "Overall, I think the SAT is more about being able to manage time and stress than about being smart."

An alumnus said, "After I went to college and witnessed various learning styles, standardized tests began to lose legitimacy in my eyes. I saw people who were very intelligent but didn't test well and people who seemed ordinary but tested like superstars."

In the long term, even students who were upset by the testing experience regained their equilibrium, not by denying the importance of the SAT but by reaching real wisdom about the testing process, especially its inequities.

It made me proud and happy to learn that students can separate test results from their own value as a person.

My fondest wish for them is that they can do the same for the whole college admissions experience.

M. F.

the tests in a reasonable way and to do their best, but try to keep standardized tests from becoming an obsession for you or them.

Some students dread receiving their scores for fear of disappointing their parents or, at the other end of the continuum, providing their parents with a reason to brag or embarrass them. Avoid both extremes. We hope that reading the history of the SAT at the beginning of this chapter has helped you gain the perspective to be the supportive parent your child needs and that you want to be. The history of the ACT is less colorful, but the same caveats apply.

A POSTSCRIPT ON THE FUTURE OF STANDARDIZED TESTING

For now, the SAT (or the ACT) is a very real part of college admissions at most—but not all—selective colleges. Slowly, over time, an increasing number of colleges are making these tests optional, leaving it up to students to decide whether to submit scores. The ACT has positioned itself as an alternative test with fewer problems than the SAT, but not everyone shares that assessment. The National Center for Fair and Open Testing (commonly known as FairTest) is very critical of standardized testing and sees little difference between the ACT and SAT in terms of its core concerns.

Standardized testing remains a very controversial area. As noted earlier in this chapter, the growing list of colleges that do not require standardized tests, or that make them optional, can be found online at www.fairtest.org. The site also provides background about the controversies surrounding the whole issue of standardized tests in college admissions. It makes for fascinating reading regardless of the conclusions you may ultimately draw.

In Fall 2008, the National Association for College Admission Counseling released the much-anticipated report of its Commission on the Use of Standardized Tests in Undergraduate Admission that was chaired by William Fitzsimmons, dean of admissions and financial aid at Harvard University. The report, which is available online at www.nacacnet.org, provides a wide range of perspectives and recommendations on the use of standardized tests in college admissions. The following statement comes from its concluding section on future directions:

Colleges individually will always try to build the strongest entering classes they can, often measured by test scores, but collectively they bear a larger responsibility to make the American educational system as good, as fair, and as socially beneficial as possible. By using the SAT and ACT as one of the most important admission tools, they are gaining what may be a marginal ability to identify academic talent beyond that indicated by transcripts, recommendations, and achievement test scores. Is this modest addition of predictive validity counterbalanced by the arguably significant social and cultural costs of the growing weight of the SAT and ACT in college admission processes?[7]

Now more than ever, colleges are being asked to consider how they would answer this question.

CHAPTER 7

Deciding About Early Decision and Other Early Options

Although most students apply to college by January 1 of their senior year and choose from among their options once they receive decisions the following spring, more and more are taking advantage of early acceptance programs. Early acceptance options require you to apply to a college early in the school year, typically by November 1 or November 15, in exchange for an early response from that college, usually by December 15.

The programs offered by different colleges differ in important ways. Some, known as early decision, commit you to attending if you are admitted. You can apply early decision to only one college since acceptance is binding. Another approach, early action, allows you to get the college's decision early, but lets you have until May 1 to make your final decision. Most early action programs permit you to apply early action to more than one college as well and even submit one early decision application. A third type, generically known as restrictive choice early action, does not commit you to attend if accepted, but it does restrict you from applying early to any other college, depending on the college's particular form of restrictive early action. If you feel you need a scorecard to keep all of this straight, you are not alone.

About 450 schools, including most of those that would be considered selective by our criteria, offer at least one of these options. About forty-five schools have both early action and early decision programs: Tulane University, St. Olaf College,

Earlham College, Wells College, and Hampshire College are examples. About seventy, including Smith College, Reed College, Claremont McKenna College, Bowdoin College, Vanderbilt University, Wesleyan University, and Tufts University, offer only early decision but have two different dates: ED I with an application date around November 15, and ED II with an application date around January 1. And a few even offer three options—Dickinson College, for example, offers two early decision dates as well as an early action option.

Early acceptance programs, and early decision in particular, have been the subject of a great deal of discussion and controversy. In this chapter, we discuss the early debate, guide you in sorting out the options, and help you decide whether an early acceptance program is right for you.

THE PROS AND CONS OF EARLY DECISION

On the surface, the rationale for early decision admission programs is simple. If you have a clear first-choice college, you can express that preference by applying early and committing to attend if admitted. If accepted, you can bypass much of the drawn-out anxiety lasting into the spring that can accompany regular decision applications. If the college says "no" (a denial), or "we are not sure" (a deferral of the decision until the regular application cycle), you can still apply to other colleges in time to meet the regular cycle deadline.

> There are so many early options to keep straight and choose from. I think the whole thing should be called "early confusion."
>
> PARENT OF A HIGH SCHOOL JUNIOR

Although early decision programs at some colleges have been around for decades, they have spread and become more popular in the last ten years. At the same time, they have become highly controversial, even rivaling debates over the SAT and affirmative action in college admissions. James Fallows, former editor of the influential *Atlantic Monthly* magazine, has forcefully argued that early decision is bad policy. In an article titled "The Early Decision Racket," he wrote that early decision programs "have added an insane intensity to middle-class obsessions about college. They also distort the admissions process, rewarding the richest students from the most exclusive high schools and penalizing nearly everyone else. But the incentives for many colleges and students are as irresistible as they are perverse."[1] These are strong words. Why has a program so seemingly well-intentioned and straightforward generated this kind of reaction?

Some Advantages of Early Decision

From a college's perspective, early decision enrolls students who are exceptionally eager to attend. The college also gets a good start at assembling a well-rounded class, since it knows that each student who is accepted early decision will indeed matriculate (that is, enroll) in the fall. There is no guesswork involved in the yield from the pool of early decision acceptances: it is 100 percent, unless a student must decline because of insufficient financial aid. Early decision reduces enrollment uncertainty for a college. It can help a college minimize the hassle and cost associated with underenrollment or overenrollment, since it is impossible to predict precisely the yield for regular decision admits. From a competitive standpoint, it takes desirable students away from rival schools.

> "I just want to go to sleep until December 15th."
>
> "I've taken up praying. I don't even believe in God."
>
> "I'd sell my soul—if I still had one."
>
> "Either the best moment in life, probably better than sex, or the worst moment, even worse than death."
>
> STUDENT COMMENTS ABOUT EARLY DECISION AND EARLY ACTION POSTED ON AN INTERNET BULLETIN BOARD

From the student's perspective, a successful early decision application can end the anxiety and uncertainty of the college admissions process by mid-December of senior year. The process appears to be an efficient way to match students who want a given college with a college that wants them, and it looks like everyone wins. But as with everything else in college admissions, the situation is not that simple.

The Major Problems with Early Decision

Critics of early decision point out that it has become something it was never intended to be—an admissions strategy that appears to increase the chances of being accepted to a very selective institution. Some selective colleges have admissions rates two or three times higher for early decision applicants compared with regular decision applicants, and they fill from one-third to one-half of their freshman classes from the early pool. As a result, the much larger pool of regular decision applicants ends up competing for fewer slots well after the early applicants—a much smaller group—have secured their places.

Critics of early decision have argued that early decision programs favor students who do not need financial aid and who have access to a support system that will assist them in identifying a top-choice college by early in the fall of their senior year so they can submit their application materials by the November deadlines. Students with limited financial means, who disproportionately attend poorly funded and overcrowded public high schools, are much less likely to meet these criteria than students from private schools or high-performing public high schools.

Students who are accepted early decision are also potentially limited in terms of their financial aid options. Although a student can be released from an early decision commitment if the college's financial aid package is inadequate, early decision does not give students with significant financial need a chance to compare financial aid offers from several schools, and perhaps even negotiate a more desirable package at one school based on the offer from another. Students whose families can pay the full sticker price of admission, in contrast, don't have this concern. Strong family and counseling support to pick that one "right" college early and submit an application in time for early decision review is crucial as well.

Does Applying Early Help Your Chances?

It has been common knowledge for many years that the percentage of students accepted via early decision is usually higher, sometimes much higher, than the percentage accepted during the regular cycle. Colleges have routinely asserted that the files of early applicants are stronger as a group than those that arrive for regular review and that differences in qualifications account for the higher acceptance rate, not differences in standards. A group of researchers at Harvard University, however, has analyzed admissions data from fourteen of the most selective colleges in the country (all of which agreed to participate under the condition that the names of the colleges would not

> I was surprised there was such a consistent result—that all of the colleges were favoring early applications. I was also surprised by the magnitude of the advantage.[2]
>
> CHRISTOPHER AVERY, PROFESSOR OF PUBLIC POLICY AT HARVARD UNIVERSITY AND COAUTHOR OF *THE EARLY ADMISSIONS GAME*

be revealed) and reached a different conclusion. Christopher Avery and his colleagues showed that early decision applicant pools, overall, were academically weaker than regular decision pools and that an early decision applicant on average received an admissions boost that was roughly equivalent to an increase of 100 points on the SAT, even when legacies and athletes were excluded.[3] These findings directly contradict what most colleges have been saying publicly for years about their early decision programs.

Although Avery's research is not without flaws and is based on data now more than ten years old, high schools with strong guidance programs have known for many years that colleges have not been candid about the boost given to those who apply early decision. Students and their counselors have watched classmates with equivalent records have very different outcomes in the admissions process due to when they applied. As a result, the number of early decision applications has gone up dramatically over the last ten to fifteen years, increasing faster than the number of applications overall.

Some colleges have also been open in telling legacy applicants that their legacy hook will be considered only if they apply early, reinforcing the idea of early decision as a strategy. The Johns Hopkins University, the University of Pennsylvania, and Cornell University, for example, tie the legacy preference to an early application. As discussed in Chapter Nine, the same situation sometimes applies for recruited athletes—they are told that they will lose their hook if they don't apply early.

Counselors cringe when they hear students say, "I want to apply early—I just don't know where," because it shows that these students feel great pressure to make a choice, perhaps prematurely, to maximize their chances of admission to a selective college without adequate thought to the qualities of the college, except perhaps its prestige. Once students do pick a school, the pressure continues, often intensely, up through the decision date. Students tend to think, often correctly, that an early decision application is their best shot at their dream school. Acceptance is greeted with great joy, while denial and deferral all too often are met with despair.

Everyone agrees that you should be absolutely sure of your first-choice college before applying early decision because it is binding—you can't change your mind after being accepted. The best way to be sure, of course, is to learn as much as possible about colleges and to visit them in person, ideally when they are in session

I didn't really know about early decision until I started hearing other kids talking about it in late October. They were all moaning about having to ask for letters of recommendation and worrying that the teachers wouldn't send them in on time. I couldn't see the point of all that drama, until someone explained to me that I might have a better chance if I applied early admission . . . like maybe if the college knew I wanted them, they would want me. So I started to feel pressure to "want" some place, but really I hadn't visited many, and the only place I really liked, I liked because my buddy was going there. I visited him once, and we went to a cool party. I mean, maybe that means the atmosphere was right for me—you know, people I could get along with—but I don't know. And my parents flipped out when I said that maybe I'd just apply early decision to Jerry's school.

Anyway, I didn't apply early decision anywhere, so now it's March, and I'm getting awfully antsy because I don't know where I will be going in the fall yet. But that is better than picking a school for the wrong reason, getting in, and then having to go there because you applied early decision. I just wish I had gotten started earlier on the whole thing.

HIGH SCHOOL SENIOR

and well before the early decision application deadline. To be a good candidate for early decision, you need to begin early, preferably by the spring of your junior year, learning about early decision options and deadlines. It also helps considerably to have the time and money to visit schools to see whether one emerges as a clear front-runner.

Suppose you like both College A and College B very much. You are a fine student, but College A is really a long shot for you, while College B is a possible for you—more like 50-50. If you apply early to College A and are not admitted, you may forfeit the advantage you would have had applying early to College B because it may have a very competitive regular application pool. You could end up with neither in the end. If you had played it safer and decided to apply early to College B, even if it was a bit less appealing to you than College A, then you might have an early acceptance in hand. But you would never know about College A, would you? This can be a tough choice.

Children and grandchildren of alumni who wish to receive maximum consideration for the legacy affiliation are urged to apply Early Decision.

UNIVERSITY OF PENNSYLVANIA INSTRUCTIONS TO UNDERGRADUATE APPLICANTS FOR THE CLASS OF 2012

I wish I would have known how early early applications were due. It seemed as though the year had just begun and I was already applying for college.

COMMENT MADE IN THE SPRING OF SENIOR YEAR

EARLY ACTION

In contrast to early decision, early action appears to offer a student the best of both worlds: no binding commitment, but still an early response from a desired college. Early action has been offered for many years. The major difference between early action and early decision is that students accepted through early action can wait until the spring to decide whether to attend—it is not binding. In the meantime, students are free to apply to other colleges through the regular process and can compare financial aid packages before making a final choice. Early action colleges have traditionally also allowed students to apply to other early programs—a maximum of one early decision college as well as other early action schools. A few early action colleges do place restrictions, however, on the other schools to which you can apply. The most restrictive is "single choice early action" used, for the time being, by Stanford and Yale. We say "for the time being" because colleges often change their policies unexpectedly. Under single choice early action, you may not apply early action or early decision to any other college (with a few exceptions such as schools with rolling admissions). In another form of restrictive early action, students may not apply early decision to another campus, although they are free to apply early action to other schools.

Students who apply early decision or early action with restrictions are expected to honor the commitments associated with those application choices. Colleges typically ask students to sign a statement as part of their application indicating that they understand and agree to the terms of that program. Some require a parent and the student's high school counselor to sign the statement as well.

SHOULD YOU APPLY EARLY DECISION OR EARLY ACTION?

In the last few years, several high-profile selective colleges, including Princeton University, Harvard University, and the University of Virginia, have eliminated their early decision or early action programs in an effort to make their colleges more accessible to low-income students and others who could not benefit from early options. "I think it will make the admissions process far more fair and equitable," said Shirley Tilghman, president of Princeton University, shortly after announcing that her school would drop early decision. "Early Decision was advantaging those who were already advantaged."[4] Very few schools have followed their lead, however, although a number have reduced the percentage of students who are admitted via early application programs, partly in response to the backlash of criticism from Avery's research. Nevertheless, for now, early applications—both early decision and early action—remain an important part of the admissions process at schools that offer them.

Early decision programs can work to your advantage if you (1) have a clear first-choice college that has emerged after careful research, (2) don't need grades from the first semester of your senior year to bolster your academic record,

COMPARING EARLY APPLICATION OPTIONS (BE SURE TO CHECK THE INSTRUCTIONS FOR SPECIFIC COLLEGES)

	Early Decision (ED)	Early Action (EA)	Restrictive Early Action
Binding?	Yes (except if financial aid is not adequate)	No	No
Allows comparisons of aid packages?	No	Yes	Yes
Allows other early applications	Yes (EA applications only)	Yes (EA applications and one ED)	Varies by college
Allows regular decision applications?	Yes (these must be withdrawn if the student is admitted ED)	Yes	Yes

(3) have the support from your parents and counselor needed to submit a strong early application, and (4) will not have to compare financial aid offers.

If all these statements apply to you and you receive a "thick" acceptance packet come December 15, your college admissions process can conclude happily months before it otherwise would. Add the bonus of an increased chance of acceptance to begin with, and early decision becomes, in Fallow's words, almost irresistible. Early action, restrictive or otherwise, is more flexible, since an acceptance does not imply commitment. An early action application is a good way to show "demonstrated interest" in a college. The admissions boost from an early action application will likely be smaller than you might receive from a comparable early decision application, but you will retain much more flexibility in your final decision making if you are accepted.

But an early application of either sort has a downside that we haven't yet discussed. The pressure to identify a single college for an early application can be intense. It can also reinforce the idea that there is only one college that is a "perfect fit" for you and that your job is simply to discover it and chase it with vigor. As more students apply early, however, more will be disappointed by denials or deferrals. For some students, the buildup has been so great, and so much seems to be at stake, that either of these last outcomes can be a major blow. Perspective can easily be lost as students face, often for the first time in their lives, what they perceive as significant failure. In contrast, at regular decision time, denials or wait-listings will probably be buffered by some good news as well. Applying to

Not everyone gets into [Elite U], but even so it's not like the 5,000 students at [Elite U] are the only ones who are happy with their college and will go on to success in life. While I eagerly hope for my deferral to turn into an acceptance, I know that I have to look at my other options as a definite possibility so my college experience is not haunted by the ghost of [Elite U].

COMMENT MADE ON DECEMBER 16 BY STUDENT DEFERRED AT AN IVY LEAGUE COLLEGE

The advantages of applying early are sufficiently great that you should at least consider applying early to a first-choice college where you would be a long shot for regular decision. [But] you can easily convince yourself that you actually have a chance of being admitted as an early applicant to a school that is well out of reach. An early application will not help you at a college where you are not close to being a competitive applicant.[5]

FROM THE EARLY ADMISSIONS GAME

several colleges also tends to negate the idea of a perfect match—you see several colleges as a good fit.

So where does this leave you? Well, it depends. If you have a first-choice college and satisfy the criteria for early decision or early action we have noted, you should seriously think about applying early. If you would be a competitive applicant, there are clear advantages to doing so. But please remember what we have said about the downside of early applications. Don't let your enthusiasm for a college lead you into succumbing to early acceptance syndrome—the belief that there is one and only one college where you can truly be happy. That is rarely, if ever, the case.

MORE THINGS TO CONSIDER

Much of what we have just presented is changing. As more students try to take advantage of the early admissions boost, some colleges are cutting back on the percentage of the freshman class admitted through the early cycle. It's like what happens when word starts to spread about a wonderful neighborhood restaurant that has always had free tables. The restaurant may need to start taking reservations that will be harder and harder to get as its reputation grows. The early admission boost is decreasing and may eventually disappear at many schools.

But what everyone else is doing or not doing shouldn't really matter. If you think a college is truly your first choice, whether there is an advantage to applying early shouldn't make any difference in your decision, as long as you are a competitive applicant. We also want to emphasize that even if you apply early decision or early action to your first-choice school, you should carefully consider where else to apply. December 15 is too late to decide on other colleges and begin your applications in the event your first choice declines or defers your application.

One of the arguments often offered in favor of early decision is that it can eliminate the need to complete additional applications. This just doesn't hold up in reality for some students. A few colleges require a pre-application, along with an application fee, that needs to be filed before the application itself. These usually must be sent in before the December 15 early action or early decision notification date. And remember, most regular decision applications are due January 1 or soon after. Beginning an application after December 15 during the holiday season isn't an appealing prospect, especially after receiving a disappointing decision from a first-choice college.

✿ Is Early Decision Right for You?

☐ I have a clear first-choice college and am completely confident that it is a very good fit for me.

☐ I have done careful research about the college that supports my choice, including most of the following: visited in-person or on the Web; studied the catalog, viewbook, and other material in detail; reviewed the college's profile in a "big book"; and talked with current or former students in person, through online chat, or e-mail.

☐ I will probably be comfortable with the financial aid that is offered to me and won't have to compare financial aid offers.

☐ My grades from first-semester senior year will not be significantly better than the rest of my record.

☐ I have taken (or will take) my standardized tests so that the scores will reach my early decision college in time for early review.

☐ My overall record places me within the admissible range for this college.

☐ I will be able to prepare and submit my application by the early decision deadline, including letters of recommendation from my teachers and counselor.

☐ I would like the extra admissions boost that early decision candidates appear to get.

☐ I would like to know for sure where I will be going to college as early as possible.

☐ I will do careful research on the rest of my college list and prepare applications to them in case I am deferred or denied in early decision.

☐ Although my early decision college is my clear first choice, I realize that I may not be accepted and that I will also be very happy with a fine education at other colleges.

Teacher and counselor recommendations and transcripts, as well as SAT or ACT scores, also need to be requested well before the due date. As a result, many students find themselves applying regular decision to their full array of college choices, although they have an early application pending. If the early application is successful, they must withdraw those additional applications. The extra effort and expense are written off as the cost of "insurance."

As noted earlier, a number of schools, mostly liberal arts schools, have two rounds of early decision, ED I and ED II. The date for ED II often coincides with the date for regular decision applications, but of course the ED II applicants get their decisions earlier, usually by mid-February, and are committed to attending if they are accepted, just as in ED I. Colleges offering two rounds of early decision say that they do this to give students more time to decide on a first choice. Although this is no doubt an important consideration that helps many students, an additional reason for a college to have a second early decision round is to receive applications from students denied or deferred on December 15 by another college. This approach gives both colleges and students two shots at making an early match.

Likely Letters and Early Notification

Colleges differ in the timing of their regular decision cycle notifications, with most notifying students between March 1 and early April in time for them to make a choice by May 1. But a few students who apply regular decision get

Greetings from Dartmouth. I hope your senior year is going well and that you are enjoying your courses and activities. My purpose in writing is very simple—we have reviewed your application and think you are an outstanding prospect for Dartmouth. I recently read your folder and was exceedingly impressed with your academic accomplishments and intellectual potential. There is no question that when we mail our final decisions at the end of March, you will be offered admission to the College. I see no reason to delay letting you know about the status of your application, and I hope this early indication will "ease your mind" a bit. The college admissions process is unnecessarily long and anxious for many students. So, relax, get back to that book you meant to read, and use this time to reflect on your plans and goals for the next phase of your education.

From a Dartmouth College likely letter for the class of 2010

Early Acceptance

I belong to a family of planners, and we like to have things resolved. What time is dinner? Who's taking out the trash? What pet are we getting? While other families decide such things on the spur of the moment, we plan, and if PETCO has only gerbils and not our choice (hamsters), we go somewhere else.

For people like us, early acceptance is compelling. Choose early? Hear back in December? Sounds wonderful—if you accept that you won't be able to compare financial aid packages.

Our family also enjoys travel, so it's no surprise that our college tours began early. My daughter checked out schools as a sophomore and gave hints to my son, who traveled junior year. Both found "favorite" colleges. By November 15, the paperwork was done.

Then came the waiting.

Brain power that could have been put to better use polishing essays for other applications (in case of denial or deferral) went into analyzing everything from postal service competency to the walking speed of our mail carrier.

Finally, the decisions came. My daughter was accepted, and life got a whole lot easier.

Three years later, my son was not as fortunate. After expending what for him was tremendous energy on his application (an audition tape was particularly daunting), he learned that he had been "deferred."

He wasn't prepared to wait.

He knew which college was his second choice. They offered a second early decision program, and he jumped for it. In February he was accepted, and that's where he enrolled.

Meanwhile, I kept waiting for him to feel bad. His first-choice school was eight miles from the beach. Second choice was in a freezing climate, 2,000 miles from his girlfriend. If he had held out for regular decision, the first-choice school might have accepted him.

But the anguish I awaited never came. He bubbled with college plans.

If the beach school had been swept into the ocean, I don't think he would have noticed.

I conclude that loyalty to a college you have never attended isn't really all that strong.

M. F.

letters early—sometimes very early—that tell them that they are very likely to be accepted, even though it is not a formal letter of admission. Known in admissions circles as "likely letters," these early notifications allow a college to adhere to the official notification date while signaling to a select group of students that the college is especially interested in them.

Colleges hope that a likely letter will increase the chances that the student receiving it will accept the official offer of admission when it arrives later. Likely letters often go to people the college is especially eager to recruit—athletes, members of underrepresented groups, and those with truly distinctive academic credentials.

Still other colleges have early notification programs where they formally admit some regular decision cycle applicants a month or so earlier than others. Swarthmore and Williams are two such colleges. Students do not apply for this kind of early notification. It is up to the college to decide. Yet another program is "early evaluation." Wellesley College offers students the option of formally requesting an early assessment of the likelihood of admission. If they apply by January 1 rather than the regular deadline of January 15, students who request early evaluation will receive a letter at the end of February that lists their chances of admission as "likely," "possible," or "unlikely." The large majority of those accepted, however, at the Ivy League and elsewhere, receive their first and only notification on the previously announced date. The Ivy League schools agree to announce their regular, but not their early, decisions, at the same time. Regardless of the timing of notification, students all have until May 1 to make a final decision.

The Advantage of Thinking Early Even If You Decide Against Applying Early

Many students habitually cut things close to the wire, and they extend that habit to the college application process. But even if you do not plan to apply "early" to a college, there are advantages to getting your application in well before the deadline. The most obvious case is if a college uses rolling admissions to select students as their applications come in, rather than waiting until they

> One of the most comical things is that close to half of our applications come in during a two to three day period right before the deadline. If you come here around December 30, you'll see the FedEx truck, Airborne Express, UPS, all lined up out here. We literally have buckets and buckets of mail that come in.[6]
>
> THOMAS PARKER, DEAN OF ADMISSIONS AND FINANCIAL AID AT AMHERST COLLEGE

can compare applications to each other. Used at many state universities, like the University of Michigan, and some less selective private colleges, rolling admission allows a college to accept qualified students up until the freshman class is full. Clearly, applying early is better than applying at or close to the deadline so that your application will be considered while there is still room.

But there are advantages to getting your application in well before the deadline for other colleges as well. Even if you are applying regular decision to a college with a January 1 deadline, you can submit your application as early as you want once the applications are available.

Getting your materials in early even if you want regular cycle review means that they will arrive earlier than the deadline "crunch" and be filed and acknowledged earlier (and be more likely to make it successfully to your folder rather than go astray). You will be notified online or via postcard that your file is complete, and you won't have to worry whether a letter or test scores will get there on time. And if something does end up missing, you'll have lots of time to get a replacement sent.

Because admissions committees start reading files that are complete soon after the closing date, you'll get a reading by staff members who are fresh and not yet fatigued by the many hundreds of files they will read during the winter. It's impossible to know, of course, if that will make any difference in the final decision, but it can't hurt. Getting applications in early also means that you can enjoy the holiday season with your family, rather than spend it worrying about applications. We think you (and your family) will be glad you took our advice.

And Humor Always Helps Keep Things in Perspective

Mike Mills, director of admission at Miami University, penned the following parody for the *Journal of College Admission*. We enjoyed it and hope you will, too.

From an Application in the Future

Term applying for: Fall 2018 _____   Spring 2019 _____   Application Fee: $250

Applying for:

Priority Decision[1] _____   Regular Decision[2] _____   Precision Decision[3] _____

Division Decision[4] _____   Revision Decision[5] _____   Provision Decision[6] _____

Derision Decision[7] _____   Rescission Decision[8] _____

[1] Yes! Beyond the tangible benefit of earlier notification, I want to receive all other attendant (albeit ambiguous) benefits of applying under this plan. I also want to keep my options open while avoiding the stigma of applying under the Regular Decision plan.

[2] I want to keep all my options open, and I refuse to be a pawn in your silly admissions game.

[3] This is exactly the school I'm looking for, and I will enroll if accepted.

[4] My parents and I fought long and hard over whether I should apply to this school, and it is your job to figure out who won.

[5] I like this school, but I may opt to attend a better school should I be admitted to one.

[6] I like this school and will attend provided you ante up with some significant scholarship dollars. I know you have the endowment to do it.

[7] I'm applying, but don't fool yourselves—you're definitely my back-up school.

[8] I'm applying, but I may and likely will cancel my application at some point in time.

Adapted from Mike Mills, "Applications We Hope Never to See," *Journal of College Admission,* Winter 2004, Number 182. Reprinted with permission. Copyright 2004 National Association for College Admission Counseling.

CHAPTER 8

Applying Well

Part I

If you've read this far in *Admission Matters*, you know that you need to do a lot of important self-reflection and research before you actually begin applying to college. But once you have done that work and developed an appropriate list of good-bet, possible, and long-shot colleges, the next step is tackling the applications themselves. You'll want to present your qualifications to college admissions committees in a way that will distinguish you from many other applicants with similar credentials. In this chapter and the next, we help you do just that. We discuss the application process in general and guide you through writing your important personal statement and other essays, both long and short. In Chapter Nine, we continue with other parts of your application and tell you how to get strong letters of recommendation, how to prepare an activities list that sets you apart, and how to shine in an interview. We also have tips for athletes, for students with special talents, and for homeschoolers.

Preparing a strong college application takes work. There's no way around that. A typical application asks many questions, and your answers tell a lot about your academic abilities, background, talents, and interests. Less obviously, your answers also send subtle messages about your degree of interest in a college and how much time and effort you have put into thinking about yourself. The best applications do both.

GETTING OFF TO A GOOD START

Although the competition for admission to selective schools is greater than ever, the actual process of filing an application has never been easier. Now almost every college not only accepts but actively encourages electronic submission of applications. Some even waive their application fees if you submit online. Colleges differ a great deal in their use of technology in the application process, but the trend is clearly toward a paperless process where materials are submitted electronically and read from a computer screen.

Gone, fortunately for good, are the days when the only way to prepare an application was with a typewriter and a bottle of correction fluid. Many parents reading this will remember how hard the old-fashioned way was. It is a major advantage to be able to update and edit your application easily until you submit it. It can now be as complete and accurate as you can make it, without having to go through the agony of starting everything over because you forgot to include something or changed your mind about how to phrase an answer.

Fight the Urge to Procrastinate

Certainly, completing a college application is not fun. It is hard to answer all those questions and distill yourself into little boxes of two hundred words or three hundred characters on a form. It also takes precious time, something often in short supply in senior year. And on top of it all, just thinking about college, as exciting as it may be, can make you nervous. *Where will I be next year? Will I have friends? Will I be happy?*

The natural tendency in a situation like this is to put off dealing with it as long as possible. Our simple advice is *don't*. Do your research on colleges early, and begin the actual job of applying. Fight the urge to procrastinate.

Everyone experiences it—including us, the authors of this book, as we tackled the job of preparing this revision and found that things didn't always go as smoothly as planned. But procrastination never helps, and it can really hurt if it means that you put your college list together hastily and it does not really fit your needs, or that you rush to meet a deadline and don't make it. Procrastination can result in missed opportunities, such as when your favorite teacher regrets that she won't have time to write your letter of recommendation because you asked her too late. It can mean less thoughtful (and usually more wordy) answers to questions,

I've always left things to pretty much the last minute, and it's never been a problem. In character, I left my most important college application to the day before it was due. I planned to rework an essay I had written for a college that had an earlier deadline, so I wasn't too worried. After spending all day Sunday putting everything together, I was ready to submit my application electronically at 9:00 PM. Then I realized the program cut off the last seven sentences of my essay. No matter what I did, I couldn't get the whole thing in. My mom looked at the essay, and we agreed that it would be really hard to cut. She suggested I look at the paper app—maybe it would fit in there. It did. I then spent the next two hours filling out the paper app by hand and doing cut-and-paste onto the form for my essay. It was after 11:00 PM when I finished. I had school the next day, but my mom mailed it for me and met the postmark deadline. I was accepted and am now a sophomore. But even I agreed I cut things too close. I could have really blown it.

COLLEGE SOPHOMORE

since you won't have time to carefully review and edit them, or benefit from feedback from others. Overall, it can mean that you don't have a chance to make your best case for admission.

The wise student starts early, makes a time line indicating what is needed and by when, and then just gets it done.

Neatness and Completeness Count!

The ease with which an application can be submitted electronically or filled out online can lead to carelessness in proofreading and failure to double-check everything for accuracy. We are all familiar with that problem in our daily e-mail. We just want to hit the "send" or "print" key and be done with it. Resist the urge. Typos, omissions, and other errors can mar an otherwise good application. In particular, you want to avoid having your great response to the question about why you want to attend Hamilton College mention that you find the University of Chicago's core curriculum exciting. The fact that Hamilton has chosen not to have any kind of core curriculum makes the mistake even more embarrassing. Errors of this kind, and worse, routinely happen when you cut and paste text from one application to another. Electronic applications make the process easier, but they can also make mistakes easier.

Mistakes can also happen when you are hastily filling out a lot of applications close to a deadline. An error-filled, incomplete application practically shouts, "I didn't take this application seriously." Why, then, should the college? So, before hitting "send," carefully proofread everything yourself and have a friend or parent proofread as well. And then proofread it again. Why be sloppy when the outcome is so important to you?

Follow Directions

Be sure to read the application carefully and answer the questions that are asked, not other ones. In an effort to economize on work, you may want to recycle answers from one application to another. This is fine, as long as you make sure that the same questions are being asked—and you are careful to remove any specific references to the first college in your answer! This is especially important in switching from an early action or early decision application to a regular one, because you may have identified your first choice in your essay.

Following directions also means being aware of limits on the length of responses and the number of recommendation letters. We talk about how to approach these limits later in this chapter and in Chapter Nine.

USING THE COMMON APPLICATION

The Common Application is an application form accepted by 350 public and private colleges and universities across the country. It was designed to simplify the college admissions process for students who would otherwise have to provide identical information in different formats to each college. A few colleges offer applicants a choice between their own form and the Common Application, including Princeton University, the University of Chicago, and Bard College. Many others now use the Common Application exclusively. This list includes Dartmouth College, Villanova University, Stanford University, Haverford College, and about 120 others. A few selective colleges (for example, Columbia University, Georgetown University, MIT, the University of Michigan, and the University of California) still don't accept the Common Application, but the number is dwindling. Be

> For years, parents, teachers, guidance counselors, school administrators, and members of the school board have been urging teenagers to abstain from sex or to use condiments.
>
> SENTENCE FROM A COLLEGE APPLICATION REPORTED BY AN ADMISSIONS OFFICER, WHO ADDED, "AT LEAST THE STUDENT USED SPELL CHECK."[1]

sure to check the Common Application Web site, www.commonapp.org, for new additions as well as for the forms themselves.

Using the Common Application can save you a lot of time, since you need only complete a single application—either online or on paper—regardless of the number of schools to which you apply. The Common App Online is particularly time-saving because you don't even have to print and mail an application. Regardless of whether they use only the Common Application, the great majority of selective colleges that use it also require a supplemental form that asks one or more college-specific questions. All schools also allow you to submit your supplement online as well. A copy of the Common Application for 2009–10, along with all related forms, is included in Appendix B. Look it over carefully. It will give you a good idea of what college applications are like in general. The latest version of the Common Application, with full instructions, can be found online through the Common Application Web site. There are modest changes every year, so be sure to use the current version, which usually becomes available in July.

> What exactly do admissions officers want to know when they ask you to write the college essay? No matter which question, we are asking what is really important to you, who you are, and how you arrived where you are. The whole college application process is really a self-exploration, and the essay is a way to put your personal adventure into words.[2]
>
> DELSIE PHILLIPS, FORMER DIRECTOR OF ADMISSIONS AT HAVERFORD COLLEGE

Students sometimes ask whether colleges prefer their own form, and if submitting the Common Application will imply that students are less interested in a college than they might really be. The fact is that colleges that accept the Common Application pay a fee for the privilege. They also pledge to treat all applications, the Common Application and their own if they still have one, identically.

Another type of generic application, known as the Universal College Application, is also available. It currently has eighty-five schools participating; forms and member colleges can be found at www.universalcollegeapp.com. Some colleges accept both the Common Application and the Universal Application, but you will find colleges on the Universal College Application list that don't use the Common Application. If your college list contains one or more schools in this latter category, consider using the Universal College Application in lieu of or in addition to the Common Application, depending on the other colleges to which you are applying: their features are similar.

WRITING AN EFFECTIVE PERSONAL ESSAY

Many college application forms, including the Common Application, require one essay or personal statement. Some require more. In this section, we show you how to approach the essay as an opportunity for self-understanding, not just as an unwelcome assignment. Although colleges differ in how much emphasis they place on the essay, it can always make a difference. Its importance may also vary for different students because of the strength of their credentials. At most schools where your grades and scores are at the top of that college's pool, a so-so essay won't be too damaging, but at a highly selective or super-selective school, it always matters, since hardly anyone is admitted by grades and tests alone.

Why Do Colleges Ask for Essays?

The essay is a way for you to personalize your application and to give it life. That's how colleges view it. Along with your letters of recommendation, your essay helps admissions officers differentiate you from others with similar records. It is a chance to share something special about yourself that will help the reader conclude that you would make a wonderful addition to the next freshman class. It can also demonstrate to a college that you can express yourself effectively and persuasively in writing—a skill that is crucial for success in college. Henry Bauld, author of a delightful book on college admissions essays, sums up the essay as follows: "It shows you at your alive and thinking best, a person worth listening to—not just for the ten minutes it takes to read your application, but for the next four years."[3]

The problem with advice like this is that it is hard to follow when you get down to yourself. You know that you should be honest, open, and tell the truth, but you realize that you are also trying to make a good impression on the readers. How can you do both? How can you avoid being stiff and impersonal, sort of like an awkward first date, as you try to make a good impression? How can you be sure you aren't making yourself too vulnerable if you admit you are not perfect? It's hard, but those are real questions to think about. In considering them, you are more likely to write a self-reflective and thoughtful essay. If you ignore the dilemma, you might err on one side or the other. Many students are so intent on being well-perceived that they write bland, uninvolving essays, thinking that as long as they are telling the truth, they are doing fine.

The Three Types of Questions

Sarah McGinty, a consultant specializing in workshops on writing college essays, points out that most college essays boil down to one of three types: some version of "tell us about yourself," some variety of "why us?" in terms of college or career choice, or a "creative" question that asks you to reflect on some topic that may appear to be only tangentially related to the college admissions process, if at all. In *The College Application Essay,* McGinty emphasizes that regardless of the form of the question, each is trying to get information about you.[4] What you choose to write tells the reader a great deal about how you think, what your life experiences have been, and what you value.

Selecting a Topic

In writing your essay, you don't try to figure out what you think colleges want to hear. Focus instead on yourself. Who are you? What makes you tick deep inside? What do you want them to know about you? Think about the qualities you want to convey, and then think about how to represent those qualities in your answer to the question. Ideally, your essay should illustrate your points through personal example, rather than simply state them; in other words, your essay should show, not just tell. Many good essays are essentially stories, based on a personal experience. Storytelling comes naturally to people, more easily than essay writing. The trick is to make your essay—your story—lively and interesting to read. You want the reader to think, "I would like to get to know this person." Or: "This sounds like a fun student to teach or have in a dorm or on a team." The problem is that you are so close to yourself that it is hard to see how a benevolent stranger reading your essay might view you.

Admissions readers like their work. Nobody does it for the money or the glory, and there is precious little power in it. They also like teenagers, and they are open-minded enough to realize that young people come in different shapes and sizes and think differently. Trusting your reader to be interested and positive is reasonable. Readers are not enemies to be tricked or gullible targets to be wowed. They

Sample Essay Topics

"Tell Us About Yourself" Essays

- What has been the most meaningful piece of advice you have ever received? Who gave you this advice and in what way(s) have you put it to use? (Colgate University, 2008–09)

- A range of academic interests, personal perspectives, and life experiences adds much to the educational mix. Given your personal background, describe an experience that illustrates what you would bring to the diversity in a college community, or an encounter that demonstrated the importance of diversity to you. (Common Application, 2009–10; one of six essay options—all six options may be found in Appendix B)

"Why Us?" Essays

- Why, in particular, do you wish to attend Bates? (Bates College, 2008–09)

- How did you first become interested in Reed, and why do you think Reed would be an appropriate place, both academically and socially, to continue your education? (This essay is instrumental in helping the admission committee determine the match between you and Reed, so please be thorough.) (Reed College, 2008–09)

"Be Creative" Essays

- Chicago author Nelson Algren said, "A writer does well if in his whole life he can tell the story of one street." Chicagoans, but not just Chicagoans, have always found something instructive, and pleasing, and profound in the stories of their block, of Main Street, of Highway 61, of a farm lane, of the Celestial Highway. Tell us the story of a street, path, road—real or imagined or metaphorical. (University of Chicago, 2008–09)

- The human narrative is replete with memorable characters like America's Johnny Appleseed, ancient Greece's Perseus or the Fox Spirits of East Asia. Imagine one of humanity's storied figures is alive and working in the world today. Why does Joan of Arc have a desk job? Would Shiva be a general or a diplomat? Is Quetzalcoatl trapped in a zoo? In short, connect your chosen figure to the contemporary world and imagine the life he/she/it might lead. (Tufts University, 2008–09; one of several optional essay topics) are often young enough to remember being in high school very clearly, and those who are older often have teenage children of their own. Treat them as human beings, and they will respond in kind.

The standard admissions prompts, both on the Common App and elsewhere, are purposely very broad to encourage individual thinking. The last thing readers want is to read five hundred words on "The Scarlet Letter" thirty times in a row, as a high school English teacher often has to do. It is true that when students write about a piece of literature, they tend to take something popular and familiar, such as the Bible, Shakespeare, or *The Great Gatsby*. Or, if they write about a person, they are likely to choose a grandparent or a famous person like John F. Kennedy or Martin Luther King Jr. These choices are fine, *if* you can present yourself well through this mechanism. But it doesn't hurt to choose something off the familiar path, as long as the choice is important to you personally. It is even all right to write about a book or type of music that the reader might not be familiar with.

It is not surprising that certain themes appear often in college application essays: "How My Summer Trip to _____ Changed My Life," for example, or "Winning (or Losing) the Race (or Game, or Election)," or "The Death of My Beloved _____." These topics, and other common ones, are not necessarily bad. In fact, there are almost no bad topics—just weak essays. A weak college essay tells the reader little about what makes the writer an interesting, unique person. The more common your essay topic, the greater your burden in writing something different from the large number of other applicants tackling the same topic. A topic more unique or personal to you, no matter how small it may appear to be, is often easier to make distinctive and interesting. Good essays have been written on topics as simple as a weekly walk with an aging grandparent, working with young children in a summer camp, and cooking a meal for a special friend. In fact, given the tremendous volume of applications at most schools, there are probably few uncommon topics any more. Searching for one is likely to be frustrating because you can never know.

One counselor we know challenges students to write about the time they saved an old lady from drowning at the beach and made the six o'clock news as a hero. Since this never happened, they naturally look puzzled. "Look," he says, "You are a normal teenager who has led a normal life with no great tragedies, thank goodness, and no Nobel Prize at sixteen either. You have to write about something in your normal life. The solution is to look inside yourself, not 'out there' for a topic."

What to Avoid

Some topics, though, are best avoided altogether, no matter how distinctive your approach. You should almost always avoid writing about sexual experiences, rape, incest, or mental illness. Don't write to express your pain. We feel a little differently about very controversial political and social issues such as abortion. Just be careful that you come across as a person of conviction, which means that you have considered opposing arguments, not as an ideologue, who knows the truth and doesn't want to hear any opposition. If you can't tell the difference, pick something less sensitive to write about. You don't know who your readers will be, and it is foolish to write about a topic that may make someone uncomfortable.

Be sure, though, that you answer the question that is asked, not some other one. Even though the questions are all asking about you, directly or indirectly, they vary in how they frame their inquiry. The only essay we are aware of that gives you total latitude in responding is the final Common Application essay option of "Choose your own topic." If you are responding to a more specific prompt, your essay should address the question the way it is asked. An essay written for one prompt can often be reworked to fit another one, however, so you may be able to use a good essay in different ways for different colleges, saving a lot of time and effort. Just be sure to modify your essay carefully each time you reuse it.

What Kind of Help Is Appropriate?

Colleges expect that the essays you submit with your application are your own work. They ask you to sign a statement to that effect on the application. This doesn't mean that you can't brainstorm essay ideas with your family, friends, teachers, and guidance counselor. Nor does it mean that you can't get comments from others once you have written a draft. In fact, most professional writers go through several drafts and get comments and reactions from others along the way. It makes good sense to write a draft, put it away for a few days, and then revisit it. William Zinsser,

> My son's girlfriend was hanging around the house bemoaning the fact that she had nothing to write about in her essay. I said, "But you like reading. You like the classics. I remember how upset you were when other kids said they didn't like *Jane Eyre*." I knew if she wrote about books, her essay would show real passion.
>
> FORMER WRITING TEACHER WHO KNOWS THAT MANY HIGH SCHOOL STUDENTS DON'T ENJOY THE CLASSICS

Essay Don'ts

- Don't write an essay that any one of a thousand other seniors could write, because they probably will *(and are probably doing just that at this very moment).*

- Avoid writing an essay that will embarrass the reader. While you definitely must risk something personally in order to write an effective essay, the risk should not place a burden on the reader. *Don't confess something too personal that you haven't completely worked through in your own mind. The risk you take should not make the reader uncomfortable.*

- Don't try to sell yourself. Rather than persuading the college that you are great, just show them who you are, what you care about, what the pivotal points in your life have been so far. *Remember you are just a high school senior who gets into a pair of shoes one at a time like everyone else. You are also a person, not a box of corn flakes. You are not "packaging" yourself. This is one of the worst metaphors in the admissions field these days, and we are embarrassed that some writers and counselors don't see anything wrong with "packaging" yourself.*

- Don't try to write an "important" essay—the definitive statement on the Middle East or race relations in America. These essays tend to come across as much more pompous than the authors intend. *Honestly, what do you have to say about the Middle East or climate change that your reader won't have heard before? On the other hand, perhaps a relative served in the army in Iraq, or you are actually involved in an environmental organization. It is the personal connection that counts, not whether you are on the "right" side of an issue. Don't assume the reader shares your views, either. You are entitled to an opinion, but be sure it is a reasoned, thoughtful one, even if you take on a hot-button issue like religion, abortion, or gay rights. Colleges are places of debate and the exchange of ideas; admissions officers want students with a variety of views, as long as they are intelligent, reasonable, and civil.*

- Don't set out to write the perfect essay, the one with huge impact, the one that will blow the doors to the college open for you. Think instead of giving the reader a sample of yourself, a slice of the real you, a snapshot in words. *Remember, essays don't often have that kind of impact. They are just one personal piece of a bigger file. Remember also that you can't put everything in your life into five hundred words. You have to select; you have to figure out what is most important; and you have to leave out some things that you like and that you would like the admissions staff to know. Then you have to make it "sing."*

Annotated in italics and adapted with permission from "What Not to Do and Why" by William Poirot, former college counselor, in C. Georges and G. Georges, *100 Successful College Application Essays*, New York: Penguin, 2002. Copyright © The Harvard Independent.

author of the fine writing guide, *On Writing Well,* says that there is no such thing as good writing, only good rewriting.[5] Almost by definition a first draft is going to be rough. So give yourself enough time to get some feedback. Your English teacher or guidance counselor can be especially helpful in making suggestions about your essay, because they are professionals who evaluate writing for a living and have seen many essays over the years. They also have natural boundaries when it comes to students' writing. They know when to stop and let the student's voice stay intact.

Parents can sometimes lose sight of this and set about trying to rewrite their child's essay. Although help with brainstorming and editing is good, wholesale rewriting is not. It can hurt much more than help. It can destroy a student's distinctive voice—something that admissions officers really want to hear—and signal that the parent doesn't think the child is up to the job. The important point, however, is that the end product should be your own work and sound like you, not like someone else two or three times your age, no matter who it is.

Pay Attention to the Shorter Essays

The typical application includes one or two five-hundred-word essays and a few questions that can each be answered in a paragraph. Many students focus all their effort on the long essays, leaving the shorter ones to the very end when they are rushed and trying to meet a deadline. But the shorter questions are important as well, because both short and long essays give the reader insights into who you are. So pay attention to the shorter questions, and edit and proofread them just as you would the long essays. The Common Application asks for 150 words on your favorite extracurricular activity: "Please describe which of your activities (extracurricular and personal activities or work experience) has been the most meaningful and why." This can be hard, since you have to be very stingy with words. Although it is probably not as important as your main essay, everything counts in the end, so take it seriously.

Many colleges include a "Why X?" question where they ask what the attraction of their individual college is. You should respond very carefully to these questions. Colleges ask these for a reason, even if you don't like them. They are trying to assess your motivation and your thoughtfulness. A good answer shows that you have carefully researched the college and thought about what you would get from, as well as contribute to, it. A vague answer shows lack of real interest or homework.

Remember that admissions staff members are experts on their own colleges. Don't tell them things that are obvious or just not very interesting: New York University is in New York, for example, and you love New York! A good answer never mentions New York; it discusses something specific about NYU that reveals something interesting about you. NYU is only the apparent subject of the essay, and you do have to write about why you like the school, but *you* are the real subject, so your essay has to be distinctively about yourself. How can you tell? Well, try to imagine a couple of your best friends who are also applying to NYU. Perhaps they like the same aspects that you do. But each of them is a different person, and their answers should differ significantly from each other, and from yours.

Supplements usually contain several additional questions requiring paragraph-length answers. Colleges know that students tend to get the most advice on the longer essays, but they think you are less likely to get heavy editing on the shorter pieces, so they might seem fresher, more direct. Even short questions to list your favorite music, movie, or current event say something about you. Everything counts.

Do I Have to Count Every Word?

Applicants often wonder how strictly they need to adhere to a word limit. The Common Application specifies an essay at least 250 words, which is about half a page of single-spaced print. That is quite a brief space in which to tell your most important story, so we recommend about 500 words, or roughly one typed page. There is no word limit, so you could write more, and there is no problem with going to 700 or so, but beyond that point, you may be taxing your reader's patience. This is not because your essay is too long for the subject, but because readers are used to spending the same amount of time on each application. It helps them pace themselves. If your application takes longer, they will try to be fair to you, but you might be irritating them too. Why take that chance?

Writing clean, stylish prose is an art. We have worked with hundreds of students on their essays, and it is rare that an 800-word essay cannot be trimmed to 600 and be strengthened in the process. So be aware of your essay's length and its effect on the reader. In some cases, such as the University of California, two essays are required, and a limit of 1,000 words total is specified. Whatever is asked, just follow the directions. This is not the place to display your feisty, rebellious side. Remember, too, that electronic applications may limit the length of your essay. Sometimes the program will allow you to type in a longer than average essay, but will truncate it before it can actually be submitted. Be sure to preview your electronic applications before submitting them to avoid this.

Steps to a Successful Essay

We conclude this section with some tips that will help you write great essays. The Resources section at the end of this book lists two excellent books that focus exclusively on writing the college essay, and there are others, too. We've given you a good start here, but we encourage you to consult one or more of these sources if you would like more detail about essay writing.

- Brainstorm either by yourself or with others about the personal qualities that you would like to convey in your essay. Look deep inside yourself. Who are you? Who are you becoming? What have you learned in your short life?

- Read the essay topics carefully. What grabs you? What would be fun to write about?

- If you have a choice of topics, select one that allows you to speak in your own voice and tell a story about yourself.

- Be sure to show by example, not just tell. Use details, even names of other people, if they are included. Make it vivid so the reader can imagine being there with you.

- Try to avoid the passive voice. When in doubt, cut extra words. Don't write a conclusion or moral at the end, like: "What I learned was . . . " The essay is short enough that it should contain its moral. You are not writing one of Aesop's fables. Think about making it easy and fun to read, not just expressing yourself. Be aware that you have an audience.

- Set your draft aside for a couple of days, and then revise it. Think carefully about whom you want to ask for advice. Ask your English teacher or counselor or both to read and comment on your essay. Your parents will probably be eager to read it as well.

- Incorporate the best suggestions into another draft. Set it aside for a couple of days again and then reread it, changing it until you are reasonably happy with it. You cannot write a perfect essay, so at some point, you have to let it go.

- Proofread your essay carefully. Then have someone else proofread it too. Why take a risk with preventable mistakes?

AN IMPORTANT TO-DO LIST

It is often said that the devil is in the details. The last thing you want to happen is for your thoughtful, carefully prepared case for admission, including a terrific essay, to be sabotaged by minor details. We offer this list to help you keep track of all those little things that can make a big difference. In Chapter Nine we talk about other parts of your application besides the essay, but we suggest that you take a quick look at this list now. When you are actually ready to apply, review it again carefully, and then double-check it several times along the way to be sure you have all the bases covered.

- *Keep close track of all deadlines—they will vary from college to college.* It is easy to forget when things are due when you have multiple applications and a lot going on at school and at home. Develop a system that will work for you and then use it to be sure everything gets done (and sent) on time.

- *Be sure to spell your name exactly the same way on all your application materials, SAT or ACT registration, and any correspondence.* If you use your middle initial, use it every time on every form for every college-related purpose. Get into the habit of doing this right at the beginning and avoid the hassle of having three copies of every college mailing arrive at your house, or test scores or recommendation letters that go astray. If your social security number is required, be sure you enter it correctly each time.

- *Make sure your e-mail address reflects your maturity.* Save imtoosexy@hotstuff-mail.com for communication with your friends, and get another address, from a reliable provider, for your college applications. Don't laugh; they do notice. And while we are on the topic of maturity, be sure that your postings on Facebook, YouTube, or similar Web sites don't contain things that would be embarrassing to you. You never know who may get access to them and at what point.

- *Keep a copy of everything you send in, including online applications and other written and e-mail correspondence.* Make sure you submit all parts of the application, along with the application fee if one is required, by the indicated deadlines. Don't wait until the last minute to file—unanticipated problems can happen near the deadline. If you are filing electronically, check online to see that both parts of your application, the basic part and any supplement, have been received.

- *Give all those who are writing recommendations for you everything they need to submit them on time.* Make up packets that include the appropriate recommendation forms (with identifying information legibly filled out at the top) and include a stamped, addressed envelope for each form with the school as the return address. Sign the waiver if the forms have one and put a Post-it note on each form with the due date. Put everything in one big manila envelope with your name and the due date for each recommendation clearly written on the outside. Do the same for the secondary school reports that you give to your counselor. Arrange to pay for the transcripts that colleges typically request, if your school has such a policy.

- *File your financial aid forms promptly, even if you and your parents have to estimate the preceding year's figures.* Keep copies of everything you use to fill out the forms. You may need to produce them as part of the data verification process.

- *Ask the College Board or ACT, or both, to send your scores to the colleges of your choice.* Both the College Board and ACT will now send only the scores you ask them to send. Each gives you a limited number of free score reports if you provide the names of the colleges at the time of testing. Later reports can be purchased online, by mail, or by phone. Be sure you send your test results in time. Allow at least three weeks for regular delivery of scores. You can pay for rush delivery, but it is expensive and unnecessary if you plan ahead, except for November scores if you apply early. This is your responsibility, not your high school's, even if they put your scores on the transcript. The scores you report for yourself on the Common Application are unofficial as well. The colleges require official scores, sent by the testing agencies.

- *Be sure to keep all correspondence that may come from your colleges after you apply.* Some may come by Postal Service and some via e-mail. You will probably get a password to access the status of your application online, as well as the final decision. Keep your password in a safe place—and remember where you put it.

- *Check the status of your application about three to four weeks after everything was sent.* It can take quite a while for forms to be opened and sorted, and information is not always immediately posted online. If a college doesn't have a Web site where you can check your application's status, be patient. The admissions staff will contact you if something is missing. It drives them crazy to get hundreds of anxious phone calls. You can always send something in again, even late, if it actually went missing in transit, and you won't be hurt by that.

- *Stay alert for phone messages or e-mail from alumni interviewers if your colleges offer such interviews.* Read the college material to see whether you have to formally request an interview (and by what date) or if you will be contacted automatically (and when). If you do not hear from someone in the time frame indicated, call or e-mail the admissions office.

- *By mid-January, request that your high school send your fall semester grades to each college that requires them as part of the regular decision application process.* Colleges typically include a "midyear report" form in the application package for this purpose. Some high schools send a new transcript; others submit the grades right on the form itself. The midyear report form also invites the counselor to note any significant additions or changes to your academic, extracurricular, or character record. Here good news can be added or problems noted. Once again, provide a stamped, addressed envelope for each college, unless told otherwise.

- *If you have a new major honor or accomplishment after you apply, send a note to the admissions office asking that this information be added to your file.* Make sure your name and social security number are clearly indicated at the top. But don't add something insignificant. It can look as if you are trying too hard.

We turn now, in Chapter Nine, to the remaining parts of your application.

CHAPTER 9

Applying Well

Part II

As we said in Chapter Eight, essays are an important way colleges learn about students beyond their grades and test scores. But many colleges go beyond what you tell them in your essays by asking for letters of recommendation, gathering information about extracurricular activities and honors, and requiring or recommending interviews. In this chapter, we talk about how to make the most of each of these opportunities to let colleges learn about you. We also provide tips for athletes, students with special talents, and homeschoolers.

GETTING GREAT LETTERS OF RECOMMENDATION

Most colleges that require letters of recommendation ask for two from teachers and a secondary school report, usually prepared by a guidance counselor, or in some cases, another school administrator. Along with your essay, these letters can make your application distinctive. Especially valuable are anecdotes that bring a paper file to life—one admissions dean referred to applicants' files as her "flat friends"—and transform numbers into a real person. Admissions officers also welcome context—descriptions of special challenges a student has faced and overcome, explanations of erratic grades or other unusual aspects of the record, evaluations of the student relative to classmates, among other things. All of this helps the admissions officer develop a fuller picture of the student and distinguishes a student from others with similar stats.

Whom Should You Ask to Write?

Although you obviously have no direct control over what your counselor or teacher writes in a letter, you can increase the chances that your letters will be helpful in making your case for admission. The most important step is approaching the right teachers. First of all, ask teachers who have taught you recently, in the eleventh grade, if possible. The tenth grade is really too far back, and the twelfth grade is probably too fresh. You may only be partway through the semester, and the teacher may not have a lot to write about yet, even if you are very enthusiastic and doing well. Second, teachers who have taught you in more demanding courses, Honors or AP for example, are good choices if you have taken such courses. They can testify to your ability to do more challenging work. That is another reason not to use a tenth-grade teacher; the work is usually not as advanced. Third, be sure to use academic teachers from English, history, math (including computer science), science, and foreign language. Colleges consider these "academic solids." Journalism, art, music, and drama might be very important to you, and even be a center-piece of your file, but you should not use these teachers for one of your required teacher references. Have that teacher write a separate, optional letter.

Students sometimes have a difficult time deciding which teachers to ask for a letter of recommendation. The most helpful letters are those written by teachers who know you the best—not necessarily the teachers who gave you the highest grades, though it is nice if both are true. A well-written letter of recommendation should include specific examples of your contributions and achievements. Like a good personal statement, it should show by example rather than simply tell. A teacher who sees you as an active and thoughtful contributor to class discussions will be more able to provide specific examples about you in writing your recommendation. So who among your teachers has seen you at your best? Where did you shine? Did you write a great paper? Did you do some independent research? Help other students with their work? Add to the class energy? That is the teacher you should ask.

Some schools with strong college guidance programs provide training for teachers in writing effective recommendations. Most schools, however, leave it up to the teachers to figure it out for themselves. Given that reality, savvy students seek out teachers who seem particularly thoughtful, who know them well, and who are themselves strong writers.

How Should You Approach a Teacher?

Writing letters of recommendation is part of a teacher's job, but it's one that can be done well or carelessly. It can be hard to know how willing a teacher will be when asked to write a letter of recommendation. You should approach your teachers early (at least one month before a letter is due, ideally more) and give them an easy way out if they have reservations about writing for any reason, including time constraints. Tell the teachers you choose that you plan to apply to several colleges and ask whether they feel that they know you well enough to write a supportive letter of recommendation. The number of colleges doesn't matter; they only have to write one, and then copy it. The response you want is an enthusiastic "Sure," "Yes," or "Of course!" If you see any hesitation, it is probably best to pick up on the cue. Thank the teacher for considering your request, but indicate that you'll be happy to ask someone else. A reluctant letter writer is unlikely to provide a letter that will be helpful, so it is best to move on to another teacher if you can. You should have a good idea of which teachers have seen you doing your best stuff in their classes, so with foresight you won't have this problem.

Providing Background Information

Guidance counselors need as much information about you as possible to write an effective letter for the secondary school report, and it is your job to be sure they have that background. At many schools, students fill out a multiple-page form that provides teachers and counselors with information about their college plans, extracurricular activities, GPA, standardized test scores, intellectual interests, hobbies, and other general background information that highlights what makes them different from other students. Your letter writers will refer to this form, so be sure to complete it accurately and thoroughly.

Your teachers may rely less on the form than your counselor does, although it will provide them with helpful background information about you. Teachers only have to be experts in what you have achieved in their classes and related activities. If they know you play soccer or sing in the chorus, that's great, as long as it is based on their personal knowledge of you. But they don't have to repeat your activities, your grades, or your test scores, because that will be found elsewhere in your file. The main point of a teacher recommendation is to give the college an idea of you as a student in the classroom. In a sense, the admissions staff are working for their college's faculty, who want to enjoy teaching you. Your current teachers are the best authorities on that.

If your high school does not provide the kind of form we are describing, you can use the one in Appendix C or make up one of your own. It is also useful to supplement the general form with specific information for each teacher to help refresh their memory of you in the classroom. Tell them how much the class mattered to you. What did you learn that you didn't know before? How has it changed your perspective on what you want to study? What have you done to follow up on this class, even if another class is not available? In other words, help teachers help you by providing qualitative information and context for your experience in their class which they might not know about. You can't tell them what to write, of course, but you can make their task easier, and the letter will probably reflect your thoughtfulness.

It will help a great deal if you provide your recommendation writers with everything they'll need at one time in a large envelope: your personal information form, the individual recommendation forms with the identifying information at the top completed by you, and due dates clearly indicated for each school. Be sure to include a stamped, addressed envelope for each recommendation. Use the school address as the return address, not your home! Most recommendation forms are similar to the one used with the Common Application. They ask a teacher to provide a written evaluation as well as complete a checklist of characteristics that compare you to other students the teacher has known. You only need to provide them with one copy of this form for your schools on the Common Application. They will fill it out once and make multiple copies. For schools that don't use the Common Application, you will have to provide the counselor and teachers the college's own forms. The questions asked on these forms are so similar that the teacher does not have to change the content for these schools.

Colleges offer teachers the option of attaching a letter to the reference form to save time rather than completing the form itself. The form should still be attached, however, with the top portion filled out, to be sure that the letter reaches your file and is treated as one of your official letters, not as an optional extra one. Although some high schools collect the letters of recommendation from teachers and submit them as part of a larger packet, most teachers send their letters directly to the colleges.

Waive Your Right to See the Letters

The Family Educational Rights and Privacy Act, known as FERPA, gives students the right to see their permanent college record unless they voluntarily waive the right to see parts of it. Since the passage of FERPA, most colleges routinely destroy these letters. Your permanent record will probably retain only your high school transcript, your SAT or ACT scores, and possibly your own part of the application. You are familiar with all of those, so there is not much point in reserving access to them. But failing to sign the waiver could signal to both your high school teacher or counselor and the college that you distrust the writer of the letter. That is a good reason not to ask someone to write for you in the first place, so sign the waiver in all cases.

How Many Letters Should You Submit?

Sometimes a college will offer a chance to submit an optional third recommendation from a coach, employer, or someone else who knows you well, in addition to the two required letters from teachers. A few colleges—Davidson College and Dartmouth College, for example—even ask for a letter from a peer. Consider sending in an extra letter if you have someone in mind who could share valuable information about you that might not otherwise get into your file. The best case is from someone outside the school setting who can comment on another side of your personality or achievements. Ideally, writers of such letters make it clear that they know you well and provide specific examples or anecdotes to back that up. But don't worry if you don't have someone who fits this bill. Most applicants, including most of those who are accepted, don't submit an extra letter. Few extra letters make much difference.

What if the application itself asks for only two? An extra letter or two from people in a position to provide a meaningful supplement to your application will be accepted and considered by most colleges even if the form doesn't explicitly say so. Be sure, though, that the writer includes your full name and social security number prominently at the top of the letter so that it can be filed correctly with the rest of your letters.

Resist starting a letter-writing campaign, however. College admissions officers have a saying: "The thicker the file, the thicker the student." By this they mean that weaker students sometimes try to pad their applications with multiple letters of endorsement, so lots of letters can make it look as if you are trying too hard. The readers might wonder, "Why can't this kid rely on the basics like everyone else?" Applications readers hate "fluff," extra stuff that clogs up a file and takes time to sort through, but doesn't add anything of substance in the end. The only really helpful letters are from people who know you well and can add something substantive to your file. A letter of support from your uncle's lawyer who met you once years ago, no matter how rich or how prominent an alumnus of the college he may be, or from the nice neighbors you babysat for so responsibly will at best be ignored and at worst annoy the admissions staff. Limit your extra letters, if you send them at all, to one or two. Sometimes less is actually more.

The Secondary School Report or Counselor Letter

Colleges also typically require a letter from your counselor—the secondary school report, or SSR for short. You should give your counselor the same background information sheet that you prepare for your teachers. In fact, it is more important for your counselor because counselors are expected to cover more ground in their letters than teachers do. So the more your counselor knows about you, the better. In addition to asking for a letter similar to the teacher letters, the form asks your counselor to rate the rigor of your program relative to that of your classmates and to provide an overall evaluation of you as a student, including class ranking if available. (Don't worry if your high school does not rank.) Colleges know that students from large public high schools often cannot get to know their counselor well, even if they try, simply because caseloads are so enormous. They see this when they visit high schools. So their expectations for the level of detail in such letters are moderate. In contrast, letters from independent high school counselors, some of whom are former admissions officers themselves, are often extremely detailed, even flowery. One admissions reader called this "private school prose" or "glosh," meaning that it was too sticky and sweet to touch, like molasses. The point is that admissions officers read in the context of the high school, including the workload of the counselor and their experience. They are trained to be fair.

However, a detailed letter can still help, so you should get to know your counselor as well as possible. This is especially important if aspects of your record or background would benefit from explanation. For example, if your first-semester grades in your junior year suffered because of a serious illness, be sure your counselor knows. Your counselor can only explain your situation when the needed information is on hand. Or if you have a learning disability that was only discovered recently and your record shows a positive jump because you are now studying more effectively, the counselor needs to know this too. The SSR, both on the Common App and most school forms, asks your counselor to indicate whether you have ever been suspended in high school, and if so, why. Obviously, it is best if your counselor can truthfully answer no. If the answer is yes, it is absolutely crucial that you disclose this information yourself in a thoughtful, regretful way that demonstrates that you have learned your lesson and there is no likelihood of the incident being repeated. Do not think of concealing an infraction. It is rarely the end of the world, if the incident is honestly reported, but the cover-up is usually worse than the crime. Think of Watergate.

The high school sends the counselor report to colleges in the same envelope as your transcript and the school profile mentioned in Chapter Two. You may need to provide your counselor with a large stamped, addressed envelope along with the appropriate form for each college just as you do for your teachers who will be writing recommendations. Be sure you put on enough postage. Also, it is now becoming easier for schools to submit documents to colleges electronically, just as you submit your applications, so you may not need envelopes for the counselor at all. Ask your counselor what the school practice is. Teachers will still usually need envelopes, however.

SHINING IN YOUR INTERVIEW

Schools vary widely in the importance placed on interviews. As we briefly discussed in Chapter Two, some require an interview as part of the admissions process, some make it optional, and some don't offer it at all. Just how important are interviews anyway, and how should you view them?

If a college doesn't offer interviews—for example, Stanford has just begun a pilot project to introduce them, and most public universities don't use them—then obviously interviews play no role in the admissions process. But what if they are offered? Our best advice is to take advantage of an interview, prepare for it, and take it seriously. But don't expect it to carry much weight in the final outcome.

The Difference Between Informational and Evaluative Interviews

Interviews fall into two main types: informational and evaluative. In informational interviews, colleges provide applicants with personalized information about their program. The main goal of informational interviews is recruitment—getting students excited about the college and its offerings. They are usually offered by local alumni who volunteer to help their alma mater, but they can be offered on-site at the college as well, often by current students at the college. Informational interviews let you ask questions and learn more about a college; they also give you a chance to demonstrate your interest in the school. Notes are rarely kept from these sessions, although the fact that you did participate will probably be kept in your file.

Evaluative interviews are trickier. Here the college is clear that the results of the interview will be part of your admissions file. Evaluative interviews may be strongly encouraged or merely optional, and they are usually offered at the college by admissions staff or by college seniors specially trained for the task, or by alumni living in your home area. Most interviews are conducted in a student's hometown by an alumni volunteer. The alum can be a recent grad, someone who graduated thirty-five years ago, or somewhere in between. The variability among interviewers—admissions staff, seniors, and, especially, alums—can make it difficult for colleges to place great weight on interview results, even when they are intended to be evaluative. The alumni do this for fun and to give something back to the college besides money because they enjoyed their college experience. Expect the interview to be positive, warm, and friendly, not an interrogation. Most of the time it will be.

How to Approach Your Interview

The admissions office may describe your interview as evaluative or informational, or it may make no distinction at all. Regardless of the description, plan to be on time. Don't arrive early at an interview in someone's home—just be there when you are supposed to be. Expect the interview to last about forty-five minutes, plus or minus fifteen minutes, depending on the interviewer and how the discussion goes. The first part of the interview is the most important. Both of us interview others for our work, and in talking as well with college alumni who interview for their schools, we have found a consistent pattern: early impressions stick. The first few minutes can set the tone for the rest of the interview, so go into it alert and ready to go. But when the interviewer seems to relax and says, "Now let me tell you the real stuff about Dream College, USA," your part of the interview is really over, and you just have to look interested from then on. Well, be careful still, but the interview does have a structure and a pace that you can anticipate.

> Somebody I interviewed once said he wanted to major in accounting. I said, "You know, that's not a major at Harvard." It went downhill from there.
>
> HARVARD ALUMNI INTERVIEWER

Dress neatly and look presentable—no jeans, sneakers, or flip-flops—but you don't need to dress up for the occasion either. If you go to the interview in someone else's car, be sure the driver parks nearby to take you home promptly after the interview. You don't want to have to awkwardly hang out in the interviewer's living room while you wait for your ride. Many schools now recommend that the alumni conduct interviews in public places such as coffee shops to reduce the discomfort of being in someone's living room. Just be on time.

 ## Some Frequently Asked Interview Questions

- What are you looking for in a college? What attracts you to this college?
- What are your top two extracurricular activities and why do you like them?
- What sort of challenges have you faced in your life so far?
- What is your favorite subject in school and why?
- How would you describe yourself to a stranger?
- What is your favorite pastime?
- How did you spend last summer and how did you grow from it?
- What book have you read that has left a lasting impression?
- What have you enjoyed most about high school?
- Do you have any questions I can help answer?

Colleges vary in how they set up interviews. Some will call to set one up very soon after you have submitted your application. Others will wait for you to call them. Some colleges have to limit the number of interviews they can offer, simply because they have too many applicants and not enough alumni in an area, so you should research this for each college, either through the Web site or by calling the college admissions office. Interviews at a college are easier to get in the summer, but beware of how busy the admissions office can be in August. In some cases, interviews are available as early as spring break of the junior year. Before you leap at the chance, though, ask yourself how much you know about the college and how ready you are for an interview. It might be better to wait for an alumni interview in the fall if you are visiting that early.

In preparing for an interview, think about how you would answer the most likely questions, like the ones shown in the box on the preceding page. You may be asked different questions, but thinking about how you would answer the ones we have provided will help you prepare. In addition, have several prepared questions ready to ask when given the opportunity (and you will always get the opportunity). It is perfectly all right to have a note card with you to remind yourself of your questions. Interviewers understand that you may be nervous. They want you to be comfortable and natural. Make sure that your questions cannot be readily answered by looking at the catalog, Web site, or application materials, such as, "Do you have an engineering program?" or "Is there separate housing for freshmen only?" Questions that show you have read the material provided by the college and thought about it are the best kind, as are questions that ask the interviewer to explain how something like the housing or advising system works.

When the interview is over, thank the interviewer for taking the time to talk with you and ask for a card or otherwise make note of the interviewer's name and e-mail or street address. A short thank-you note or e-mail sent after the interview is a nice gesture.

HIGHLIGHTING WHAT YOU'VE ACCOMPLISHED

As discussed in Chapter Two, extracurricular activities, community service, and work experience are important ways to demonstrate your passions, initiative, and leadership skills. Depending on exactly what your activities are, however, the

Tips From an Alumni Interviewer

I am an alumni interviewer because I care about students, and I believe I can give them a good interview experience. Since alumni interviewers are basically untrained, unknown "staff," I realize that our opinions do not count highly in the selection of students. We're there to report the few bad apples, emphasize a few who are truly exceptional, and to be friendly contact people to everyone else.

These tips are drawn from my experience.

1. *It's fine to ask logistical questions in advance of the interview.* Take down the interviewer's phone number, in case you have further questions or get lost. Don't be surprised if, for safety reasons, your interviewer suggests meeting in a public place, like Starbucks, which could be busy and noisy.
2. *Don't assume that your interviewer knows much about you.* Colleges differ in how much information they dispense. I never receive any information about grades or SAT scores—and, frankly, I prefer not to know. An interview gives the student an opportunity to be more than a number.
3. *Although it is helpful to prepare answers for a few obvious questions, don't spend hours on this task.* Use your time, instead, to prepare thoughtful questions about the college that can't be answered by the catalog or Web site.
4. *Ask about your interviewer's own experience at the college.* This gets you off the hot seat for a while, and you may gain a new perspective on the school.
5. *Remember that the interview is not only to evaluate your potential and make friendly contact.* Admissions offices want to know you are really interested in the school. If you don't show any prior knowledge of my college, I may assume that it's not near the top of your list.
6. *Don't be afraid to let your passion show.* I still remember one student who said, "I know it sounds crazy, but I want to be the next Steven Spielberg." I wrote a report to the college that captured his dreams.

Final note: I consider it a privilege to interview the wonderful applicants who come my way. When they get denied, I'm disappointed, too.

M. F.

🌿 Interview Checklist

☐ Make sure you have the exact details of the interview time and location and arrange reliable transportation. If something goes wrong and you are late, don't blame the interviewer. Just apologize for the misunderstanding or for the delay.

☐ Carefully review the material you have about the college (online and paper) to make sure you know about its programs and special features.

☐ Think about your answers to possible questions, including the most important, "Why are you interested in this college?"

☐ Prepare your own thoughtful questions about the college to ask your interviewer.

☐ Dress neatly and appropriately for the setting. Dressy clothes are not necessary, but jeans and shorts are best avoided.

☐ Shake hands when you meet the interviewer and try to maintain eye contact throughout the interview.

☐ Try to relax and enjoy the conversation.

☐ After the interview is over, thank the interviewer for taking the time to speak with you. Shake hands again and ask the interviewer for a business card or other contact information.

☐ Send a short thank-you note in the next few days. A written note is nice, but e-mail is fine, too.

typical college application form can make it hard to fully convey your strengths. Most forms, including the Common Application, have a small grid that asks you to list each of your activities, the years when you participated in them, and the number of hours per week and weeks per year you spent on them. The grid also asks you to fill out any positions held, honors earned, or athletic letters awarded for each activity.

The space is small, however, and it may be hard to do your activities justice so briefly. The solution is simple. You can create your own supplementary form that presents the same information in a more user- and reader-friendly way. If the application form is adequate for your needs, however, you don't have to produce a separate activity sheet. Use one only if you need it, and certainly don't include one if the instructions specifically tell you not to do it. Some colleges are very clear that they don't want extra materials like a résumé, but others are OK with it. Some forms, including the Common Application, request that you complete the application grid even if you submit a separate activity sheet.

If you do prepare a separate activity sheet, keep it short—one or two pages if possible—and follow the general format used on the application itself. Use the extra space you now have to write two or three sentences that capture the essence of your involvement in each activity if it is not obvious from its name. Be sure to note "see separate activity sheet" on the application form so that the reader will know to look for it. An easy-to-read activity summary can be a valuable addition to a college application. Just be sure it is compact, neat, and clearly identified by your name and social security number.

If you submit your application online, you may have to send in your activity sheet by regular mail. Attach a note requesting that this supplementary information be added to your application file.

SPECIAL TALENTS

Students seeking admission to selective drama, art, music, theater, or dance programs are expected to audition or submit portfolios and CDs for review. These programs vary widely in their intensity and selectivity. Many liberal arts colleges and research universities have strong arts programs as part of their regular curricular offerings. In addition, a number of schools specializing in the performing and visual arts offer degrees in the arts as part of an arts-focused liberal arts program. And some highly specialized schools, known as conservatories, have as their sole mission the training of professionals at the highest level. Programs vary widely in their requirements for admission, so you should check into specific requirements as early as possible. The beginning of junior year of high school is not too early to begin to prepare.

But what if you simply want to bring your special talent to the attention of an admissions committee? Colleges differ in their approaches. About seventy colleges on the Common Application now use an Arts Supplement, through which you can submit your special materials. That number is likely to grow. Pomona College and Occidental College, for example, explicitly ask on the application

Activity Sheet Format

A separate activity sheet gives you the flexibility to organize your information as you want and to present detail where it would be helpful. You can decide to include some categories as-is, combine others, and simply omit those that are not relevant to your situation. Limit the details to a couple of sentences or a short paragraph at most.

Categories to Consider

Extracurricular activities (includes athletics)

Awards and honors

Hobbies and special interests

Summer activities

Work experience and internships

Community involvement

Other activities

Be sure your activity sheet has your name, address, and social security number at the top. Arranging information in columns makes it easy to follow. The format given here (we've included a sample entry) works well for most categories, although you'll need to modify the headings somewhat for a couple of them.

Extracurricular Activities

Activity	Grade (9, 10, 11, 12)	Hours per week/ Weeks per year	Description
French Language and Culture Club	10, 11, 12	5/40	Secretary (11); president (12). Led development of foreign language semiannual newsletter at high school

whether you wish to submit arts material for review and invite you to send such material with your application. Some colleges are quite detailed about what you should send. Although CDs and portfolios of art slides may be sent to the admissions office, the relevant academic department reviews them, so there may be an earlier deadline to allow for the extra processing time. When the evaluation comes back to the admissions office, it is added to the student's file. Other campuses, such as Colgate University, ask students to send their materials directly to a specific faculty member for review. The evaluation is then sent to the admissions office to be included with the rest of the application.

Regardless of how the review is obtained, the result is the same. In each case, the admissions office receives a professional assessment of your materials. If the evaluation indicates exceptional ability in a given area, your talent may serve as a significant admissions hook, especially if it is in short supply at the college. If the evaluation of your work isn't particularly strong—if you are just good, not great, at the piano—it won't hurt you, but it probably won't help much either.

If you are in doubt about how to submit evidence of your talent, you should call or e-mail the admissions office. These are common questions, and anyone can help you. The earlier you do this the better, since it often takes a good deal of time to prepare your portfolio or audition materials. Although planning ahead is a good idea for everyone, it is especially important if you want to make your special talent part of the application process.

THE STUDENT ATHLETE

As noted in Chapter Two, athletic talent can be the biggest hook of all when it comes to admission at a selective college. If you are an exceptionally strong athlete and want to play in college, you should read this section.

The more than eight hundred colleges that are part of the National Collegiate Athletic Association (NCAA) are divided into three divisions. Division I houses the most athletically competitive programs and, with eighteen exceptions, all offer athletic scholarships. The Big Ten schools (actually eleven since Pennsylvania State University joined the conference) are all Division I, as are Stanford, the Ivy League, and many others. Division II schools, which offer some scholarships, are less competitive both athletically and academically than most Division I schools.

They tend to be regional universities like the University of Wisconsin, Parkside, and California State University, Chico, as well as private colleges that draw students primarily from their local area.

Division III schools are more selective academically than Division II schools but less competitive athletically. Liberal arts colleges like Bowdoin College, Amherst College, and Lafayette College are in Division III. So are some selective universities like Emory University, New York University, and Carnegie Mellon University. Division III coaches want to win just as much as the well-publicized Division I schools. Almost every college takes athletic recruitment seriously, with a few exceptions like the University of Chicago and Cal Tech. A complete list of NCAA membership by division can be found at www.ncaa.org.

Coaches are always looking for athletic talent. Sometimes that talent comes to their attention when high school students are nationally ranked in their sport or when they receive other sports-related honors. Coaches keep track of such students with an eye toward actively recruiting them when it comes time for college admission. These students are fairly rare, however, and probably don't need this book. Far more often, talented student-athletes bring themselves to a coach's attention by expressing interest through correspondence that provides relevant athletic and academic statistics.

> Dealing with college coaches in the fall of your senior year is flattering but nerve-racking. A coach may call and write every week, insisting that you're the 6' 2" center she needs for her basketball team . . . but you don't know how many other 6' 2" centers she has on her call list as well, and she only needs one for next year. If you delay, and another of those players commits, your phone will go stone cold, and you'll never even know what happened.
>
> COLLEGE FRESHMAN HEAVILY RECRUITED TO PLAY WOMEN'S BASKETBALL

The NCAA sets rigid guidelines that govern student eligibility as well as the recruitment process. Strict rules govern when and how often a coach can contact a prospective athlete, as well as what can and cannot be reimbursed if an athlete comes to campus for an interview. The rules ensure that eager coaches do not overwhelm young athletes. You can find the guidelines that govern the division you are interested in at the NCAA Web site noted above. By and large, the rules bind the coaches more than the students, but you should know what they are just to be safe.

The Role of the College Coach

At many colleges, coaches are given a number of slots they can fill with their highest-priority recruits. They can submit additional names, but those athletes won't get priority from the admissions office beyond the merit of the rest of their nonathletic credentials. The problem for recruited students, however, is that they rarely know in advance where they rank on a coach's list. It is OK to ask, however, and an honest answer can be helpful. Coaches have to recruit more students than they actually need, since they have no guarantee all will enroll. This is one reason for an increasing emphasis on using early action and early decision for athletes. A coach may tell you that your status as an athletic recruit can help you only if you apply early, but not in regular. This can put you in a bind. Sure, you like this school, but are you ready to commit to it, to the exclusion of all others? This is the dilemma of the recruited athlete: to take advantage of being recruited at the risk of foreclosing the college search experience. There is no right answer for everyone. Nonetheless, a coach's influence, even at Division III schools, can be crucial. Another problem for the recruit is that coaches may not know their full potential talent pool until the recruiting season is over. A student who is high on the list at an early stage may be bumped down by talented late arrivals.

The Academic Index, or AI for short, is a formula that has been used since the early 1980s by Ivy League colleges to ensure that the academic credentials of recruited athletes do not deviate too much from the credentials of their college classmates. Computed from SAT or ACT scores and class rank, the AI is used to ensure that a recruited athlete's academic record falls within the broad parameters of the prior year's freshman class. In addition, only a few athletes whose AIs fall significantly below the mean of the preceding year can be admitted.[1] Although their admissions processes give a big boost to athletes on a coach's list, Ivy League colleges have agreed to accept common constraints on just how big that boost can be. A number of other colleges have established constraints as well.

Start Early and Be Informed

If you are a strong athlete interested in playing in college, you should talk to your high school or club coach about your level of ability early in your junior year. We find this unfortunate, we admit. At the early stages, we would like you to emphasize your personal and academic growth, not your three-point shot, but we are also realistic. Begin your college search early so that you can identify colleges that both meet your academic and social needs and can offer the opportunity to play your sport at the right level for you. Contact college coaches, providing a short athletic and academic résumé, by the end of your junior year if you are not contacted first. And be sure to register with the NCAA Clearing House at www .ncaa.org by the end of your junior year to ensure your eligibility if you plan to play in Division I or Division II.

The NCAA Web site provides a wealth of information about athletic recruiting. You and your parents should read it carefully so that you will know what to expect and what is expected of you. If a college coach will only guarantee you a place if you agree to apply early decision, consider the implications. Accept the offer if you know you want to attend that school and will be happy there. Do you want your whole choice of college to revolve around sports? If not, placement on the coach's list is no bargain. A strong athlete who is not recruited may be able to play as a "walk-on" to the team after being admitted via the regular admissions process. The point is to be in control of your own decisions as much as possible.

A young athlete at my child's private school was superb in her sport. An Ivy League coach showed intense interest and encouraged her application so forcefully that the private school's counseling staff thought it was a done deal. The girl was denied early decision. Turns out that the coach was new and inexperienced, and had encouraged the girl without checking with admissions to see if she had an admissible profile. She didn't make the Ivy League grade for athletic recruits.

MOTHER OF TWO ATHLETIC RECRUITS

Recruiting puts kids under tremendous pressure to apply ED. Most coaches told my daughter that the only influence they had was in the early decision cycle—if she waited and applied regular decision, they could not help her. I don't know if that was the truth, or just a ruse so that the coach would know which students were serious enough about the college to merit further attention.

PARENT OF A HEAVILY RECRUITED ATHLETE

TIPS FOR HOMESCHOOLERS

Over the last twenty-five years, homeschooling has become an increasingly popular option for U.S. families. Homeschoolers are very difficult to count, but a recent Department of Education survey estimated that about 1.5 million students are homeschooled in the United States. Families homeschool for many reasons—the most often cited are concerns about school environment, a desire to provide religious or moral instruction, and dissatisfaction with the academic instruction available in other schools (including a wish to provide a more challenging curriculum). If you are a homeschooler or parent, this section will help you prepare for and apply to college.

Despite the proliferation of online college courses and even some graduate programs that can be done entirely online, most homeschoolers still prefer the idea of a real college education. Very few opt for homeschooling beyond high school. Overall, this book is perfectly useful for any homeschooling family. As you approach the college application process, our basic advice is that you should try to emulate the behavior of a regular high school applicant as much as possible. Colleges have become much more receptive to homeschooled applicants than they were even a decade ago. Most colleges now have at least some experience evaluating the credentials of homeschooled students, and some have even developed formal admissions guidelines and policies for homeschoolers. There is excellent, more detailed advice available from some college Web sites (for example, you can search for Home-Schooled Applicant Guidelines at Stanford University, Homeschool Admission Guidelines at Claremont McKenna College, and Homeschool Applicants at Lawrence University) to find suggestions on how to proceed that will fit almost any college.

Similarities and Differences

Everything we have said in *Admission Matters* about self-inquiry, visiting colleges, writing essays, preparing for standardized tests, and deciding on a balanced list of colleges applies to homeschoolers as much as to regular students. On several points, however, the experience of homeschoolers does diverge significantly, and special care needs to be taken.

Grades and Transcripts: Colleges like to see grades, but they only mean something in a comparative context. Even in a regular high school, having all A's doesn't mean too much if half the class gets all A's. Similarly, if you are the only one in the class, and your parents are your teachers and give you all A's, it is hard for a college admissions officer to make too much of that. Colleges do want you to have taken a broad array of courses in high school, including laboratory science and foreign language. While they may grant you some flexibility because you followed your passion for birds for a year but didn't take a basic biology course, or read nothing but Greek and Celtic mythology without a regular English class, you can only take this so far. Basically, you have to think about meeting the college halfway. It can help if you have supplemented your homeschooling with some regular courses from a high school, community college, or online, something that allows your record to be evaluated relative to other students in a class.

Test Scores: With less emphasis on your grades, standardized testing is often more important for you than it is for regular applicants. It seems to fly in the face of the purpose of homeschooling to emphasize standardized tests, but they can help a college evaluate your mastery of your curriculum. SAT Subject tests are an especially good way to do this. Even if your colleges do not normally require them, taking SAT Subject Tests in several areas can strengthen your application. Some homeschooled students prepare for and take AP exams to show the rigor of their coursework.

Recommendations: Is your mother your "guidance counselor"? Can she write an "objective" letter on your behalf that will be persuasive to a college admissions officer? This can be difficult, but most colleges will want such a letter. Anything you can do to supplement your file with recommendations from others who have taught you will help. Here courses taken at a high school or community college can be especially valuable.

Activities: Stereotypes die hard, but some admissions officers may believe that homeschoolers are loners and don't socialize well. There is no basis for this, of course, but it is important to be aware of it when preparing for college. You should make a concerted effort to be a normal teenager, to get out and do things in the community. It is not important what you do, and the admissions office will understand that you didn't have a school band or yearbook staff to belong to, but it is helpful to show some energy and social experience.

Interviews: While we think it is a good idea for all students to take advantage of an interview with an admissions officer or alumni interviewer, we strongly recommend that homeschooled students participate in an interview if one is available. In fact, some colleges require that homeschoolers interview as part of the application process. An interview gives you an opportunity to talk about your experience as a homeschooler, to discuss your aspirations, and to display your social and communication skills firsthand.

Record Keeping: Keep good records of your education, including what textbooks you used, what books you read for English, what special projects you worked on—this last one is a special advantage for homeschoolers, who can demonstrate more easily than regular high school students that they can pursue projects on their own and take responsibility for their own education. Colleges admire this trait, but they will want details. Explaining why you chose to homeschool, how you went about it, and how you feel about it now will all be important elements of your personal essay and other parts of your application.

Start Early

As a sign that homeschooling has arrived in the mainstream of the college admissions process nationally, since 2006 the Common Application has included a "Home School Supplement" that you can find in Appendix B. Homeschoolers are no longer square pegs seeking to fit into the round holes of the standard college applications. The Home School Supplement is a form completed by your homeschooling supervisor (most often your parent) that asks why you homeschooled, what grading system was used, and what distance education or traditional secondary school or college courses you may have taken. It also provides a structure for a transcript.

We cannot stress too strongly that homeschoolers need to start much earlier than regular high school students in finding out what colleges will want from them, in terms of a transcript, required coursework, testing, recommendations, a portfolio, and the like. Each college is likely to be different, even if their applications look the same. A homeschooler has to take the application process just as seriously as anyone else, and perhaps even more so, since the normal sources of information found in a high school counseling office are less likely to be available.

YOU'VE FINISHED YOUR APPLICATIONS—NOW WHAT?

Completing your applications is a major milestone in the college admissions process. Although you will still have a few things left to do (for example, checking on the status of your application and participating in interviews), the bulk of the work is behind you. Take a deep breath and celebrate!

If you have built your college list well, you will have at least one and probably several good choices come April. Now you can get back to being a fully engaged student, doing well in your classes and continuing to be involved in meaningful activities. These are your last few months of high school, so enjoy them. It has been a long haul, and you're almost there. But don't take it too easy. Colleges will still want to see your final grades in June.

CHAPTER 10

Paying the Bill

The news is mixed when it comes to paying for college. The good news is that for many students, the cost of tuition, fees, room, and board printed in the college catalog is only loosely related to what the student actually pays. Although no one pays more than the "sticker price," many students pay less, sometimes much less, depending on their family's financial situation and their campus's financial aid policies. The not-so-good news is that financial aid can be complex and confusing, and in some cases disappointing, if you don't understand how it works both in general and at the specific colleges where you are applying. The additional tough news is that the nation's economy is weaker than it has been in a generation or more, placing financial strain on both families and colleges.

Finding adequate financial aid is going to be more difficult in the years ahead than in the recent past. Nevertheless, the basic principles and objectives of the financial aid system are intact and will change only in degree. Colleges are still firmly committed to helping those who need financial aid because they want diverse student bodies and because, collectively, they adhere to the principle that financial need should not be a barrier to higher education. Aid budgets may shrink, but they will not be eliminated, and the federal government is likely to compensate somewhat as it works to stimulate the economy. The advice in this chapter holds for both good times and bad. It includes the tools you need to understand the different kinds of financial aid and how they are awarded. We show you how you can roughly calculate how much aid you might expect to receive, and we explain why the actual amount may be more or less depending on a college's financial aid policies and practices. We also share our thoughts about the role of financial considerations in developing a college list and in making a final decision. If your family can easily cover the cost of your education, you can safely skip this chapter. Otherwise, it will pay to read it carefully.

> Financial aid allowed us to send our daughter where she wanted to go, a private school in the East. With three children, we couldn't have done it without that help. Financial aid really helped our middle-class family.
>
> PARENT OF COLLEGE SOPHOMORE

HOW DO COLLEGES DETERMINE YOUR FINANCIAL NEED?

Need-based aid is financial assistance awarded on the basis of a family's demonstrated need, the difference between the cost of attending a particular college (including tuition and fees, room and board, transportation, and books and incidentals) and what a student and family can reasonably be expected to pay for such costs (the *expected family contribution,* or EFC for short). Need-based aid is designed to reduce or eliminate financial need as a barrier to attending college. The determination of what a family can afford, however, is not left up to the family, for obvious reasons. Colleges have objective ways of measuring how much a family can reasonably contribute to its child's education. An underlying principle is that parents and students have a primary responsibility to contribute to the cost of a college education, according to their ability, before receiving financial aid.

> I thought we would qualify for need-based aid, but the calculations showed we didn't. It was probably just wishful thinking on my part.
>
> PARENT DISAPPOINTED BY THE RESULTS OF THE NEED ANALYSIS

Forms and More Forms

All applicants for need-based financial aid, regardless of where they live or where they are applying, must complete the Free Application for Federal Student Aid, or FAFSA. Beyond that, the forms you'll need to submit will depend on the colleges to which you are applying and your home state. Some students will have to

The Key Equation for Financial Aid Based on Need

Cost of attendance
– Expected family contribution
———————————————
= Financial need

complete the College Scholarship Service Financial Aid PROFILE, or CSS PRO-FILE, or a supplementary form from their home state, or both. Students applying to certain colleges, mostly private ones, may also need to complete another form, which the college itself prepares and administers. Thus, colleges vary from requiring one form, the FAFSA, to up to four forms (the FAFSA, a state form, the PROFILE, and a form of their own). Additionally, at some schools, forms may be required for particular students such as those whose parents are divorced or those who do not need to file taxes.

The Free Application for Federal Student Aid

The FAFSA is a need analysis form that all colleges use to calculate the expected family contribution for purposes of determining eligibility for federal financial aid. It is also used to determine eligibility for most state-based aid, for many private awards, and for institution-based aid at many colleges. The FAFSA includes the majority of a family's income and assets. However, it excludes untaxed social security income and does not consider home equity as an asset, among other things. In addition, in the case of divorce, the FAFSA does not take into account the income and assets of a noncustodial parent, but it will include the income and assets of a stepparent. The FAFSA includes questions about the size of the family and the number of family members currently in college, and it assumes a certain basic level of household expenses. Calculation of need using the FAFSA is known as the "federal methodology."

The FAFSA can be submitted between January 1 of the year a student plans to start college and June 30 of the following year. (For example, the 2009–10 FAFSA can be submitted between January 1, 2009 and June 30, 2010.) It requires detailed information from the parents' and student's federal income tax return for the preceding calendar year, current asset information, as well as the list of colleges to which a student will be applying.

It is a good idea to file the FAFSA as early as you can, even before your tax returns are completed. Most schools have priority due dates, some as early as January 20, and some schools award aid based on "first filed—first awarded." The FAFSA allows you to use estimates of the figures that will appear on your tax return. You submit the FAFSA online (at www.fafsa.ed.gov) or in paper form directly to the government agency. Later, you can amend the estimates when you have the final figures from your returns. The online version is easy to use and gives you immediate feedback about any errors you may be making in entering your data. Confidentiality is assured either way.

> I didn't find the FAFSA as daunting as some people said it would be. It's time-consuming, but it's not difficult. You need to gather all your records and your tax returns in one place. From there on it's pretty straightforward.
>
> MOTHER OF TWINS WHO HAD
> TO FILE TWICE

After your FAFSA is filed and processed, you will receive your Student Aid Report, or SAR, indicating your expected family contribution based on the federal methodology. It can take three to four weeks to get your response if you submit your FAFSA by mail, but a week or less if you do it online. Once you receive your SAR, review it carefully for any errors and report them immediately. Complete information about the FAFSA, along with the application, can be found at www.fafsa.ed.gov. You submit your FAFSA just once; copies of your SAR are sent electronically to the campuses you designate on the form. For the online version, only ten schools can be added at a time. After the first ten have been processed, you can return to the program, delete the original schools, and add any remaining schools you are applying to.

College Scholarship Service Financial Aid PROFILE

Several hundred private colleges as well as a small number of public colleges also require financial aid applicants to complete another form known as the CSS PROFILE. The PROFILE is used by colleges to determine aid eligibility from college-based resources. Some states and a number of foundations and other groups that award special scholarships also require the PROFILE.

The PROFILE takes into account all the sources of income and assets used in the FAFSA, and asks for additional information such as the value of home equity, parental funds in the name of siblings, and amounts withheld from wages for medical spending accounts. These additions generally increase the expected family contribution in those cases where they apply. On the other side of the ledger, however, the PROFILE calculations consider some of a family's expenses such as medical and dental costs and private school tuition. Normally, schools that require the PROFILE will also require the noncustodial PROFILE, thus taking into consideration the income and assets of a noncustodial parent. A need calculation using the CSS PROFILE is known as "institutional methodology" to distinguish it from the federal one.

The College Board, the administrator of the SAT, also administers the PROFILE. Information about the PROFILE can be found at www.collegeboard.com. Unlike the FAFSA, which uses the same application for everyone, the PROFILE is customized for each family with additional questions requested by the colleges to which the student is applying for aid. Individual colleges can choose from among a large number of additional questions dealing with things such as foreign assets, the cash value of life insurance plans, or the value of Section 529 plans established for the student by someone other than the student's parent. The extra questions that appear on a student's form will vary depending on the colleges a student lists when registering for the PROFILE.

The PROFILE can only be submitted online (https://profileonline.collegeboard .com). Unlike the FAFSA, which is free, students pay a fee to register for the CSS PROFILE and then a fee for each college to which the results are sent. In 2009–10, the registration fee was $9, with an additional charge of $16 per college. The PROFILE is available by October 1, and colleges typically require students to submit the PROFILE within a few weeks of their application deadline. As with the FAFSA, the CSS PROFILE is usually completed with estimated numbers. Since you cannot make changes to the Profile after it is submitted (except for adding schools), the colleges themselves will update the numbers after they receive tax forms from the family.

The good news is that the FAFSA, the PROFILE, and the various state forms are submitted only once; you list the colleges that should receive the information, and the forms are sent electronically by the processing agency. However, you

Differences Between CSS PROFILE and FAFSA Calculations of Expected Family Contribution

- PROFILE includes home equity and business value as family assets. FAFSA does not include home equity nor business value unless the business has one hundred full-time employees or more.

- PROFILE expects a student to make a minimum contribution, usually through summer work. FAFSA does not require a minimum contribution from the student.

- PROFILE schools usually require the noncustodial PROFILE and thus include information on income and assets of a noncustodial parent. FAFSA does not include this information.

- PROFILE collects information on private elementary and secondary school tuition, medical expenses, and so on and allows the campus-based financial aid officer considerable discretion in evaluating special financial circumstances. FAFSA does not ask for these costs though a letter explaining such costs can be written directly to the school, and the costs may be taken into consideration.

- PROFILE includes additional child tax credit, earned income credit, untaxed social security benefits received for all family members except the student applicant, tuition and fees deduction, amount withheld from parents' wages for dependent care and medical spending accounts, and the amount of foreign income exclusion. FAFSA does not include these amounts.

will have to keep careful track of which forms your schools request. For example, the University of Virginia requires the FAFSA and a college-specific form. The University of North Carolina asks its applicants to submit the FAFSA and the PROFILE. Also be sure to pay attention to any supplemental forms that a school may require.

In all cases, you need to keep track of submission deadlines. If you plan to apply early action or early decision, colleges will typically ask you to submit the PROFILE and their own institutional form, if any, soon after the application deadline and then follow up with the FAFSA later, after it becomes available on January 1. Getting your forms in as early as you can is always wise.

THE VERIFICATION PROCESS

Verification is a process designed to ensure the accuracy of the submitted financial aid information. The federal government selects about 30 percent of FAFSA applicants for verification, most of them randomly. A small percentage of verifications are targeted because of inconsistencies or other anomalies reported on the form. If you are selected, the college you have chosen to attend will ask you to submit a verification worksheet, federal tax returns, and perhaps other supporting documents. It is a good idea to keep copies of all your financial aid application information in one place so you can get to it easily.

Although the FAFSA verification process affects less than a third of applicants, many private colleges require that all financial aid applicants submit tax forms and supporting documentation. Be sure to check the financial aid application instructions carefully so that you will be aware of these requirements.

WHY DO NEED-BASED PACKAGES DIFFER FROM COLLEGE TO COLLEGE?

You may be surprised to learn that your aid offers will differ, sometimes by a sizable amount, even at colleges that offer only need-based aid and that promise to meet the full need of all admitted students. Although all colleges must use the FAFSA to compute the EFC (expected family contribution) for federal financial aid, they may use the PROFILE and their own forms to determine need for institutional aid. Additionally, different colleges may interpret your need differently; you can't know what your aid will look like, either in amount or type of aid, until you have your offer in hand.

This wasn't always the case. For more than thirty years, a group of twenty-three high-profile selective colleges known informally as the Overlap Group would meet each spring to agree on the need-based financial aid packages for students who were being admitted by two or more of them.[1] The goal of the Overlap Group was to meet student financial need without engaging in counterproductive bidding wars that would interfere with their ability to use their funding for the neediest students.

Then in 1989, after an investigation of the Overlap Group, the federal government called its practices a violation of antitrust laws that amounted to "price fixing." The meetings were permanently discontinued in 1991. With the demise of the Overlap Group, member colleges once again could make financial aid offers independently of one another. This free market approach to financial aid awards has led to a good deal of variability from college to college in the size of aid awards for the same student.

> Increasingly, there is evidence that students and their parents are confused by the substantial disparities in the reports they receive from financial aid experts at different campuses of the costs of educational expenses that families will reasonably be expected to pay.[2]
>
> HUNTER RAWLINGS, FORMER PRESIDENT OF CORNELL UNIVERSITY

HOW CAN YOU ESTIMATE YOUR FINANCIAL NEED?

It is a good idea to do a quick FAFSA analysis to get an idea of how much need-based aid you might qualify for under federal methodology. Although the FAFSA itself can't be filed before January 1, you can use online calculators at any time to get a ballpark idea of your EFC. The College Board Web site, www.collegeboard.com, has a very helpful and easy-to-use FAFSA calculator. It also has a PROFILE calculator, though individual schools may follow their own guidelines in interpreting the PROFILE calculations. The Department of Education has also established a Web site, www.fafsa4caster.ed.gov, that can provide you with an early estimate of your eligibility for federal financial aid. When you are ready to complete the FAFSA itself, FAFSA4caster will transfer your data to the actual FAFSA application, making the process much easier.

You and your family may be pleasantly surprised to learn that your expected family contribution is lower than you thought it would be. Some families, however, may find that the government expects them to contribute more than they had planned. As a general rule, the estimated EFC using federal methodology will probably be the lowest estimate of your EFC and hence the most generous estimate of your financial need. The PROFILE usually, but not always, calculates a higher EFC, meaning less need, because it includes income and assets specifically excluded from the FAFSA. For example, a family with substantial home equity or a noncustodial parent with financial resources may find that its EFC is significantly higher using the institutional methodology.

WHAT GOES INTO A FINANCIAL AID PACKAGE?

The financial aid that a student typically receives from a college consists of different kinds of assistance from federal, state, and college-based resources. The particular combination you will receive to meet your need is known as your financial aid package. Need-based financial aid packages usually have three parts. A typical package has grant funds, work-study funding, and student loans. Grants are considered gift aid, while work-study funding and student loans are often referred to as self-help.

Grants

Grants are awards you don't have to repay. They are tax-free when used to cover the cost of tuition, fees, books, and supplies. There are no special conditions to receiving a grant other than remaining in good academic standing. (Grants can also be awarded for reasons other than need, and we discuss these in the section on merit aid.) Need-based grants come from three primary sources: the federal government, state governments, and college resources. Currently, the federal government has four major need-based grant programs:

- *Pell Grants* ranged from $890 to $4,731 a year for 2008–09 depending on need. For 2009–10, the maximum award will total $5,350. In recent years, about 90 percent of Pell Grant recipients have had family incomes below $40,000.

- *Federal Supplemental Educational Opportunity Grants (FSEOG)*, currently ranging from $100 to $4,000 per year, are designed for students with exceptionally high need. Priority is given to Pell Grant recipients.

- *Academic Competitiveness Grants (ACG)* are additional grant money for Pell Grant recipients who have completed a "rigorous high school curriculum." The grant is $750 for freshmen and $1,300 for sophomores (as long as they maintain at least a 3.0 GPA).

- *National Science and Mathematics Access to Retain Talent Grants (SMART)* are additional grants of $4,000 per year awarded to Pell Grant recipients who are juniors or seniors, have a cumulative GPA of at least a 3.0, and are majoring in engineering, mathematics, physical science, biological science, computer science, technology, or certain limited "critical foreign languages."

Work-Study

Work-study programs provide part-time jobs to students who can then apply their earnings to tuition or living expenses. The earnings are not included in the EFC calculation. Work-study jobs are usually on or near campus and vary in their time commitment. Most work-study programs are subsidized by the federal government, which provides matching funds to colleges to pay for them. The federal program encourages work that performs a community service and work related to a student's area of study, although not all jobs meet one of those criteria. Students are paid at least the minimum wage, and freshmen typically work about ten hours a week when classes are in session, a load that is usually manageable.

Loans

Loans are borrowed money that must be repaid with interest. To qualify as financial aid, a loan must have an interest rate below the current commercial rate and have favorable repayment terms. Financial aid loans may be taken out by students or parents, and may be guaranteed and often subsidized by the federal or state government. When a loan is subsidized, interest charges and repayment do not begin until six months after the student graduates, leaves school, or drops below half-time enrollment. The repayment period, once it starts, is usually ten years. There are several federal loan programs:

- *Perkins Loans* (to students) are fixed-rate, low-interest loans (5 percent) offered by participating schools to students with the greatest need. The federal government subsidizes these loans by paying the interest on them while the student is still in school. When repayment begins, you repay the loans directly to the college.

- *Stafford Loans* (to students) are fixed-rate, low-interest loans that take two forms: subsidized and unsubsidized. Subsidized loans are made on the basis of financial need and have a fixed rate of 5.6 percent as of July 1, 2009. The rate will lower to 4.5 percent and 3.4 percent in each of the following years. Unsubsidized loans are available to students independent of need, but the government does not pay the interest while the student is in school. The interest rate is fixed at 6.8 percent. The student may defer payment of the principal, but unless the interest is paid while the student is in school, it will accrue and be added to the principal.

- *PLUS loans* (to parents) allow parents to borrow up to the total cost of education for each child, minus any student financial aid that is awarded. The interest rate is fixed at 7.9 percent for schools that use the Federal Direct Loan Program and 8.5 percent for schools that use outside lenders. PLUS loans are made without regard to financial need, but parents must have a positive credit history to be eligible. PLUS stands for Parent Loans to Undergraduate Students.

Stafford Loans and PLUS loans are offered through two different sources of funding: either directly from the government through the Direct Loan Program, or through the Federal Family Education Loan Program (FFELP), which uses banks and other private lenders. Colleges choose to participate in one program or the other, but it makes little difference; the terms and conditions of the two are nearly identical except for some administrative details.

HOW IS YOUR PACKAGE PUT TOGETHER?

Grants are clearly the most desirable source of funding, since they require no extra work and do not need to be repaid. Almost all colleges, however, include some form of self-help as part of their financial aid packages. What varies is the proportion of the aid package that is self-help. Colleges with large endowments can usually afford to award a larger portion of the package as grant aid. For example, in 2001 Princeton University announced that it would no longer include loans in any of its financial aid packages, a first among major institutions. Work-study and grant funding would be the only components. By 2008, nearly fifty other colleges had pledged to eliminate loans from financial aid awards for some or all of their accepted students.

Although no-loan schools are the notable exception to the general rule that colleges include loans in a financial aid package, many colleges can and do exercise discretion in awarding aid. Two students may have identical need and receive the same amount of aid, but it may be packaged very differently. If a college is particularly eager to recruit a student, it may offer a higher percentage of grant money in the total package, making it more desirable to the recipient. Colleges also have flexibility in determining the final EFC—much more with institutional methodology than with federal methodology—based on the professional judgment of the financial aid staff.

When you eventually compare packages from different colleges, you'll need to look at both the individual components of the package and the total package amount. Be sure to check the college's figure for the cost of attendance, including tuition and fees, room and board, books, incidentals, and transportation. An unrealistically low estimate of these costs is equivalent to less financial aid, even if the awards are the same size. When you receive your aid offer, all the components of the package will be itemized and listed separately, and you will be asked to accept or reject each part if you choose to attend that college. If the package is inadequate or less than another you have received, you or your parents can ask the financial aid office to review your case for possible adjustment. We talk more about how to approach this in a later section of this chapter.

> In general, when awarding money from programs they administer but do not fund (i.e., federal programs), colleges give priority to the neediest of the able. When awarding money from their own funds, colleges give priority to the ablest of the needy.[3]
>
> ANNA AND ROBERT LEIDER, AUTHORS OF *DON'T MISS OUT: THE AMBITIOUS STUDENT'S GUIDE TO FINANCIAL AID*

WILL YOUR NEED FOR FINANCIAL AID AFFECT YOUR CHANCES OF ADMISSION?

Only a small number of private colleges have the financial resources to admit students without regard to need and then to meet the full demonstrated need of those admitted. These colleges are referred to as "need blind" in admissions and "full need" in their financial aid policies. Most of them direct all of their available financial aid, with the exception of athletic scholarships where offered, to students demonstrating financial need.

Other colleges have policies that are "need aware" or "need sensitive" to some extent. These colleges have sufficient resources to make most, but not all, of their admissions decisions independent of financial aid considerations.

Even need-aware colleges offer financial aid, of course. Those affected by need-awareness are usually only a small portion of the applicants, and you can't know if you will be one of them. All colleges would like to be need-blind; that is their goal. If you apply to a need-aware college and need little or no financial aid, you may enjoy a small admissions advantage over someone with a similar record who needs substantial aid. This is especially true if you are a borderline candidate. Colleges that cannot afford to offer support to all their students will offer the support they do have to the most compelling students in their applicant pools. But the admission advantage associated with being able to pay the full cost of college is usually quite small—not anything to count on if you have it or fret about if you don't.

> The College also remains committed to admitting students without regard to their financial resources, though, in any given year, we may have to admit a small portion of a class with some concern for their financial need.[4]
>
> PAUL THIBOUTOT, DIRECTOR OF ADMISSION, CARLETON COLLEGE, EXPLAINING HIS NEED-AWARE POLICY

Carleton College, Washington University in St. Louis, Colorado College, and Union College are among the many colleges that are presently need-aware to some extent. Policies can change, however, based on a college's financial situation. Carleton College had been need-blind for many years until it could no longer afford to be. Brown University, in contrast, moved from a need-aware to need-blind admissions policy for the first time for the class of 2007.

Read the information about a college's financial aid policies carefully. You can usually find it posted on the Web along with other admissions-related information and included with printed application materials. If a college states that it meets the full need of all admitted students but doesn't state that it has a need-blind policy, it probably admits some percentage of its freshman class on a need-aware basis. If a college says it is need-blind in its admissions policy but doesn't commit itself to meeting the full need of those admitted, some students may find a gap between the college's financial aid award and what they actually need to attend. That gap has to be filled somehow if they choose to attend that college.

WHAT ABOUT MERIT-BASED AID?

More and more colleges, especially those that seek to build their reputations, are offering aid that is not based on need. Known as merit-based aid, these awards are often given to students in recognition of particular abilities, talents, or other criteria. Recipients may also have financial need, but need is not the basis for the award. There are three major sources of funding for merit awards: states, the colleges themselves, and private individuals and groups. The federal government has no merit awards for undergraduates. Merit grants are often referred to as scholarships.

Colleges have learned that merit aid in the form of a $5,000 or $10,000 scholarship can encourage students with little or no financial need to accept an offer of admission at an institution they might otherwise decline. This kind of "tuition discounting" can help a college increase its yield. A large merit scholarship, often a full ride, extended to a student with an outstanding record may result in a catch for the college—an academic superstar whose presence can help raise standards and contribute positively to intellectual life on campus.

Some less selective public research universities like the University of Oklahoma and Iowa State University have pursued this approach by aggressively targeting National Merit Finalists (see Chapter Six for more information about the National Merit Scholarship Program). These students may receive a generous scholarship if they inform the National Merit Scholarship Corporation that the university is their first choice and if they subsequently apply and enroll. National Merit Finalists usually have stronger academic profiles than the typical enrollee at such an institution and are thus seen as very desirable potential students.

Non-need-based financial aid is a controversial topic in higher education. Some colleges, usually the most selective, argue that all of their aid should be need-based to ensure that financial need is not a barrier for students. Other colleges want to be able to give scholarships to academically talented students with

I talked to several parents who had not considered private schools because they thought the cost was prohibitive. Well, that's not always true. The most selective schools don't give merit aid, but others do. We were really fortunate that our kids were high achievers and worked hard in high school. They got a lot of merit-based aid.

MOTHER OF FAMILY NOT ELIGIBLE FOR NEED-BASED AID WITH TWO CHILDREN IN PRIVATE COLLEGES

We want kids who are good at dancing, who are good at collecting butterflies, who are good at basketball. At the point where we have the capacity to attract students with the magnetism Harvard does, we'll be happy to follow Harvard's [need-based] policies.[5]

STEPHEN TRACHTENBERG, FORMER PRESIDENT OF GEORGE WASHINGTON UNIVERSITY no financial need, while still awarding most of their aid to those with demon-strated need. The debate over the two approaches to aid is sure to continue, and in fact shows signs of intensifying as colleges compete for students with special qualities they seek and as the demand for need-based aid grows in a challenging economy.

Some schools award financial aid based on a combination of need and merit. Before these schools award institutional aid, a student must demonstrate a certain amount of merit based on grades, rigor of courses taken, test scores, and other factors. Students with high need can be admitted and receive only federal aid, because their merit standing is not outstanding enough to receive need-based institutional aid. Other students with high need and high merit might be awarded full need. Boston University and the University of Puget Sound, for example, make awards on the basis of combined merit and need.

Seeking Scholarships

Scholarships from non-college-based sources are an additional source of finan-cial aid. They represent a very small percentage of the total amount of money available for financial aid overall, but they are definitely worth pursuing. Awarded to students for a variety of reasons—academic achievement, talent, writing competitions—these scholarships are generally sponsored by organizations, foun-dations, and businesses. Local Rotary Clubs and Lions Clubs, for example, award scholarships to high school students in communities across the country, and some large businesses offer scholarships for their employees' children. These awards are typically paid directly to a college to offset the cost of attendance. The amounts vary widely, from a few hundred dollars to several thousand. Most are fairly small, maybe $1,000 or less, but even those can add up to make an important difference. Local scholarships typically have fewer students competing for them than do national awards, and hence the chances of winning one are generally higher.

A number of states have their own merit scholarship programs as well; these programs vary in generosity and how they can be used. HOPE scholarships, for example, cover full tuition at any state-supported institution for all Georgia stu-dents with a minimum GPA. The Florida Bright Futures Scholarship Program has several options, one of which covers 100 percent of tuition and fees at public or private institutions for Florida high school graduates who meet certain academic and community service criteria and who choose to stay in-state for college.

Although most state scholarships are applicable only to in-state institutions and sometimes to a particular campus, others are more flexible and can be applied anywhere a student chooses to attend.

If a student receives an outside scholarship in addition to a need-based package that contains federal aid, federal law requires that the aid package be reduced by the amount of the scholarship, since financial aid may not exceed demonstrated need whenever federal funds are involved. Colleges are usually willing to substitute the scholarship, dollar for dollar, for all or part of the self-help components of the aid package rather than the gift aid component. This means that although a scholarship will not increase the actual amount of your package, it can make your package more desirable. Colleges vary somewhat in their policies and flexibility with regard to the treatment of outside scholarships, so it is worth asking the financial aid office of each college that admits you how such a scholarship would be handled.

> We encouraged our kids to apply for community-based scholarships. They are easier to get because you're only competing against people from your own local area.
>
> SAVVY PARENT OF FRESHMAN AND SENIOR

Should You Use a Scholarship Search Service?

High school seniors and their parents often receive letters from businesses offering to help the student find or apply for financial aid. These letters may look very official and suggest that the student and family must participate in a special program to find out about financial aid opportunities.

It is easy to see why such businesses exist. Many families feel overwhelmed by the process of sorting out the many different kinds of financial aid available. A service that promises to ferret out thousands of dollars in awards in return for a fee of a few hundred dollars may seem like a good investment. But is it?

Financial aid experts generally agree that no family needs to pay for help finding financial aid. At best, these services provide information about funding programs that is already in the public domain. At worst, they may be shady businesses that defraud or exploit vulnerable families. The Federal Trade Commission cautions families to be aware of the following approaches that can signal a scam:

- "The scholarship is guaranteed or your money back."

- "You can't get this information anywhere else."

- "I just need your credit card or bank account number to hold this scholarship."

- "You've been selected by a 'national foundation' to receive this scholarship," or "You're a finalist" in a contest you've never entered.

Most financial aid, whether federal, state, or college funded, is awarded through college financial aid offices after you've applied, completed your FAFSA and any other need analysis forms, and been accepted. Information about private scholarships is readily available, for free, from many sources. The counseling office at your high school is the first place to look. It can be particularly helpful as a source of information about scholarships awarded by local businesses and community organizations, in addition to national programs. Several Web sites, which make their money through advertising rather than fees, also provide good information about scholarship opportunities. Two sites definitely worth checking out are www.finaid.com and www.fastweb.com.

> I'm not saying there aren't people out there who are legitimate private counselors [for aid], but we try to direct families to where they can get help without spending unnecessary dollars.[6]
>
> DALLAS MARTIN, PRESIDENT OF THE NATIONAL ASSOCIATION OF STUDENT FINANCIAL AID ADMINISTRATORS

FINANCIAL AID AND YOUR DECISIONS

Parents and students need to talk openly and honestly about how much they, as a family, are willing to contribute to the cost of college through savings and borrowing, especially in times of financial uncertainty. It does little good for a college to calculate that a family can contribute $10,000 a year to a student's education when the family is either unwilling or unable to contribute that amount.

Thinking About Financial Aid Before You Apply

The uncertainties of financial aid (both up and down) are such that you should not let aid considerations determine where you apply. But if you are worried

Questions to Ask Colleges About Financial Aid

- What percentage of incoming freshmen receive financial aid from federal, state, or institutional resources?
- Does the college meet the full need of all admitted students?
- Does the college offer merit aid, or does it offer need-based aid only?
- Is this college need-blind or need-aware?
- How will an outside scholarship affect my financial aid package?
- Assuming my need remains the same after freshman year, will the composition of my financial aid package change?
- What are the academic requirements for continued financial aid?

about your family's ability to comfortably handle the Expected Family Contribution computed through the FAFSA, it would be wise to include at least a couple of colleges that you could afford and, of course, where you have a good chance of admission. Think of them as your financial good-bet colleges, which can provide some much-needed security. In the end, a private school with high tuition may actually cost your family no more than a less expensive state school because of generous financial aid. But you can't know that in advance.

College-based merit aid is a bit of a wild card in the financial aid equation. If a college offers such aid, that's great, but it is hard to predict your chances of getting it or how much you might receive. You should certainly not count on it. The College Board Web site, www.collegeboard.com, is just one of several that shows whether a college offers merit aid and how much it offers. It is worth checking out the colleges you are interested in to see their practices. If a college offers merit awards and your record is strong compared to that of an average freshman at that school, you're a good prospect. The stronger your record, the better your chances

> It was clear early on that our kids would not qualify for need-based financial aid. So then we became pretty adept at looking through the Web sites to identify which institutions gave merit-based aid.
>
> PARENT OF TWO COLLEGE STUDENTS
> WHO RECEIVED SIGNIFICANT MERIT AID

of getting a large merit award. We encourage you to think about this when you build your college list, but don't let it drive all your decisions.

Evaluating Aid After You've Been Accepted

Comparing financial aid offers can be an important part of your decision-making process once you have your letters of admission in hand. As noted earlier, financial aid packages can vary widely, not only in total amount but also in their components. Financial aid letters also differ in the way they present information, so you should transpose them into a common format before you begin. The Financial Aid Comparison Worksheet in Appendix D will help you do this.

First, take a careful look at the total cost of attendance for each school. Is it realistic, or does it omit or underestimate some key expenses such as travel home? Another worksheet, in Appendix E, lets you compare how colleges estimate cost of attendance. Since the cost of books, room and board, incidentals, and travel is a key factor in determining your financial need, an unrealistically low figure will mean that you will have additional expenses that are not covered by your financial aid package.

Then carefully compare the total cost of attendance and the total amount of your aid packages as well as the components. The total amount of aid is important, but so is the composition of the package. And all of this is relevant according to the total cost of the college. When completed, the worksheet in Appendix D will show you the breakdown as well as the total amount of each aid package. Rather than concentrating on the amount of gift aid offered, take a close look at the total amount of out-of-pocket costs the family must pick up. This may include the expected family contribution, student loans, work-study, student summer contribution, and any amount of gap, or unmet need. Two schools may offer the same amount of total aid, yet one may offer a much higher percentage of the package as grants that do not have to be repaid. From a purely financial perspective, assuming the cost of attendance is the same at the two schools, the package with a higher percentage of gift aid is more desirable. Your financial aid offer will allow you to accept or reject each individual component.

Be sure you know each college's policies on financial aid for subsequent years. Almost all schools will require you to reapply for aid each year. Even if the amount of aid will remain the same (assuming no change in your family's financial circumstances), will the package change? Will packages in subsequent years contain a higher percentage of self-help aid? You should consider all these questions as you review your financial aid offers.

Students and parents often ask if they can appeal a financial aid offer. Although most colleges resist negotiating revised packages, they are usually open to reviewing their offer in light of new information. You may, in fact, be able to work out a more favorable package at a given college based on changes in your family's financial situation, a possible error in how your financial information was interpreted, or even an offer at another college. You should appeal your financial aid offer diplomatically and without any hint of arrogance or entitlement.

Adjustments to reflect new circumstances or clarification of previously submitted information are the easiest ones for colleges to accommodate. Perhaps your mother's self-employment income suddenly dropped, or the college did not adequately consider the expense of caring for your elderly grandparents. You or your parent should respectfully ask the financial aid office to review your package, making clear the basis for your request and your sincere interest in attending the college. You'll be asked to put your request in writing, and you may be asked to document your circumstances.

It's more difficult for colleges to make adjustments based on offers from other colleges, and some will simply not do so. As a general rule, though, a college is more likely to increase your offer based on one from another college if it routinely competes with that college (or aspires to compete with it) for students. A highly selective college, for example, will be more inclined to match a package offered by another highly selective college than a package offered by a less selective school. A school that only offers need-based aid will not try to match

Too many parents jump quickly into negotiation mode, trying to play one school's offer against another's. If they sense you are just trying to get a better deal and you are treating it like a car, even if there's flexibility on their end, they're not likely to show it.[7]

STEPHEN PEMBERTON, PRIVATE COLLEGE CONSULTANT

A number of elite privates give substantially different packages depending on how much they want you.[8]

MORTON OWEN SHAPIRO, FORMER PRESIDENT OF WILLIAMS COLLEGE

a merit offer from a less selective school. Similarly, a college may be more likely to increase its financial aid offer if you have exceptional academic qualifications or other talents relative to its overall pool of admitted students. In these cases, it is better for you to be seen as a big fish in a small pond rather than a small fish in a big pond.

ANOTHER WORD ABOUT EARLY DECISION

In Chapter Seven, we noted that one of the major criticisms of early decision programs is that they commit students to attending a college without giving them a chance to compare financial aid packages. Since packages can vary significantly, especially when merit awards are involved, this is a real concern if you hope to maximize your financial aid offer. Ironically, those with the greatest need may have the least to be concerned about when applying early, since colleges able to meet the full need of accepted students will provide packages to cover the total cost of tuition, room and board, and other expenses. Those with less need, however, must accept that colleges vary in how they define need and how they propose to meet it. It is precisely those students who will want to compare aid packages and for whom early decision may be unwise, even if attractive for other reasons.

You do not lose all flexibility, however, if you apply early decision. You may still request that a college review your early decision financial aid package if the award amount is genuinely insufficient for you to be able to attend. Adjustments are often made, and if the package does not meet your need, you can decline the offer and choose one of the colleges to which you have applied regular decision. But you cannot hold on to your early decision aid offer until April and then decide to attend if, in the end, it turns out to be the best.

PLANNING AHEAD WHEN YOUR CHILD IS YOUNG

This chapter has discussed financial aid issues that face families in a student's senior year. At that point, a family's income and assets are usually a given. But what if you are reading this book when your child is much younger? What can you do to prepare for the financial responsibilities of a college education? We want to mention briefly some important but often overlooked points about saving for college.

More detailed advice on the topic can be found on financial aid Web sites and in books on financial planning. Laws and practices can change quickly, however, so it is important to seek the most current information at the time you are making your plans.

- It may be advantageous to save money for college in a parent's name rather than in the student's name. Currently, federal need analysis formulas count parent assets at a much lower rate than student assets. Saving money in the parent's name also has the advantage of keeping it under parental control until it is needed. But parental income is usually taxed at a higher rate than children's income, so you have to estimate the relative gains in this context.

- Section 529 College Savings Plans, available in each state, are worth a careful look. Although contributions are after-tax, they grow tax-deferred in the parent's name. When used for postsecondary educational expenses, earnings are currently tax-free, both at federal and state levels. In addition, many states provide income tax deductions for all or part of the contributions of the donor.

- Education IRAs (Coverdell Education Savings Accounts) are a good way for some families to save for college expenses. Contributions are nondeductible, but earnings accumulate tax-free and remain tax-free if they are used for college. Coverdell ESAs can also be used for qualified elementary and secondary education expenses. There are annual contribution limits, as well as limitations based on income.

Some observers have complained that financial aid policies do not encourage families to save, since savings reduce the amount of aid for which a student is eligible. Although it is true that savings (over an asset protection amount) will reduce the amount of financial aid your child may receive, you have no guarantee about which colleges will accept your child or what their financial aid policies will be. The more money you can save toward a college education, the greater your flexibility in choosing colleges and in dealing with the vagaries of financial aid. Not all parents can save enough money for college, however, and aid policies are designed to help their children. But those who can and do save are, in a very real sense, making an investment in their children's future—one of the best long-term investments a parent can ever make.

A SPECIAL NOTE ABOUT FINANCIAL AID IN TOUGH TIMES

As of fall 2008, the country has fallen upon difficult economic times—and no one really knows how long or how deep those economic challenges will be. But we don't have to tell you that; it is all around us, and all of us are affected. Colleges are affected too. Many of them have instituted major cost-cutting by deferring maintenance and building projects, trimming travel and other discretionary expenses, and not replacing retiring staff. As in any budget crunch, every part of a school's finances is affected. All colleges have recently seen their endowments shrink dramatically, and thus the payout from those endowments has shrunk as well. Along with tuition, endowments are a primary source of financial aid funds for most colleges.

The wealthiest colleges (which are also among the most selective) announced early in the financial crisis that they would protect financial aid at all costs. But few colleges have endowments that will let them provide financial aid as if they were unaffected by the economic downturn. One university that had recently declared itself able to do need-blind admissions has said that, with great reluctance, it will have to reexamine that policy. And even wealthy schools may have to alter how packages are put together. Their budgets are finite, and they want to stretch them as best they can.

We believe that all the advice we have provided in this chapter still holds in the ongoing crisis. Remember that the vast majority of financial aid comes from government (federal and state, in some cases) and from the colleges themselves. They will still have money, but you need to be proactive in getting your forms in as early as possible (and certainly by the deadline) and in filling out the forms accurately and completely. And as we discussed earlier, there are also many sources of financial aid beyond the government and the colleges. Being aggressive and alert about these resources can also serve you well, although the amounts of most of these scholarships are modest. And no doubt competition for these funds will be more intense. You will have to seek them out and apply for more than you might have before.

The other reality of tough times is that we must all economize. Students may have to find a paying job in the summer (if they can) rather than work for a nonprofit or do worthy community service. They may have to work more hours during the school year. This is no fun (unless it's an interesting job, and some are), but there may be no valid alternative. Each family will also have to carefully weigh the importance of financial aid and the cost of college in deciding on an appropriate college list and ultimately in the final choice after the acceptances are in. Now, more than ever, it is important to have a financial good-bet college on your college list. It is also a good time to think about where your own credentials would make you an especially desirable applicant for a college relative to the overall applicant pool—if they offer merit aid, those colleges would be more likely to make you a generous aid offer.

But overall, our advice is simple. Don't panic. Be deliberate, realistic, and focused on making good choices for your college list that will ensure that you have some financially viable options in the end. Many students are in the same situation, and there is some comfort in knowing that you are not alone.

CHAPTER 11

Making *Your* Decision After the Colleges Make *Theirs*

Up to this point, *Admission Matters* has focused on the process of choosing colleges and preparing strong applications. We now want to shift attention to the end of the process and talk about how to approach the choices you and your family will have to make once the colleges' decisions come in. For students applying early action or early decision, closure may come quickly. Colleges usually notify students mid-December (or mid-February, for those pursuing the ED II options offered by some colleges). Many colleges with rolling admissions, most often public universities such as the University of Pittsburgh, Indiana University, and the University of Minnesota, also provide fast turnaround in just a few weeks or less. But for students applying regular decision (including those deferred from an early cycle), it will be the middle or end of March before most decisions are available. Ivy League colleges are usually among the last to announce their decisions, observing a common notification date in late March or the beginning of April.

HOW WILL YOU BE NOTIFIED?

Whether applications were submitted early or during the regular cycle, hope and its twin, anxiety, naturally rise for parents and students as the notification date nears. More and more, colleges are notifying students electronically to speed up the process and reduce uncertainty about when decisions will be received, since regular mail can be unpredictable. Colleges that post their decisions online typically announce the precise date and time when this information will be available. At the appointed hour, thousands of students across the country sit tensely in front of their computers checking for the final outcome.

Students expecting to receive their decisions via regular mail have a tougher time predicting exactly when their notifications will arrive. For many families, the familiar sight of the mail carrier or FedEx driver is filled with anticipation. The "thick" packet—the one containing an acceptance letter along with enrollment forms and other information—is the one that everyone hopes to see. The "thin" business size envelope is usually (but not always) the bearer of disappointing news.

> Early action and early decision letters should arrive next week. We feel that it is very important for students to treat other members of the community, and themselves, well—no matter what the results. Students who are admitted should consider the feelings of those who may not have been admitted or who have not applied early. Intense displays of happiness in public are not the most advisable behavior. Conversely, no one expects a student who did not get admitted to be happy about that. But intense public displays of anguish also can be a burden to others. We recommend that students try very hard to receive the decisions off-campus.
>
> POSTING ON PRIVATE SCHOOL WEB SITE IN EARLY DECEMBER

THE SPECIAL CASE OF EARLY DECISION

The wait for an early answer is often an emotionally intense time. By the very nature of the process, the student has been asked to make a major investment in a college as the "top choice." A lot seems to be riding on the outcome. When the outcome is a happy one, students and families are elated. When the outcome is not favorable, they can be severely disappointed, even if they knew it was a long shot.

Students can easily get caught up in their own feelings and forget that their friends and fellow students are dealing with their own concerns over the admissions

I applied early action to Harvard. That's where my sister goes, but I didn't get in. The letter came on Wednesday, and I was pretty upset for a couple of days. By Friday I was OK. Then the weekend came, and I just kind of forgot about it. Just because I didn't get into Harvard doesn't mean that there's anything wrong with me. It also helped that my sister had been rejected by Princeton and Yale. That showed me how random things could be. The other thing that really helped was that those who did get in did not run around screaming "Oh, I got in early. My life is great!" That would have made it much worse for those of us who didn't get good news. Everyone was really respectful of everyone else. There were a lot of terrific kids who got rejected or deferred. It was like "Join the club." We kind of shared the pain.

HIGH SCHOOL SENIOR

process. We encourage everyone to save overt bursts of emotion, whether shrieks of joy or tears of disappointment, for a private setting. Some schools prohibit students from using on-site computers to access admission results for just this reason.

We also urge parents to respect their children's privacy for decisions received at home, whether they arrive via e-mail, regular mail, or are posted on a college's Web site. Some students may want family members present. Faced with possible disappointment, however, some prefer to be alone to absorb the decision. Parents should take their cue from their child and be there, literally or figuratively, to offer support regardless of the outcome. If the news is disappointing, parents should be sure not to add to their child's burden with displays of anguish or anger. This is good advice not only for the early acceptance cycle but also for the regular cycle notifications that come later.

Accepted!

If your early application is a binding one, a "thick" packet or Web-based equivalent brings your college search to an early, happy conclusion. If your acceptance packet does not include financial aid information, it will follow shortly, and if the offer covers your need, you are expected to submit your intent-to-enroll form and deposit by the deadline indicated. You must also withdraw all other pending applications. Unmet financial need is the only grounds for not attending a college that admits you under binding early decision. If your financial aid package provides less money than you will need to attend, contact the financial aid office immediately to explain the situation in detail and respectfully request that your financial aid package be reviewed. Perhaps something can be worked out. Remember, though, that there may be a difference between what a college believes a family needs and what the family wants. The two may not be totally reconcilable. The family, however, makes the final decision about whether the early decision financial aid package is sufficient to allow the student to attend.

Financial aid issues aside, colleges rely primarily on an honor system with regard to binding enrollment, since they cannot legally force you to attend against your will. Guidance counselors also serve as enforcers of the rules. Some selective colleges using early decision may share their acceptance lists as a way to police compliance with the binding policy. If your name were to show up on two early decision admit lists, you would be in trouble with both schools. Students who are not released from their binding commitment and who choose not to enroll at their early decision college may find some other doors closed to them. The vast majority of ED admitted students, however, never even remotely think of declining their early decision acceptance, or if they do, the "buyer's remorse" passes quickly.

An early action acceptance can also bring your college search to a happy ending. But under the terms of early action, you have until May 1 to formally decide whether you will attend. For students whose early action school is clearly their first choice, it is courteous (although certainly not mandatory) to withdraw other applications from the regular decision process and to refrain from submitting any new ones (especially if financial aid is not an issue). The reason is simple: the more applications in the college pipeline, the lower the percentage of applicants who can be accepted by any given college. If you know for sure where you will be going in September, share your good fortune by giving your fellow students (locally and nationally) a better chance for a regular decision admission at one of the colleges they would like to attend.

But an early action acceptance may not end your college search. You may be interested in other colleges as well and want more time to make a decision. You may also want to see what your other financial aid packages may look like when you receive other acceptances in the spring. In that case, you'll have to wait until the regular cycle decisions are made. You can do so, however, knowing that you already have an acceptance from a school you would be happy to attend.

Denied or Deferred

Many early applications end happily, but a lot do not. As more and more students seek the benefits of an early application, colleges have to deny or defer more of them to leave room for regular cycle admits. Colleges differ in their approach to dealing with applicants they do not accept. Some, like Georgetown University, defer all or most of them, denying only those who clearly don't meet the qualifications for admission. A deferred application is considered again along with the applications submitted during the regular cycle. Other colleges prefer to make hard decisions sooner rather than later, denying many qualified candidates they know they would deny in the regular cycle anyway, and deferring just a small percentage who look competitive for the final round. After years of deferring no one, Northwestern University deferred a small number for the first time in fall 2008; Stanford University also defers only a small percentage. If there is a trend, it is in the direction of denying more students in the early round rather than fewer. The continued staggering growth in the regular cycle applicant pool makes it harder to get the files read if there are too many deferrals. Colleges that deny students during an early cycle do not allow them to resubmit their application for the regular cycle for the same year.

The problem with an early application denial is that it usually occurs in isolation, and also at holiday time. Because of all the restrictions, students usually apply early to only one college, and those who receive denials have no simultaneous acceptances to ease the blow. But a denial does not mean that you weren't a strong applicant or that you weren't qualified to attend. It simply means that the admissions staff decided not to admit you—nothing more and nothing less—and that your application will not be considered further. Given the vagaries of the college admission process, it is best to accept such a decision as the luck of the draw and move on. This may in fact be a blessing in disguise because it is a reality check. You were denied outright at Yale early, so what does that mean for your other super-selective choices? This is a good time to reassess that list one more time, trim some of the long shots, and perhaps add a possible or good bet to compensate. If you follow our advice, your other applications of good-bet, possible, and long-shot colleges will be ready to go or already submitted.

What You Can Do If You Are Deferred

Students who find themselves deferred still face uncertainty about the final outcome, and it is hard to predict the chance of admission during the regular cycle. Statistically, it is never very high. The regular pool is likely to be large and strong, and the admissions staff feels an obligation to treat everyone fairly. The admissions office may provide information in your letter about the percentage of applicants who were deferred. If not, they may tell you if you call and ask. You can also see whether your high school counselor can find out from the admissions office how close you came to admission. Some colleges will provide this information, and it can help you assess your chances in the regular cycle. But if you can't get this information, don't worry. Just knowing your chances isn't going to increase them.

What can you do to increase your chance of admission if you have been deferred? A letter reaffirming your strong interest in the college is a good idea. Asking your high school counselor to send a similar note with your midyear grades is also appropriate. If you have received any significant new honors (this is rare, of course) or participated in any noteworthy activities since you first applied, you should include this information in the letters you and your counselor send. Finally, finishing the fall semester strongly can only help. During the regular cycle, unlike the early review, colleges will have access to your fall semester grades. If those grades are good, it will help you. In fact, that may be one reason you were deferred: so that they could see your semester grades. In the absence of information to the contrary, the best approach to dealing with deferral is to assume that your chances of being admitted during the regular cycle are the same as they would have been had you first applied regular decision. No more and no less. Major changes in your file are fairly rare after December, and you should never count on a deferral turning into an offer of admission.

Be prepared whatever the outcome. Because most early application outcomes cannot be predicted with certainty, students applying early must have a well-developed list of additional schools in reserve, with applications ready to go (or, if you are proactive, well-organized, and impatient, already sent out by the time a decision arrives on December 15). Depending on how optimistic you were about your early application to begin with, it can be psychologically quite deflating to be denied or deferred. You want to avoid, if at all possible, having to complete new applications when your confidence may be shaken.

Above all, don't get discouraged! Try to remember that the outcome depends not only on your submitting a strong application, but also on the quality and number of other early applications the school received that year. It also depends to a great extent on the priorities of each admissions office. All of these are out of your hands. Focus on what you can control. If you have prepared your college list wisely, you will have good choices at the end, regardless of the outcome at any particular college.

WHEN IT IS YOUR TURN TO DECIDE

Mid-December, as intense as it may be, is just a dress rehearsal for the spring, when the regular admission cycle results start dribbling in. This time, many more students are waiting for responses from even more schools—and everything is drawn out over a longer period. But now, after waiting for many months to hear their decisions from colleges, students and families once again have a chance to make decisions of their own.

Choices Can Be Tough to Make

The process of making a final decision to attend a college will vary, not surprisingly, from student to student and from family to family. A lot depends not only on personality and decision-making style but also on the specific choices. Students admitted to their top-choice schools with sufficient financial aid or no need for aid have a pretty easy decision to make.

Other students may have several desirable choices, with financial aid sometimes weighing heavily in the final decision. Because many highly selective colleges offer only need-based aid or very little merit aid, less selective colleges can compete for strong students by offering attractive merit aid packages, sometimes even full rides, which go above and beyond calculated need. It can be hard to turn down a good school that offers a free or almost free education in favor of another, no matter how attractive and prestigious, that would cost your family much more. Many students, particularly those with little or no demonstrated financial need, make this choice in the end.

Sometimes students facing a difficult decision find it helpful to make a list of pros and cons for each college. We suggest revisiting the priorities that emerged when you completed the questionnaire at the end of Chapter Four. Thinking through what is really important to you is critical, now more than ever. Your priorities may have changed over the past few months. Now that you know your choices, prestige may no longer play such an important role because the high-prestige schools turned you down. Or you may have a better idea of the major you want to pursue because a senior year course has changed your academic direction. Or you may be more willing to go farther from home, or you may feel more comfortable not needing to do this. All of these are valid factors to consider.

> I've asked people ahead of me in school, "How did you choose?" They all said, "I walked on campus and I just knew." Well, I need something more concrete. I don't ever just know about anything. I don't have gut instincts on major life decisions.
>
> SENIOR APPROACHING DECISION TIME

You may, however, prefer to bypass lists and go with gut instinct. Both approaches can work and, in fact, elements of both may be best of all. The selection priorities will be different for each person, but make sure they are sound. One young man we know likes to plan ahead. Characteristically, he took a long view in choosing to attend a particular Ivy League college. "Thirty-five percent of legacy applicants get in," he said. "If I say yes to [Ivy U], I'm saying yes for my children; I'm saying yes for everyone down the line." Had this been a major factor in his decision (it wasn't), he would have been on shaky ground. No one knows whether the practice of legacy preference will exist in twenty-five years, let alone whether his children would even want to attend that university.

Colleges ask that students declare their intentions, one way or the other, by May 1, the widely observed candidate reply date. It is courteous to respond as soon as you have made your decision—not only to the college you plan to attend, but to the others as well. All colleges overadmit because they know some students will go elsewhere. As discussed in a later section, your decision not to attend a college may open up a spot for a student on the wait-list. The earlier a college can determine it has space, the sooner it can send the happy news to this student.

> What I did was flip a coin, and wherever it landed, I tried to decide how I felt about that. Every time it landed on [College X], I got a gut feeling that I wasn't going to feel comfortable on that campus.
>
> SENIOR WHO DECIDED TO ATTEND [COLLEGE Y]

Dealing with Disappointment

While many students are excited by the task of choosing a college in April, many others are disappointed. If you are admitted to only one or two good-bet colleges but denied or wait-listed by the others, you may not be excited by any of your choices. It isn't fun to be told no by a school you were really enthusiastic about. When several say no, it is even harder. Remember, though, what we emphasized in Chapter Three. Many factors in the college admissions process are beyond your control and have no bearing on who you are as a person. Realizing how uncertain the outcome can be at highly selective colleges can make it easier to accept each outcome gracefully—whether it is an acceptance or a denial.

Even students with several acceptances may find themselves uncomfortable as they second-guess whether they made the right choices to start with. Having become a reality, none of the colleges look good, and some students start to wonder whether they should have aimed higher.

These reactions and others like them are normal. The important thing is to move beyond

> My parents knew I was nervous, so they sat me down and said, "Look, you've done everything you can do." But when the rejection letters came in, I still felt like every mistake I'd made in the last four years of high school was coming back to haunt me.[1]
>
> HIGH SCHOOL SENIOR

I applied early decision to [Elite University] although I didn't really think I'd get in. It was a big stretch for me, but you never know. I was rejected, which made me unhappy, but then I got over it. What was hard was getting rejected later at less competitive schools. The schools I got into I could have gotten into without working so hard. People who played a lot and weren't so serious about school got in there, too. I really wanted to have that happy acceptance thing, when I would open the mail and jump up and down and call my mom to tell her the great news. I missed that. But I learned that if you don't get in where you want to go, it's not the end of the world. I'm not a religious person, so when people say everything happens for a reason, I'm like, "Yeah, well." But I think in this case, everything did happen for a reason. I'm really happy here.

COLLEGE FRESHMAN

that first shock of rejection. Dwelling on the negative, as well as on what-ifs and if-onlys, keeps you from moving on. All colleges, no matter how highly rated or well regarded, have faults. And all colleges, even the most humble by most measures, have good points. If you have done your research carefully at the outset, your choice will be a good one no matter what you choose. In fact, it is not the college that makes the difference in your future contentment; it is your degree of commitment to making it work for you. The choice is your first step of that commitment. One young woman we know was denied by all colleges except her one good bet. Although disappointed, she took a positive approach. Ten weeks into her freshman year, she enthusiastically reported how happy she was with her college, even though she had had no choice. She loved her classes, her new friends, and the college itself. Each year many students have similarly happy endings after a disappointing start.

Remember also that choosing a college is not an irrevocable act. Students can and do transfer after freshman or sophomore year. Some students transfer from their first-choice schools, even an early decision school, and some from their good bets. Doing well in the last semester of high school and during your freshman year will enhance your transfer options, although some colleges are as selective for transfer students as they are for freshmen. And not all colleges accept transfers. We don't recommend choosing a college to attend as a springboard to transferring to another one. This is a recipe for being an unhappy freshman. We hope you will find the good points of your college and vow to make the best of it. If it doesn't work out, then you can think about transferring, but first give your college an honest try.

SPRING ADMITS

Inundated with more good applicants than they can accept, some colleges have found a creative solution so they can admit a few more students each year. They offer a group of students the opportunity to enroll as freshmen starting in the spring semester rather than in the fall. A college can do this because it knows that some students will not return for spring semester. Students withdraw due to health, adjustment, or family problems, and a few seniors usually graduate early. The spots opened up by the departures create space for students willing to start midyear.

Making the Final Choice

Teens know instinctively that you become your own person by making your own choices. Yet, when college admission letters arrive, many students find themselves just plain stuck.

A student with several acceptances suddenly faces a complex dilemma. It's better than the uncertainty of waiting, but it's not an easy time.

In April, I interviewed students who were struggling to decide.

"Paul" stood out. He sighed fifty times in our ten-minute conversation. Trying to decide between a liberal arts college and a large university, he favored the small school—until the big one invited him to join an honors program.

No matter how carefully students have ranked their choices, they may be jolted by last-minute developments like this. And now parents sometimes express opinions they carefully withheld before. Paul confided, "Dad's trying to be objective, but he's biased toward the big school."

The big school was closer to home.

Indeed, distance from the "nest" looms large for both parents and students. One student explained, "In September, everyone was excited about the idea of going away. But people got closer to each other during the year. They put away their grudges—like who did what to whom in sixth grade. They lost the desire to escape."

Some students wonder if they analyzed themselves correctly when they prepared their college list. One talented young vocalist viewed her singing as just one of many extracurricular activities. Yet when a top women's college accepted her, she asked plaintively, "Do I want to spend four years in a chorus with no male voices?"

New details attract students as they make their final selection ("One school will wash, dry, and fold my clothing!" exclaimed a young man.) Most students told me that in-person visits were the best way to decide.

In May, I called Paul back. He didn't sigh even once when he reported that he chose the larger school.

"There's still some hesitation," he explained. "Did I choose the right place? But I'm really looking forward to college." I could almost hear his smile.

"It's a great feeling," he said, "to have it decided."

M. F.

Colleges offering spring admission encourage students to use the fall semester well, either through coursework at another college or through other enriching activities. Middlebury College and UC Berkeley have offered spring admission for many years. Middlebury calls spring arrivals "Febs"—for the month of February, when the spring semester starts. Brandeis University and Wheaton College (Massachusetts) now offer spring starts as well. A few other schools offer students a first semester at an overseas location: Skidmore in London and Colby in Dijon, France, for example. The disadvantage of a midyear start is obvious—you don't have the opportunity to experience the first exciting semester of college life with your future classmates. On the plus side, though, after just a few months you will join them, when you would not otherwise have had a chance. You usually don't apply for spring admission; if a school cannot accept you for the fall but expects to have room in the spring, it will advise you of that in your admission letter. Middlebury even asks on the application if you would like to be considered for spring admission, so you can express your willingness at the outset. They look for outgoing, flexible students who will adjust easily.

> The scary thing is that no one in our family, adult or child, has the slightest clue which school would be best. They all have pros and cons. Sometimes I think it might be a relief to get rejections from all but one to avoid having to make these incredibly difficult decisions.
>
> A PARENT AT DECISION TIME

TAKING ANOTHER LOOK

Most colleges host special "admit" days or weekends in April before the May 1 Common Reply Date. Even if you have visited a college before, going to an admit weekend can be fun and a good way to get a feel for the campus. It can be especially important, though, if you have not visited before.

Finally, the pressure is off, and you can enjoy being courted. Everyone realizes that the parties and food might be better than usual on this special weekend, but you'll still get to know the campus better because you can meet so many students, including other "pre-frosh," your potential classmates.

Normally, students must pay the cost of travel to admit weekends. In some cases, though, a campus may be particularly eager to recruit a student and will offer to pay all or some of the expenses up to a certain dollar limit. This applies mostly to underrepresented minorities or students from low-income families. If you are not offered financial assistance but find that the cost of travel is a hardship, consider asking the admissions office whether the campus can help with your travel costs. The answer may be no because of budget limitations, but it cannot hurt to ask.

Admit days, especially when you stay overnight, give you a good chance to talk to current students about what the college is really like, as well as get a sense of who might be joining you in the freshman class. It is worth rereading the section on college visits in Chapter Five to refresh your memory of what to look for. Some colleges also encourage parents to attend the admit days and even offer special programs for them (although no dorm housing!), and all colleges welcome them regardless of whether formal events are provided. It's fine for parents to go along on an admit weekend—as long as they make sure to leave their children lots of space.

REVISITING FINANCIAL AID

Once you have all your acceptance and financial aid offers, you may also want to make your top-choice college aware of any offer that is significantly larger than the one it sent you if the differences in the aid packages may affect your final choice. Also make its admissions staff aware of any changes in your financial situation that might increase your eligibility for aid. Courteously requesting a financial aid review to see whether anything more can be done is both appropriate and smart. Be prepared, of course, for a negative answer. Colleges can more easily make adjustments when new information or a new interpretation of existing information results in a calculation of greater financial need. They can sometimes make adjustments even without such new information as the result of a second hard look, but these cases are less common, and this might happen only for the applicants the college is most eager to recruit. Don't expect a college that offers only need-based aid to adjust its package to offset a merit scholarship at another college. At the same time, don't let a no discourage you from continuing to consider the college as an option, if you are excited about the college and it is within financial reach.

> I want to look at the academics and which college really fits my academic goals the most. Visiting becomes more important. Getting a feel for the people that go there. Making sure that they're compatible. Do I want to live in New Jersey? In Southern California? How much of a stretch do I want from my current lifestyle?
>
> SENIOR TRYING TO MAKE A DECISION BETWEEN TWO VERY DIFFERENT BUT EXCELLENT COLLEGES

HOW WAIT-LISTS WORK

A wait-list consists of applicants who are not admitted outright but who are notified that they will be considered for admission if space becomes available later in the spring. What should you make of a letter that essentially puts you in limbo? Being placed on a wait-list means that your file will be considered again if the college has fewer acceptances than it anticipated when mailing out offers of admission. Because no college gets a yes from every admitted student, they all accept more than they can accommodate. On the basis of past experience, they calculate an estimated yield from their offers. Then they wait until after the May 1 deadline to see how many students send in their deposits. Because of competition for good students, colleges know that some of their wait-listed students are likely to be wait-listed at other, comparable colleges. So they may even take students from the wait-list before May 1 to get a head start on their rivals. Sometimes they may take students in stages: twenty prime candidates before May 1 and thirty more on May 10, when they have a firmer fix on the yield. The process is very similar to the way airlines fill their planes. It is common to overbook a plane, since some passengers will be no-shows. If empty seats remain when the plane is ready to leave, those seats can be filled by standbys who know that they may or may not get a seat, but have been patiently and hopefully waiting.

If more students accept admission than planned, the college may have to increase the number of freshmen in each dorm room, convert student lounges into bedrooms, use trailers or motels for temporary housing, or drastically cut the number of transfer students who will be offered admission that spring. All of these have happened. Estimating yield is very hard to do. One enterprising campus we know purchased smaller dorm room furniture when it found it had to house three students in rooms meant for two. And of course, if a college finds itself in an oversold situation, it does not take anyone from the wait-list.

Who Goes on the Wait-List?

Over the last few years, wait-lists have gotten longer, as colleges find predicting yield more difficult. This reflects, for the most part, the increasing number of highly qualified candidates who apply to several selective institutions. A wait-list decision can mean that a candidate was fully qualified to attend and would indeed have been admitted if only the college had the room. It can also be a gentle way

I was put on the wait-list. The dean sent me a very nice letter that said, "After long and careful consideration, the admission committee has decided to place your name on the waiting list. . . . I congratulate you on your fine record of accomplishments, which deserve a much more fitting recognition than I can provide right now. I hope you will remain interested in our college and that you will choose to hold a place on our waiting list. I also hope that I may ultimately have a chance to offer you a place in our entering class."

Accompanying the letter was an attachment stating that about 1,000 students were placed on the wait-list, that about 300 to 400 were expected to remain on it, and that over a ten-year period the average annual number of acceptances from the wait-list was less than 30. At least they were up-front about how tough it would be.

WAIT-LISTED STUDENT

for a college to say no to a weaker candidate it finds difficult to deny outright for other reasons, such as a legacy applicant. And as discussed in Chapter One, a few colleges will even place an exceptionally qualified candidate on the wait-list if they strongly believe the student will receive and accept an offer elsewhere.

Because of a combination of all or some of these factors, many wait-lists are as big as the entire freshman class, or bigger. The "Principles of Good Practice" of the National Association for College Admission Counseling say that each college should tell you how many applicants have been placed on the wait-list for your year and for each of several previous years, along with the number on the wait-list eventually offered admission, but you may have to ask. One university stands out for its steadfast refusal to do this; it is rumored to offer a spot on the wait-list to many thousands of students every year. The number admitted from a wait-list can vary greatly, from zero to low single digits to several dozen or more. It all depends on the ability of a college to predict its yield accurately in the first place. The importance of predicting yield is one reason colleges have embraced early decision so readily, and why some colleges consider demonstrated interest in making their admissions decisions.

The domino effect from wait-lists can be sizable, widespread, and disruptive to colleges. As students accept admission from the wait-list at a college, they withdraw from another college, which now finds itself with empty spots that they, in turn, must fill from their wait-lists. A college with a full class on May 1 may have space on May 15 after losing some students to other colleges. And so on.

Steps to Increase Your Chance of Acceptance from the Wait-List

A letter notifying you that you have been placed on the wait-list includes a post-card asking whether you wish to stay on the wait-list. What should you do? No single answer fits everyone. Don't fall into the trap of automatically thinking that the college that didn't take you at first is automatically better than any that accepted you. It was just a different admission process. Usually, less than half of those placed on a wait-list opt to remain. If you find your other college choices more attractive, then it obviously makes little sense to remain wait-listed. But if the wait-list college is still an appealing option, you may want to respond positively, knowing that your chance of moving from the wait-list is low. You should also inquire about a college's policy regarding financial aid for students admitted from the wait-list. Will aid be available if you have financial need? In some cases, it won't. You have to ask. Make sure you send a deposit to one of the colleges where you have been accepted outright by the May 1 reply deadline.

> I didn't like being wait-listed. It felt like a consolation prize. Why would they wait-list so many people when clearly they're letting in very few? It seemed so pointless.
>
> SENIOR WHO WAS WAIT-LISTED BY HARVARD UNIVERSITY AND DECLINED TO REMAIN ON THE LIST

Although airline standby lists are ordered in some kind of priority so passengers can assess their chances of getting a seat, wait-lists are usually unranked. This means that openings are not filled from the list in any prearranged order. There may be some broad tiers with a preferred group at the top, but the college usually won't tell you which group you are in. The reason they don't order the wait list is that they don't know who will stay on it, so ordering it would be a lot of extra work, and they don't know what the composition of the final class will be. They want to retain the flexibility to add the prospective students they want. So as openings occur, a college may examine its whole freshman class along geographic, gender, racial, and many other dimensions and fill any perceived gaps from the wait-list. The student who came closest to admission during the regular review cycle will not necessarily be chosen from the list when openings occur. Each admissions officer may have the chance to nominate a few students for consideration.

Usually, a wait-list sees little movement until colleges have a clear grasp of their yield from those already accepted, and that generally doesn't happen until after May 1. Mid-May through early June is the busiest time for wait-list notifications. Wait-listed students who are accepted are usually notified first by phone, followed by written confirmation with a two-week, or sometimes much shorter, deadline for reply. If you tell the caller you are no longer interested, the college will move on to another wait-listed student and repeat the process. Most selective colleges officially close their wait-lists by the end of June and notify those who have not been accepted accordingly. Many have very little activity from the wait-list after Memorial Day.

If you decide to remain on a wait-list, it is wise to discuss your continued interest in the college with your high school counselor. Tell your counselor whether the college is your first choice. Your counselor may be able to help your cause by contacting the college and conveying support for you as well as your enthusiasm for the college. A letter from you expressing your interest as well as any new accomplishments will be necessary. Don't rely on your counselor to do this for you. But again, movement from the wait-list at a selective college is a long shot at best. Don't let hope of admission, which could even come well into the summer,

I tell my wait-listed kids to put their wait-list schools out of their mind and pick one where they have been accepted because chances are pretty good that this is where they will go. If they find out later that they've won the lottery, that's great, and they can deal with it then. But they need to start forming new attachments. I'd also encourage parents to foster that attitude.

INDEPENDENT COUNSELOR

It is a great way to shape the class and meet our institutional priorities. Maybe we could use a few more artists or a few more math or science researchers.[2]

DICK NESBITT, DIRECTOR OF ADMISSION AT WILLIAMS COLLEGE, REFERRING TO THE WAIT-LIST. FOR THE CLASS OF 2012, 1,066 WERE PLACED ON THE LIST AND 42 WERE EVENTUALLY OFFERED ADMISSION.

What Can You Do If You Are Wait-Listed at Your Top Choice?

- Return the reply postcard indicating you want to remain active on the wait-list. It is OK to remain on more than one wait-list.

- Write a letter to the dean of admissions to say that you are still very eager to attend. Include any significant new information since you last wrote: grades, awards, and so forth. If it is your clear first choice, say so up front. But you cannot do this at more than one college.

- Ask your counselor to call or write the admissions office conveying your enthusiasm and supporting your desire to attend the school.

- Consider sending an additional recommendation or letter from a teacher or another person who knows you well. But don't overdo it to the point that it looks like a campaign.

- Carefully select a school from among those that have admitted you and send in your deposit.

- Recognize that most students placed on the wait-list at selective colleges are not ultimately admitted. Once you have taken the steps indicated here, put the wait-list out of your mind and focus on the college you will probably be attending in the fall. If you are eventually admitted from a wait-list, you might be very happy with your May 1 choice, and want to stick with it. Telling a college where you were wait-listed that it is your first choice is not binding like early decision.

spoil your excitement about college. Sometimes closure, even if it means deciding to attend a college lower on your list, is far better than the emotional limbo of staying on a wait-list. You know yourself best—be sure to weigh the wait-list option carefully before deciding what to do.

In any case, remember to send your intent-to-register form, along with your deposit, to your preferred college from among your acceptance options. If you subsequently decide to join a college that accepts you from the wait-list, you will need to send a deposit as well to that college. You will forfeit your deposit at the first school, but it may be worth it if you end up where you really wanted to go. Some deposits are quite large, so be careful.

Deposit Ethics

Students are expected to send a deposit to hold a spot at only one college by May 1. Holding more than one spot, known as double depositing, deprives others of the potential opportunity to move from a wait-list. If you are offered a spot from a wait-list and accept, you'll have to inform the first college you accepted of your change in plans as quickly as possible. A phone call isn't enough—they will want it in writing. Your letter doesn't have to be long unless you want it to be; a simple note informing the college of your new plans is sufficient. This happens all the time, so don't be bashful or embarrassed about your change in plans. The important thing is to notify the college quickly. The place you release will then generate an opening for a student on that school's wait-list, continuing the cascading effect. Double-depositing is not ethical, and if either college finds out, you can lose your place at both colleges.

> Colleges are looking for a 100 percent yield from any students they take off the wait-list, so they are going to be looking for commitment. The key is for students to demonstrate as much honest interest as they can and indicate that if offered admission they will definitely enroll. They are the students the admissions office will most likely look at first.
>
> EXPERIENCED HIGH SCHOOL COUNSELOR

A WORD ABOUT SENIORITIS

Senioritis typically strikes students right after they receive their college acceptances, sometimes earlier. For those accepted early, it may occur in mid-December, but for most others it attacks in mid-April. (Wait-list status may confer immunity, however.) Teachers know to expect senioritis, but they dread it nonetheless. Students start performing significantly below their pre-infection levels. High school may not seem to matter very much once the big hurdle is behind you.

We encourage you to avoid falling victim to this disease. This advice has several reasons—perhaps one or more will resonate with you. First, colleges accept you on the explicit condition that your performance for the remainder of the year will remain at its prior level. The last official part of your college application process is having your final transcript sent to the college of your choice at the end of the school year. Colleges review these to identify any marked departures from previous performance.

Colleges will send letters of varying degrees of harshness to students whose grades have dropped dramatically, asking for an explanation. A serious decline may result in a strongly worded letter threatening that the student's admission is in jeopardy. Colleges reserve the right to put conditions on your enrollment (requiring summer school classes, for example), or they may even rescind your admission entirely if your performance deteriorated drastically or if you dropped demanding courses without good reason. True, the drop in grades has to be pretty striking and without mitigating conditions for an offer of admission to be withdrawn, but a college can and will do it given the appropriate circumstances. Why risk everything when you have worked so hard to reach this point?

Your high school record will be with you forever. While your grades in high school may not matter much once you have graduated from college, you may want to transfer to a different college at some point. A record that deteriorated in the second half of your senior year will not help your case. Finally, and maybe most important, continuing your best effort (or close to it) shows respect for your parents, your teachers, your counselors, and especially yourself. Show your appreciation and maturity by continuing to be a good student. Almost everyone will cut you a little bit of slack—just don't abuse it.

CELEBRATE AND ENJOY!

With your college choice behind you, you can enjoy the remaining weeks of your high school career. You can look forward to the Senior Prom, graduation, and more and more commonly, an alcohol-free all-night party or trip for the entire senior class. Make the most of this time to cement the bonds with your classmates. Some of them may turn out to be lifelong friends. Others will be people you will see only at class reunions every five or ten years. With the passage of time, you will remember most of them fondly, even if they aren't close friends now.

CHAPTER 12

What Matters Most

Advice to Parents and Students

We wrote *Admission Matters* to help families navigate the college admissions process, showing how the role of the student and the role of the parent are complementary yet different. The idea was to provide you with the information and practical advice you need to work together to achieve a good outcome.

In this final chapter, we offer some parting thoughts that summarize and capture the heart of what this book is about. It may be helpful to read this chapter more than once as you go through the college admissions process. It is easy to get caught up in the whirlwind and lose perspective, but this chapter will remind you what matters most. The chapter is divided into two parts. The first part is for parents; the second part is for students. Like the rest of the book, you should read both parts, not just the part intended for you. We think everyone will benefit.

SOME PARTING THOUGHTS FOR PARENTS

What your child will remember long after the college admissions process is over is the support you provided.

Your relationship will last for the rest of your lives. This year or more is a tiny portion of your overall time as parent and child. Keep that in mind as you think of imposing your own ideas or detaching completely from the process. Above all, don't do anything that might damage your future relationship. Whatever it is that seems so important at this moment, in the long run, it really isn't so crucial. Earlier in this book we mentioned a father who steamed open his daughter's newly arrived SAT scores when she was away at camp. It was a long time ago, but both parties remember it to this day. Don't do it!

It can be hard to accept that your almost-grown child has ideas and preferences that differ significantly from your own. This is especially true when it comes to college choice, when so much seems to be at stake. Your child may want to experience a different part of the country—you may want your child to be close to home (or vice versa). You may feel an education at a liberal arts college is best—your child may be looking forward to the excitement of a large research university (or the reverse). The list goes on and on. The bottom line is that although your child should respect your views and may ultimately embrace them, the final choices—where to apply, what to put in the application, and where to go after acceptance—should be the student's.

Ideally, you want to be able to look back after the final college choice is made and savor knowing that you provided emotional and practical support for your child that contributed to a successful outcome. It may take your child a while to appreciate your good intentions and acknowledge your contribution.

The parent's role is to support, advise, and listen, except when it comes to money.

You can support your child in the college admissions process in many ways: sharing your own thoughts and experiences; encouraging research into colleges including visits where feasible; and providing useful feedback and organizational support. But you need to realize that your child must own this process—it is the student, not the parent, who is applying to and ultimately attending college.

It is critical, however, that you be up-front about financial considerations.

As discussed in Chapter Ten, colleges use a complex formula to determine your aid package and thus your "expected family contribution," the amount they believe a family should be able to pay to help support their child's education. This is rarely an amount that parents are eager to pay. Doing some early calculations and being frank about what you are prepared to contribute financially to your child's education is imperative to avoid disappointment later on. This is not as easy as it sounds. Most parents keep their family finances to themselves. Discussions of big expenses are often reserved for the adults in the family. This may have to change now. Most teenagers, we have found, are realistic if you treat them as intelligent adults. They know that these are tough times economically. They understand you have a mortgage or rent to pay and younger siblings to put through school, and that your own retirement plan may not be as flush as it was during recent boom times, or that jobs may be (or have been) lost. Trust your children; they will respond.

This is not the time to live vicariously through your child, however tempting that may be. Try not to use college admission to validate your parenting skills.

Most parents of high school seniors are forty years old or older. Participating in the process with their child allows them to re-experience, or perhaps experience for the first time, a uniquely American rite of passage. However, if you catch yourself saying "We're applying to college," you may be overly involved. Even the most confident children may fear they will disappoint a parent if they do not get into their parent's alma mater or dream college, or if they do less well than a superstar older sibling. Wise parents try not to inadvertently contribute to that fear by their words or actions.

Parents sometimes lapse into the belief that all their parenting efforts over the last eighteen years will be held up to scrutiny during the admissions process. The parents of the student who is accepted by one or more prestigious colleges have done a good job, while parents of students who apply to less prestigious institutions or who are denied by brand-name colleges didn't do their job quite as well. Put bluntly, these inferences are ludicrous, but they frequently reside just under the surface. The bumper stickers and T-shirts that proclaim things like "Proud Mom of a Yalie" put them into words. So does the seemingly endless supermarket check-out line and carpool chatter about where Suzie has applied early, or where Tommy got accepted. All of this sends subtle messages that put teens under great pressure and promote values that are at best superficial and at worst actually harmful. A wise parent learns to be upbeat even when the news is disappointing and modest when the news is good. Think of the difference between "My child got into X" and "My child is going to get a fine education at Z."

Remember that at many first-rate institutions with reasonable acceptance rates your child can get a fine education and be happy.

Most people know surprisingly little about the amazing array of institutions of higher education in the United States. One counselor challenges audiences to see if they collectively can name more than three hundred colleges. If they come up short, they have to pay him. If they go over three hundred, he has to pay them. Nobody takes him up on the challenge. Try it, just for fun. See how many you can name without a guidebook. Most parents can name a few local colleges, most of the Ivy League and their peers, and some schools whose football games are televised nationally, but that's about it. As part of the college admissions process, you can support your child by learning about colleges you may not be familiar with and helping your child realize that a successful college experience is the result of a good fit between college and student—and that while there is no perfect fit, many good ones are possible. Many wonderful colleges accept a much higher percentage of their applicants than those considered very selective. By all measures, these colleges offer an education that is every bit as good and maybe even better than some highly selective, brand-name institutions. Helping your child explore options and supporting the resulting choices can be immensely rewarding.

Help your child with organizational matters and be a good sounding board and editor during the application process—but don't do the work for your child.

The actual process of applying to college can be daunting. There are forms galore, short and long essays to be written, score reports and transcripts to be sent, and so on, all by looming deadlines. When asked what they would do differently if they had a chance to start over, many high school seniors say that they would have started the whole process earlier and procrastinated less. Procrastination is a normal human reaction in face of an unappealing task—think of writing a will or paying taxes. But it is just a bad habit, not a sin. And it can be foreseen. As a parent, with your greater experience as an adult, you can encourage your child to get started early and to keep track of what has been done and what remains to be done. Some teens resent this; they have always been able to complete their work by the deadlines, so they are convinced they can do the same now. The problem, though, is that college applications are probably much more complex than any task they have undertaken before—and more hangs in the balance. College deadlines are also more severe and inflexible than those imposed in high school.

Students should be encouraged to organize their materials and set deadlines for themselves. Remember that a child who decides to apply early action or early decision will have to get everything together by November 1 or November 15—a very early date indeed, especially if preparation begins on October 1. What kind of help can you provide? Proofreading of applications and help with essay ideas and constructive criticism can be very helpful. (Just be aware your efforts may not be enthusiastically welcomed!) At all costs, however, resist the urge to rewrite the application yourself, even if your child seems willing or even eager for you to do that. Admissions readers get pretty good at telling an authentic student voice from one that has been doctored in a major way by adults.

You can also assist with organizational matters if you have those skills and your child welcomes the help. Volunteer, for example, to address and stamp the envelopes in which your child's teachers send in their letters of recommendation. You can register your child for the SAT—it's your credit card, after all. It is fine for you to get the maps from AAA for the college trip, as long as you don't pick the colleges too. Make the organizational tasks easier and less time-consuming so your child can concentrate on the hard parts. Of course, some teens enjoy these organizational tasks because they're easy to do and yield a sense of accomplishment. Make the offer to help and let your child decide.

Model ethical behavior and integrity.

Our children learn many lessons from us, including those we never explicitly teach. Children learn by observing others, and the most powerful role models are parents. The pressure to do everything possible to ensure success in college admissions is powerful, even if it means compromising integrity along the way. Resist this temptation. The college admissions process is a major opportunity for parents to model ethical behavior and integrity for their children. Use it accordingly.

Don't offer inappropriate help with the application itself ("editing" an essay to the point of essentially writing it yourself, for example), and don't permit your child to seek it elsewhere (paying someone to write the essay). Similarly, discourage exaggeration of activities or accomplishments. Admissions officers look for consistency between what students have written about themselves and what teachers and counselors say about them. Why take a risk by embellishing too much?

But the fear of getting caught in a fabrication is the least of the reasons to encourage honesty in the application process. Our society has too many people who believe shaving the truth is not only OK but also the smart thing to do. Young adults need to know that their integrity is their most precious asset. Parents can reinforce that lesson through their actions and advice.

Everyone wants to be accepted for their own efforts and for who they really are. Allow that for your children. You don't want them to start freshman week thinking, "I'm not the person who was on my application. This school doesn't really want me."

Accompany your child on college visits, but stay in the background.

As we have said before, probably the best way for a student to get the feel for a college is to visit it. Where possible, encourage your child to visit a number of campuses, perhaps in conjunction with vacation, and go along if you can. Going to some nearby colleges of different sizes can help give your child an idea of the kind of college that might be the best fit. When it comes time to look seriously at colleges, you can help schedule tours and encourage your child to have an interview if one is available. But remember that the visits are for your child's benefit. Encourage, and perhaps even do so strongly, but let your child make the final call about visiting a given campus.

Help your child make realistic choices.

One of the major themes of this book is that admission to selective colleges can be quite unpredictable. Your child can have a wonderful record yet be denied at a given college, while another student with a weaker record is accepted. You never learn why, but in the end, it doesn't matter. If you understand the difficulty and uncertainty of selective college admissions, you can help your child consider a good range of colleges. This means you have to keep your own vicarious ambitions to yourself as much as possible.

If your child is interested in a super-selective college and would be a competitive applicant, then it is fine to apply. But your child should understand that admission to colleges that select less than 20 percent of their applicants is a long shot for almost everyone, simply because of numbers. After the final decisions arrive, support your child by sharing the disappointment at the denials and the joy over the acceptances. Model poise over the former and humility for the latter. Every parent knows that if the worst thing that ever happens is being denied admission to a college, then their child will have a long and happy life. If the family made the list with care at the outset, the outcome should be happy regardless of the particulars.

Be supportive as your child makes the final choice.

When the decisions arrive, your child may be elated or disappointed, or some-where in between. Allow the child space for sorting it out and making the final decision. Offer your perspective where appropriate, but remember that within the boundaries of financial constraints and family responsibilities, the choice is your child's, not yours.

Rejoice with your child.

Regardless of the outcome, express your love and let your son or daughter know how proud you are of the young adult he or she has become. Savor the moment.

SOME PARTING THOUGHTS FOR STUDENTS

Parents want the best for you and want to help. Let them, within boundaries.

Although parents differ widely in their knowledge, abilities, and resources, almost all want to help a college-bound student however they can. Be gracious and communicate with your parents so that they can help appropriately. The trick is to define boundaries for what is helpful, what is intrusive, and what is counter-productive. Each family is different—so you'll have to work this out together with help from this book.

Parents can sometimes make great suggestions about colleges to consider. They can also be your companions on trips to see colleges in person. And they can sometimes be good editors, proofreaders, and clerical assistants, depending on their background, as you prepare your applications. The more both you and your parents know about the college admissions process, the easier it will be to agree on what form their help should take. Encourage them to be partners with you. If they see you taking charge maturely, they will be much less likely to feel that they have to be constantly on your case.

Recognize that launching a child into adulthood is emotionally difficult for many parents—help them get through it.

Sending a child off to college is bittersweet for many parents. They share your delight at your prospects for a wonderful future, but at the same time they can't help feeling a sense of loss. The child they have loved and nurtured for eighteen years is now a young adult, ready to leave home for a new life in which parents will play a much less prominent role. Try on occasion to put yourself in your parents' place. Something as simple as an occasional heartfelt "thank you" in response to help that is offered can make all the difference to a parent struggling with a changing role.

Share something about the high school scene with your parents. Most know surprisingly little about the pressures at school, and they are often unaware of the many discussions about college that go on between you and your friends. If you help your parents understand the environment you navigate every day, they will appreciate why your experience of the college admissions process may be very different from theirs.

The most important part of the college admissions process is choosing schools that would be a good match. Be as honest as you can with yourself about your interests, preferences, strengths, and weaknesses as you consider colleges.

A recurring theme throughout *Admission Matters* is that a successful college experience is all about fit—finding a college that is a good match for you. The most important, and probably hardest, part of the process is self-assessment—an honest self-evaluation of your interests, preferences, strengths, and weaknesses. The next toughest part is doing the necessary research to find colleges that are a good match based on your self-assessment. Part of that match includes a determination of the likelihood of acceptance. You want to be sure to have a range of colleges on your list to ensure that you will maximize the likelihood of a good outcome.

Have eight first choices.

Well, the number doesn't have to be eight, and they don't all really have to be equally your first choice. But the idea is to be sure that you would be happy to attend every single college to which you apply. This includes the good-bet applications as well as the long-shot ones. Joyce Mitchell, a high school counselor who has written her own book on college admissions, has made the "eight first choices" rule a cornerstone of her advice to students. It is good advice. Because you cannot predict the response from long-shot colleges, having several first choices including at least one that is a good bet scholastically and is also a financial good bet virtually guarantees a happy outcome. You should use the "eight first choices" rule even if you apply early decision, since it may not work out.

Don't procrastinate at any point in the process.

When you ask college seniors what they would do differently if they could relive their college application experience, the most common response is, "I would start earlier and not procrastinate." Procrastination is a normal reaction to a stressful process. But it really does make things worse. Leaving applications to the last minute invariably means rushed decisions, mistakes, and potentially missed opportunities, not to mention needless stress. Establish a reasonable time frame for your efforts, setting deadlines for yourself along the way. Having and meeting deadlines will also reduce stress on your parents. Do this for them, as well as for yourself.

Get and stay organized; keep everything together, and make copies of everything you send in.

The college application process generates an astonishing amount of paper, even with the trend to doing more online. Copious brochures and college catalogs arrive early on. Later, multipart applications have to be completed, reference forms submitted to teachers and counselors, and transcripts requested. Making things worse, different colleges have different requirements and deadlines. Staying on top of it all can be a real challenge, but it is a challenge that is important to meet. A simple filing system in a cardboard box is all you need, along with a record of each school's requirements and deadlines that you can check off as you meet them. And be sure to make a copy of everything you send in, even online applications. Colleges rarely lose materials, but you don't want to take any chances. Starting over when you thought you were done is no fun.

Talk to your friends, but remember that each person is different.

Peers can be wonderful sources of information. For example, a friend may return from a trip to another part of the country, excited about touring several colleges you never heard of, and open your eyes to new possibilities. But a good choice for one person, even a good friend, may not be a good choice for you. When someone offers an opinion of a college, whether good or bad, try to find out what's behind it. Get to the facts, then see how those facts fit with your own needs. And respect the choices of others. A good-bet college for one person may be a possible or even a long shot for another.

Enjoy your senior year. College applications are important (that's why you are reading this book), but they should not be allowed to take over your life.

College admissions can easily become the focus of your senior year. There is so much to do, and so much seems to be at stake. But the senior year in high school should also be special in other ways—sharing adventures with old friends, enjoying a fleeting year of being "top banana," and beginning to enjoy the freedoms that come with being an adult. Balance is key. A wise student takes the college application process seriously but doesn't let it overwhelm everything else. If you approach things calmly and rationally, and in a timely way, you can achieve the dual goals of having an array of fine college choices and a senior year filled with wonderful memories.

End the college admissions process on a high note.

When the final decisions from colleges come in, you get to decide. Do so carefully. Your choice may or may not be the one you hoped or thought you would make when you began the process, but if you have followed our advice, it will be a good choice. Celebrate with your family and friends, and begin to plan for your new life as a college student (but remember you still have to successfully complete your senior year).

Thank your teachers and counselors again for writing letters for you and tell them where you got in and didn't. Visit them to say "hi" when you return home over winter break during your freshman year, or send them cards if you can't see them in person. Above all, thank your parents for all they have done and still do for you, and tell them that you love them. Do this along the way, but especially when the process is over.

Epilogue

We end our book with a wonderful letter to students that Fred Hargadon, now-retired dean of admission at Princeton University, had for many years included with Princeton's application packet. Dean Hargadon's long and distinguished career in college admissions spanned thirty-five years and three major institutions: Swarthmore, Stanford, and Princeton. We believe the letter contains important messages for all applicants to selective colleges, not just those who applied to Princeton, and Dean Hargadon kindly allowed us to reprint it here. We've taken the liberty, with his permission, to lightly edit it to omit Princeton-specific references so that it would be clear that it applies to everyone.

 A Letter from the Dean of Admission to All Prospective Applicants for Admission to the Class of _____

In a favorite book of mine, *The Phantom Tollbooth,* one of the delightful characters the reader meets up with is the Dodecahedron (named after a mathematical shape with twelve sides). He introduces himself in the following manner: "My angles are many. My sides are not few." Those words have always struck me as a pretty good description of the admissions process not only at this university, but at many similar colleges and universities as well. In any event, as you approach the college admissions process, with its "many angles" and "not a few sides," I've been thinking about what sort of advice might be useful to share with you were

---

we able to have a conversation about your applying to colleges. While a printed letter may be a poor substitute for a conversation, I've simply jotted down a few of the observations I'd most likely make if I had the opportunity to talk with you in person.

First of all, I'd tell you that I don't envy you the task of trying to determine to which colleges you should apply, or trying to estimate your chances of admission at any particular college, or, ultimately, having to make a choice about where to enroll from among those to which you are offered admission. I can tell you that I don't think there are any shortcuts (not even Harry Potter's "Sorting Hat"), to finding good answers to these questions, and that since this is one of the more significant decisions you will make in your life, it's worth as much time and effort and homework as you can put into it.

Following the old adage, "well-begun is half-done," I'd like to suggest that you begin your college search by taking some time to think hard about why it is you want to go to college in the first place and about what, once you get there, you hope to gain from those four years. The more thought you give now to what it is you think you want to learn and experience in college, the better informed will be your choice of colleges to which to apply. Otherwise, you're likely to find yourself in the situation akin to that of trying to decide whether to drive, fly, or take a train without first deciding where you want to get.

Set aside some quiet time in order to reflect frankly on your strengths and weaknesses: think about what it is that you now know, are especially interested in, do well, or just plain enjoy and therefore would like an opportunity to continue to pursue in college; and about what it is, on the other hand, that you don't know (but think you should) or don't do particularly well (but hope to learn to do better) and therefore also want to pursue in college.

I'd even go so far as to recommend that you sketch out a tentative plan of what it is you wish to accomplish in college (not a plan of what you want to do after college, but in college), keeping in mind that you're likely to alter it as you go along. You probably will find yourself making some changes in it even between now and next year. It just seems to me that the better the handle you try to get now on at least some of the ways in which you hope to change and grow as a result of your college experience, the better you will be able to identify those colleges that appear most likely to meet your needs. (For example, whether your goal right now happens to be becoming a doctor, or an engineer, or a writer, you might decide that you also want to leave college having become bilingual, or having mastered a musical instrument, or having gained more than a superficial appreciation of art, or having taken up the sport of rowing. I regret, for instance, that I didn't spend some of my time in college learning to play the piano, however thankful my friends may be that I didn't. As someone once wisely pointed out, the person you will spend most of your life with is yourself, and therefore you owe it to yourself to become as interesting as possible.)

While it's not unusual for students to talk of their "first choice" college, I think it's a rare individual for whom it can be said that there exists but a single, best college. Even if, as the result of the homework you do on colleges, you arrive at a point where you accord enough preference to one college to consider it your "first choice," your final list ought to include a number of colleges, any one of which you'd be happy to attend if admitted. Keep in mind that most students end up very much liking the college they attend, regardless of whether it had been their "first choice" when they applied.

It's also a good idea to focus at least as much attention on the overall quality of a college as on the quality of the particular department or academic area in which you may now be especially interested. Experience indicates that a fair number of students ultimately major in an academic area other than the one they had in mind when entering. This happens for any number of reasons. Some students simply find that the more they learn about what is involved in studying a particular subject, the less satisfying it becomes. Some find a different, but closely related, field more to their liking. More often, it happens that it is only after they get to college that students become familiar with one or another field of study, and subsequently find themselves more attracted by it than by their initial interests as freshmen. The point is that you will want to take into account the possibility of a change in your own interests while you are going through college, and therefore you ought to feel reasonably confident that the colleges to which you are applying are ones which will offer you an excellent education across the board. You should also try to imagine how well a given college will meet your needs and interests as a junior or senior, not just what it offers you as a freshman.

You need to be realistic, too. There are no absolutely perfect colleges. I've never met a student for whom every classroom experience, every faculty member, or every out-of-class experience turned out to be ideal. A good way to approach the colleges you are looking into is to think of each of them as a set of probabilities. And, depending upon your interests and the kinds of experiences you hope to have, you should try to get some sense of the probabilities of satisfying those interests or of having those experiences at one or another of them. For instance, what are the probabilities of being in classes of one size or another, or of getting to know at least some faculty members well, or of undertaking independent research, or of participating in one or another extracurricular activity? These are the sorts of questions you ought to be asking.

There isn't any quick or easy way that I know of in which to fully know what a particular college is like, despite the proliferation of commercial publications that purport to give you capsule summaries or the "inside" story. Colleges and universities are dynamic and complex institutions, if for no other reason than the fact that one-quarter of the student body is new each year. While some information is relatively easy to come by (size, costs, course offerings, and the like), many of the factors you may wish to weigh and compare are simply not so easily measured and assessed. For instance, I'd be surprised if on any given day, let alone over the course of four years, any two students at my university experience this place in quite the same way. There are many paths, both academic and nonacademic, through any single college, and almost every student travels more than one of those paths during the course of his or her four years.

In any event, try to avoid falling into the trap of thinking about one or another college solely in terms of a few descriptive adjectives or traits. And remember that any college is going to be at least slightly different than it now is simply by virtue of your enrolling there. If at all possible, you should visit the campuses of the colleges in which you are most interested, attend classes, and talk with some currently enrolled students. Rather than rely on any single source of information, seek out a number of different sources, always keeping in mind the fable about the seven blind philosophers, each of whom, upon touching a different part of an elephant, described the seven quite different animals they thought it to be. So, too, is the same university likely to be perceived, at least in part, quite differently by its various members.

Neither you nor your parents will be able to ignore the fact that some colleges (including mine) are more expensive than others. Even if I were not representing one of those institutions, I'd still be telling you that I don't think it wise to cross any college off your list just because it appears to cost a small fortune to attend. In the first place, while we all know that cost is not a perfect indicator of quality, it is also true that a first-rate college education does not come cheaply. Second, a number of colleges and universities make their admission decisions completely without regard to whether an applicant will need financial aid.

Keep in mind the following: first, you can always turn down a college's offer of admission should the amount of financial aid it awards you appear inadequate; second, the one sure way not to gain admission or not to receive financial aid is by deciding not to apply in the first place.

Now, about applying for admission. What you will quickly learn over the next few months is that with regard to many of the questions you are likely to have about various aspects of the admission process, there is no single set of answers that apply for all colleges. Do colleges require personal interviews? Some do and some don't. Do colleges treat your SAT results as a combined score or treat the component scores separately? Some do the former, some the latter.

You will find these differences frustrating in at least two respects. First, you will have to treat each institution (and therefore each application) individually. That's not so bad when you think of it, given that we assume you want the colleges to treat your application individually. Second, a particular college's practice with regard to how it treats your high school transcript or your test scores, and so forth, may not be in accord with your preference in such matters. After all, it's only human nature for an applicant to want colleges to place the greatest weight on those factors he or she shows up best on and the least amount of weight on those factors he or she shows up less well on. My advice is simply to roll with these differences, especially since there is not much you'll be able to do about them anyway. A good rule of thumb here is simply to make sure that you meet each college halfway in completing its application.

I think it helps to understand from the outset that the context within which a college views an applicant (say, as one of a large number of similarly qualified applicants from across the country) is bound to be different from the context within which that applicant is viewed locally. Moreover, the context within which an applicant is viewed by one college is also bound to be different from the context within which that same applicant is viewed by another college, given not only that applicant groups are not completely identical from one college to another but also that the sizes of their respective freshman classes may vary considerably. Lots of times this explains why an applicant is offered admission by one college and not another.

Nor is there a single scale (or at least none that makes sense to us) against which colleges are able to precisely rank-order applicants from one to whatever number of thousands it is who apply. There are simply too many variables. For instance, similar grade point averages may represent quite different levels of achievement across thousands of high schools or even across different departments within the same school. And think of the number of possible combinations of SAT scores as well as the various SAT Subject Test scores. That is why we treat each application individually, and why we make every effort to take into account the enormous variation in academic and extracurricular opportunities from one school to the next, from one community to the next, from one state to the next, and from one country to the next. Experience suggests that excellence does not always and everywhere come in uniform dimensions.

While it is true that, all other things being equal, the better one's academic credentials, the better one's chances of admission, it is not the case that every student we admit will have higher test scores or a higher grade point average or a higher rank-in-class than those who are not offered admission. Colleges like mine are "selective" in two ways: first, every year, more well-qualified students apply than it is possible for us to admit to a freshman class as relatively small as ours, and therefore we have to make a lot of difficult choices; second, in setting out to enroll a freshman class that is characterized by a variety of academic and non-academic interests, exceptional skills and talents, experiences, aspirations, and backgrounds, we exercise judgments relating to factors other than just quantitative ones. We are aware that an important part of a student's education here is derived from the mix of students he or she will live with, study and play with, and come to know.

In other words, you should realize that in applying to a college with more qualified applicants than there are places available in the freshman class, there will be some factors affecting the ultimate decision on your application (primarily, the number and nature of all the other applications) over which you have no control and for which you should not feel responsible. Too often, applicants not offered admission automatically assume that there are specific deficiencies or faults in their applications when in fact that simply isn't the case. No college enjoys the prospect of disappointing qualified applicants, but applicants who are not in some measure prepared for the possibility of being disappointed are being unrealistic. (When all is said and done, I happen to believe that the saving grace of college admissions as a whole in this country is the fact we don't all agree on precisely the same students to admit in a given year.)

Elsewhere in the application materials, I have suggested that in completing your application, you should just be yourself, rather than attempting to match some imagined ideal candidate you think we have in mind. And I confess that every time I offer that advice, I remember the comment Mark Twain made: "Telling a person to be himself is the worst advice you can give to some people!" Still, that's my advice.

In thinking about what you hope to gain from college, you might also want to consider the possibility of taking a break between school and college—deferring your entrance to college, in other words. Every year, about two dozen or so of the students to whom we offer admission choose to defer their entrance for a year, some just to work, some to travel abroad on an American Field Service or similar program, some to continue private music study, and so forth. I mention it here just so you are aware that it is an option.

Not one of us who annually reads and rereads the thousands of applications for admission believes either the process or our ultimate decisions to be perfect, whatever criteria for perfection are used.

Ultimately, however, to the best of our limited abilities we make those decisions. While I can't guarantee you admission should you apply, what I can do is to assure you that we will evaluate your application with an open mind, respect for you as an individual, and no small measure of humility.

As you go through this year, try to retain a sense of perspective and even a sense of humor. I know how important where you attend college is to you, but I also know that students often see as critical those differences between attending one college and another which, in many cases, are very slight. Whatever you do, don't let the college application process so preoccupy you that you miss out on all that your school has to offer you during your senior year. OK, that's not all of the advice I'd like to give you, but it's about the limit of one letter and I hope that some of it is useful.

Happy trails.

FRED HARGADON, DEAN OF ADMISSION

Appendixes

Appendix A
College Research Worksheet

(Make copies of this form and complete one for each college you are seriously considering.)

Name of School _____ Location _____

Admissions Phone and E-mail _____ Campus Web Site _____

Testing Requirements (circle all that apply):

Required: SAT   ACT   ACT Writing   SAT II _____

Recommended: SAT   ACT   ACT Writing   SAT II _____

Optional: SAT   ACT   ACT Writing   SAT II _____

Freshman Class Profile:

GPA: % in the top 10% of class _____ % in the top 20% of class _____

    % in the top 50% of class _____

applications _____   % admitted _____

early applications _____   % admitted _____   % of class filled early _____

SAT: mid-50% math _____   mid-50% critical reading _____   mid-50% writing _____

ACT: mid-50% composite _____

Total # undergraduates _____   Total # students on campus _____

Academic Profile:

Circle one: Research University   Liberal Arts College   Other _____

Majors of interest to you: _____

_____

continues on next page

Academic Profile, *continued*

Curriculum requirements (general education, senior thesis, etc.): _____

_____

Special programs of interest (honors program, arrangements with other colleges, etc.):

_____

_____

Overall impression of academic pace and rigor: _____

_____

Other: _____

_____

Campus Life

Campus Housing: Guaranteed for _____ years

Details (process for assignment, housing options, % living on campus): _____

_____

_____

Characteristics of Student Body (single sex, geographic and ethnic diversity, liberal/
conservative, etc.): _____

_____

_____

Social Life and Activities (% in sororities and fraternities, intramural and club sports, recreational
facilities, clubs of special interest, etc.): _____

_____

_____

Other: _____

_____

Special Interests

Intercollegiate Athletics: Your sport: _____ NCAA Division: _____

Coach's name and contact info: _____

Arts, Music, or Special Academic Focus:

Area: _____ Contact: _____

Area: _____ Contact: _____

Other: _____

Financial Aid Policies

Circle all that apply: Guarantees to meet full demonstrated need   Offers merit aid

Need-blind admissions   Need-based aid only

Financial Aid Deadlines: FAFSA _____ CSS Profile _____ Other(s) _____

Application Process

Circle all that apply: College-specific form   Pre-application

Common Application   Common Application Supplement

Application Deadlines: Early action _____ Early decision _____ Regular _____

Rolling _____ Fee _____

Interview: Required   Optional   Not offered

Details: _____

_____

Other Notes _____

_____

Appendix B
Common Application 2009–10

2009-10 FIRST-YEAR APPLICATION

For Spring 2010 or Fall 2010 Enrollment

APPLICANT

Legal name _____
       Last/Family/Sur *(Enter name **exactly** as it appears on official documents.)*   First/Given   Middle (complete)   Jr., etc.

Preferred name, if not first name (choose only one) _____   Former last name(s), if any _____

Birth date _____ ○ Female ○ Male   US Social Security Number, if any _____
              mm/dd/yyyy   *Optional, unless applying for US Federal financial aid with the FAFSA form*

E-mail address _____   IM address _____

Permanent home address _____
                           Number & Street   *Apartment #*

_____
         City/Town   *State/Province*   *Country*   *ZIP/Postal Code*

Permanent home phone (_____) _____   Cell phone (_____) _____
             Area Code   *Area Code*

If different from above, please give your current mailing address for all admission correspondence.

Current mailing address _____
                         Number & Street   *Apartment #*

_____
         City/Town   *State/Province*   *Country*   *ZIP/Postal Code*

If your current mailing address is a boarding school, include name of school here: _____

Phone at current mailing address (_____) _____   (from _____ to _____)
                      Area Code   *(mm/dd/yyyy)*   *(mm/dd/yyyy)*

FUTURE PLANS

Your answers to these questions will vary for different colleges. If the online system did not ask you to answer some of the questions you see in this section, this college chose not to ask that question of its applicants.

College: _____   Deadline: _____
                                                            mm/dd/yyyy

Entry Term: ○ Fall (Jul-Dec)   ○ Spring (Jan-Jun)

Decision Plan: ○ Regular Decision   ○ Rolling Admission   Do you intend to apply for need-based financial aid?   ○ Yes ○ No
               ○ Early Decision   ○ Early Decision II   Do you intend to apply for merit-based scholarships?   ○ Yes ○ No
               ○ Early Action   ○ Early Action II   Do you intend to be a full-time student?   ○ Yes ○ No
               ○ Restrictive Early Action   ○ Early Admission   Do you intend to enroll in a degree program your first year?   ○ Yes ○ No
                                     juniors only   Do you intend to live in college housing? _____
                                                      Academic Interests: _____

Career Interest: _____

DEMOGRAPHICS

○ US citizen
○ Dual US citizen
○ US permanent resident visa (Alien registration # _____)
○ Other citizenship (Visa type _____)
List any non-US countries of citizenship_____
_____

How many years have you lived in the United States?_____
Place of birth _____
        City/Town   *State/Province*   *Country*
First language _____
Primary language spoken at home _____

Optional The items with a gray background are optional. No information you provide will be used in a discriminatory manner.

Marital status: _____
US Armed Services veteran?   ○ Yes ○ No

1.   Are you Hispanic/Latino?
○ Yes, Hispanic or Latino (including Spain)   ○ No
    Please describe your background _____
2.   Regardless of your answer to the prior question, please select one or more of the following ethnicities that best describe you:
○ American Indian or Alaska Native (including all Original Peoples of the Americas)
    Are you Enrolled? ○ Yes ○ No If yes, please enter Tribal Enrollment Number _____
    Please describe your background _____
○ Asian (including Indian subcontinent and Philippines)
    Please describe your background _____
○ Black or African American (including Africa and Caribbean)
    Please describe your background _____
○ Native Hawaiian or Other Pacific Islander (Original Peoples)
    Please describe your background _____
○ White (including Middle Eastern)
    Please describe your background _____

AP-1/**2009-10**

FAMILY

Please list both parents below, even if one or more is deceased or no longer has legal responsibilities toward you. Many colleges collect this information for demographic purposes even if you are an adult or an emancipated minor. If you are a minor with a legal guardian (an individual or government entity), then please list that information below as well. If you wish, you may list step-parents and/or other adults with whom you reside, or who otherwise care for you, in the Additional Information section **online**, or on an attached sheet **if applying via mail**.

Household

Parents' Marital Status (relative to each other): ○ Never married ○ Married ○ Widowed ○ Separated ○ Divorced (date _____)
mm/yyyy

With whom do you make your permanent home? ○ Parent 1 ○ Parent 2 ○ Both ○ Legal Guardian ○ Ward of the Court/State ○ Other

Parent 1: ○ Mother ○ Father ○ Unknown   **Parent 2**: ○ Mother ○ Father ○ Unknown

Is Parent 1 living? ○ Yes ○ No (Date deceased _____)   Is Parent 2 living? ○ Yes ○ No (Date deceased _____)
mm/yyyy   *mm/yyyy*

_____   _____
Last/Family/Sur   *First/Given*   *Middle*   *Title (Mr./Ms./Dr., etc.)*   *Last/Family/Sur*   *First/Given*   *Middle*   *Title (Mr./Ms./Dr., etc.)*

Country of birth _____   Country of birth _____

Home address **if different** from yours   Home address **if different** from yours

_____   _____

_____   _____

_____   _____

Home phone (_____) _____   Home phone (_____) _____
Area Code   *Area Code*

E-mail _____   E-mail _____

Occupation _____   Occupation _____

Name of employer _____   Name of employer _____

College (if any) _____   College (if any) _____

Degree _____ Year _____   Degree _____ Year _____

Graduate school (if any) _____   Graduate school (if any) _____

Degree _____ Year _____   Degree _____ Year _____

Legal Guardian *(if other than a parent)*

Relationship to you _____

_____
Last/Family/Sur   *First/Given*   *Middle*   *Title (Mr./Ms./Dr., etc.)*

Home address **if different** from yours

_____

_____

Home phone (_____) _____
Area Code

E-mail _____

Occupation _____

Name of employer _____

College (if any) _____

Degree _____ Year _____

Graduate school (if any) _____

Degree _____ Year _____

Siblings

Please give names and ages of your brothers or sisters. If they have attended or are currently attending college, give the names of the undergraduate institution, degree earned, and approximate dates of attendance. If more than three siblings, please list them in the Additional Information section **online**, or on an attached sheet **if applying via mail**.

Name	*Age*	*Relationship*

College Attended _____

| Degree Earned | | Dates _____ |
| or Expected | | *yyyy-yyyy* |

Name	*Age*	*Relationship*

College Attended _____

| Degree Earned | | Dates _____ |
| or Expected | | *yyyy-yyyy* |

Name	*Age*	*Relationship*

College Attended _____

| Degree Earned | | Dates _____ |
| or Expected | | *yyyy-yyyy* |

AP-2 / **2009-10**   © 2009 The Common Application, Inc.

ACADEMICS

Secondary Schools

Current or most recent secondary school attended _____

Entry Date _____ Graduation Date _____ School Type ○ public ○ charter ○ independent ○ religious ○ home school
mm/yyyy *mm/dd/yyyy*

Address _____ CEEB/ACT Code _____
Number & Street

_____
City/Town *State/Province* *Country* *ZIP/Postal Code*

Counselor's name (Mr./Ms./Dr., etc.) _____ Counselor's Title _____

E-mail _____ Phone (_____) _____ Fax (_____) _____
Area Code *Number* *Ext.* *Area Code* *Number*

List all other secondary schools, including summer schools as well as summer and other programs, you have attended, beginning with 9th grade.

School Name & CEEB/ACT Code	Location (City, State/Province, ZIP/Postal Code, Country)	Dates Attended (mm/yyyy)

If you received college counseling or assistance with your application process from a community-based organization (such as Upward Bound, Questbridge, HEOP, etc.), please specify. _____

If your secondary school education was or will be interrupted, check all that apply and provide details in the Additional Information section or on an attached sheet.

○ did/will graduate late ○ did/will change secondary schools ○ did not/will not graduate
○ did/will graduate early ○ did/will take time off ○ did/will receive GED Date: _____ (Official scores must be sent from the testing agency.)
mm/yyyy

Colleges & Universities List all colleges/universities at which you have taken courses for credit; list names of courses taken, grades earned, and credits earned in the Additional Information section **online**, or on an attached sheet **if applying via mail**. Please have an official transcript sent from each institution as soon as possible.

College/University Name & CEEB/ACT Code	Location (City, State/Province, ZIP/Postal Code, Country)	Degree Candidate? Yes No	Dates Attended (mm/yyyy)	Degree(s) Earned
		○ ○		
		○ ○		
		○ ○		

TESTS

Be sure to note the tests required for each institution to which you are applying. The official SAT, ACT, TOEFL, MELAB and/or IELTS scores from the appropriate testing agencies should be sent as soon as possible.

ACT Tests

Date taken/ to be taken	English	Math	Reading	Science	Composite	Writing	Date taken/ to be taken	English	Math	Reading	Science	Composite	Writing

SAT Reasoning Tests

Date taken/ to be taken	Critical Reading	Math	Writing	Date taken/ to be taken	Critical Reading	Math	Writing	Date taken/ to be taken	Critical Reading	Math	Writing

SAT Subject Tests

Date taken/ to be taken	Subject	Score	Date taken/ to be taken	Subject	Score	Date taken/ to be taken	Subject	Score
Date taken/ to be taken	Subject	Score	Date taken/ to be taken	Subject	Score	Date taken/ to be taken	Subject	Score

AP/IB Tests

Date taken/ to be taken	Subject	Score	Date taken/ to be taken	Subject	Score	Date taken/ to be taken	Subject	Score
Date taken/ to be taken	Subject	Score	Date taken/ to be taken	Subject	Score	Date taken/ to be taken	Subject	Score
Date taken/ to be taken	Subject	Score	Date taken/ to be taken	Subject	Score	Date taken/ to be taken	Subject	Score

TOEFL/IELTS/MELAB

Date taken/ to be taken	Test	Score	Date taken/ to be taken	Test	Score	Date taken/ to be taken	Test	Score

© 2009 The Common Application, Inc.

AP-3 / **2009-10**

Honors Briefly list any academic distinctions or honors you have received since the 9th grade or international equivalent (e.g. National Merit, Cum Laude Society).

Grade level or post-graduate (PG)					Honor	Level of Recognition			
9	10	11	12	PG		School	State/ Regional	National	Inter- national
○	○	○	○	○	_____	○	○	○	○
○	○	○	○	○	_____	○	○	○	○
○	○	○	○	○	_____	○	○	○	○
○	○	○	○	○	_____	○	○	○	○
○	○	○	○	○	_____	○	○	○	○

ACTIVITIES

Extracurricular Please list your **principal** extracurricular, community, volunteer and family activities and hobbies **in the order of their interest to you**. Include specific events and/or major accomplishments such as musical instrument played, varsity letters earned, etc. **To allow us to focus on the highlights of your activities, please complete this section even if you plan to attach a résumé.**

Grade level or post-graduate (PG)					Approximate time spent		When did you participate in the activity?		Positions held, honors won, or letters earned	If applicable, do you plan to participate in college?
9	10	11	12	PG	Hours per week	Weeks per year	School year	Summer		
○	○	○	○	○	_____	_____	○	○	_____	○

Activity _____

| ○ | ○ | ○ | ○ | ○ | _____ | _____ | ○ | ○ | _____ | ○ |

Activity _____

| ○ | ○ | ○ | ○ | ○ | _____ | _____ | ○ | ○ | _____ | ○ |

Activity _____

| ○ | ○ | ○ | ○ | ○ | _____ | _____ | ○ | ○ | _____ | ○ |

Activity _____

| ○ | ○ | ○ | ○ | ○ | _____ | _____ | ○ | ○ | _____ | ○ |

Activity _____

| ○ | ○ | ○ | ○ | ○ | _____ | _____ | ○ | ○ | _____ | ○ |

Activity _____

| ○ | ○ | ○ | ○ | ○ | _____ | _____ | ○ | ○ | _____ | ○ |

Activity _____

Work Experience Please list **paid** jobs you have held during the past three years (including summer employment).

Specific nature of work	Employer	School year	Summer	Approximate dates (mm/yyyy - mm/yyyy)	Hours per week
_____	_____	○	○	_____	_____
_____	_____	○	○	_____	_____
_____	_____	○	○	_____	_____
_____	_____	○	○	_____	_____

WRITING

Short Answer Please briefly elaborate on one of your extracurricular activities or work experiences in the space below or on an attached sheet (150 words or fewer).

_____

_____

_____

_____

Personal Essay Please write an essay (250 words minimum) on a topic of your choice or on one of the options listed below, and attach it to your application before submission. **Please indicate your topic by checking the appropriate box.** This personal essay helps us become acquainted with you as a person and student, apart from courses, grades, test scores, and other objective data. It will also demonstrate your ability to organize your thoughts and express yourself.

- ○ **1** Evaluate a significant experience, achievement, risk you have taken, or ethical dilemma you have faced and its impact on you.
- ○ **2** Discuss some issue of personal, local, national, or international concern and its importance to you.
- ○ **3** Indicate a person who has had a significant influence on you, and describe that influence.
- ○ **4** Describe a character in fiction, a historical figure, or a creative work (as in art, music, science, etc.) that has had an influence on you, and explain that influence.
- ○ **5** A range of academic interests, personal perspectives, and life experiences adds much to the educational mix. Given your personal background, describe an experience that illustrates what you would bring to the diversity in a college community, or an encounter that demonstrated the importance of diversity to you.
- ○ **6** Topic of your choice.

Disciplinary History

① Have you ever been found responsible for a disciplinary violation at any educational institution you have attended from 9ᵗʰ grade (or the international equivalent) forward, whether related to academic misconduct or behavioral misconduct, that resulted in your probation, suspension, removal, dismissal, or expulsion from the institution? ○ Yes ○ No

② Have you ever been convicted of a misdemeanor, felony, or other crime? ○ Yes ○ No

If you answered yes to either or both questions, please attach a separate sheet of paper that gives the approximate date of each incident, explains the circumstances, and reflects on what you learned from the experience.

Additional Information If there is any additional information you'd like to provide regarding special circumstances, additional qualifications, etc., please do so in the space below or on an attached sheet.

_____

_____

_____

_____

SIGNATURE

Application Fee Payment If this college requires an application fee, how will you be paying it?
○ Online Payment   ○ Will Mail Payment   ○ Online Fee Waiver Request   ○ Will Mail Fee Waiver Request

Required Signature

○ *I certify that all information submitted in the admission process—including the application, the personal essay, any supplements, and any other supporting materials—is my own work, factually true, and honestly presented. I authorize all schools attended to release all requested records covered under the FERPA act, and authorize review of my application for the admission program indicated on this form. I understand that I may be subject to a range of possible disciplinary actions, including admission revocation or expulsion, should the information I've certified be false.*

○ *I acknowledge that I have reviewed the application instructions for each college receiving this application. I understand that all offers of admission are conditional, pending receipt of final transcripts showing work comparable in quality to that upon which the offer was based, as well as honorable dismissal from the school. I also affirm that I will send an enrollment deposit (or the equivalent) to only one institution; sending multiple deposits (or the equivalent) may result in the withdrawal of my admission offers from all institutions. [Note: students may send an enrollment deposit (or equivalent) to a second institution where they have been admitted from the waitlist, provided that they inform the first institution that they will no longer be enrolling.]*

Signature ✎ _____   Date _____
mm/dd/yyyy

AP-5 / **2009-10**

CURRENT COURSES

Current year courses—please indicate title, level (AP, IB, advanced honors, etc.) and credit value of all courses you are taking this year. Indicate quarter classes taken in the same semester on the appropriate semester line.

First Semester/Trimester

Second Semester/Trimester

Third Trimester
or additional first/second term courses if more space is needed

_____   _____   _____

_____   _____   _____

_____   _____   _____

_____   _____   _____

_____   _____   _____

_____   _____   _____

_____   _____   _____

_____   _____   _____

2009-10 TEACHER EVALUATION

For Spring 2010 or Fall 2010 Enrollment

TE

TO THE APPLICANT

After completing all the relevant questions below, give this form to a teacher who has taught you an **academic** subject (for example, English, foreign language, math, science, or social studies). **If applying via mail**, please also give that teacher stamped envelopes addressed to each institution that requires a Teacher Evaluation.

Legal name _____

          Last/Family/Sur *(Enter name **exactly** as it appears on official documents.)*   First/Given   Middle (complete)   Jr., etc.

○ Female
○ Male

Birth date _____ Social Security # _____

      mm/dd/yyyy   (Optional)

Address _____

      Number & Street   Apartment #   City/Town   State/Province   Country   ZIP/Postal Code

School you now attend _____ CEEB/ACT code _____

> **IMPORTANT PRIVACY NOTICE:** Under the terms of the Family Educational Rights and Privacy Act (FERPA), after you matriculate you *will* have access to this form and all other recommendations and supporting documents submitted by you and on your behalf after matriculating, unless at least one of the following is true:
>
> 1. The institution does not save recommendations post-matriculation *(see list at www.commonapp.org/FERPA).*
> 2. You waive your right to access below, regardless of the institution to which it is sent:
>
> ○ Yes, I do waive my right to access, and I understand I will never see this form or any other recommendations submitted by me or on my behalf.
> ○ No, I do *not* waive my right to access, and I may someday choose to see this form or any other recommendations or supporting documents submitted by me or on my behalf to the institution at which I'm enrolling, if that institution saves them after I matriculate.
>
> Signature ✎ _____ Date _____

TO THE TEACHER

The Common Application membership finds candid evaluations helpful in choosing from among highly qualified candidates. You are encouraged to keep this form in your private files for use should the student need additional recommendations. Please submit your references promptly, **and remember to sign below**.

Teacher's name (Mr./Ms./Dr., etc.) _____ Subject taught _____

                              Please print or type

Signature ✎ _____ Date_____

                                                      mm/dd/yyyy

Secondary school _____

School address _____

          Number & Street   City/Town   State/Province   Country   ZIP/Postal Code

Teacher's phone (_____) _____ Teacher's e-mail _____

      Area Code   Number   Ext.

Background Information

How long have you known this student and in what context? _____

What are the first words that come to your mind to describe this student? _____

List the courses you have taught this student, noting for each the student's year in school (10th, 11th, 12th; first-year, sophomore; etc.) and the level of course difficulty (AP, IB, accelerated, honors, elective; 100-level, 200-level, etc.).

_____

TEACHER EVALUATION 1

TE-1/**2009-10**

Ratings Compared to other students in his or her class year, how do you rate this student in terms of:

No basis		Below average	Average	Good (above average)	Very good (well above average)	Excellent (top 10%)	Outstanding (top 5%)	One of the top few I've encountered (top 1%)
	Academic achievement							
	Intellectual promise							
	Quality of writing							
	Creative, original thought							
	Productive class discussion							
	Respect accorded by faculty							
	Disciplined work habits							
	Maturity							
	Motivation							
	Leadership							
	Integrity							
	Reaction to setbacks							
	Concern for others							
	Self-confidence							
	Initiative, independence							
	OVERALL							

Evaluation Please write whatever you think is important about this student, including a description of academic and personal characteristics, as demonstrated in your classroom. We welcome information that will help us to differentiate this student from others. (Feel free to attach an additional sheet or another reference you may have prepared on behalf of this student.)

TO THE APPLICANT

After completing all the relevant questions below, give this form to your secondary school counselor or another school official who knows you better. **If applying via mail**, please also give that school official stamped envelopes addressed to each institution that requires a Secondary School Report.

Legal name _____   ○ Female
　　　　　　　*Last/Family/Sur (Enter name **exactly** as it appears on official documents.) 　First/Given　　　　　Middle (complete)　　　　Jr., etc.*   ○ Male

Birth date _____ Social Security # _____
　　　　　　　mm/dd/yyyy　　　　　　　　　　　　　　　　　　　　　　　　　　　　　*(Optional)*

Address _____
　　　　　Number & Street　　　　Apartment #　　　　City/Town　　　State/Province　　　Country　　　　ZIP/Postal Code

School you now attend _____ CEEB/ACT code _____

Current year courses—please indicate title, level (AP, IB, advanced honors, etc.) and credit value of all courses you are taking this year. Indicate quarter classes taken in the same semester on the appropriate semester line.

First Semester/Trimester	Second Semester/Trimester	Third Trimester *or additional first/second term courses if more space is needed*
_____	_____	_____
_____	_____	_____
_____	_____	_____
_____	_____	_____
_____	_____	_____
_____	_____	_____
_____	_____	_____
_____	_____	_____

IMPORTANT PRIVACY NOTICE: Under the terms of the Family Educational Rights and Privacy Act (FERPA), after you matriculate you *will* have access to this form and all other recommendations and supporting documents submitted by you and on your behalf after matriculating, unless at least one of the following is true:

1. The institution does not save recommendations post-matriculation *(see list at www.commonapp.org/FERPA)*.
2. You waive your right to access below, regardless of the institution to which it is sent:

○ Yes, I do waive my right to access, and I understand I will never see this form or any other recommendations submitted by me or on my behalf.
○ No, I do *not waive* my right to access, and I may someday choose to see this form or any other recommendations or supporting documents submitted by me or on my behalf to the institution at which I'm enrolling, if that institution saves them after I matriculate.

Signature ✎ _____ Date _____

TO THE SECONDARY SCHOOL COUNSELOR

Attach applicant's official transcript, including courses in progress, a school profile, and transcript legend. (Check transcript copies for readability.) Use both pages to complete your evaluation for this student. **Be sure to sign below.**

Counselor's name (Mr./Ms./Dr., etc.) _____
　　　　　　　　　　　　　　　　　　　　Please print or type

Signature ✎ _____ Date _____
　　mm/dd/yyyy

Title _____ School _____

School address _____
　　　　　　　　　　　City/Town　　　　　　State/Province　　　Country　　　　　　　　　　　　　ZIP/Postal Code

Counselor's phone (_____) _____ Counselor's fax (_____) _____
　　　　　　　　Area Code　　　　　Number　　　　　Ext.　　　　　　　Area Code　　　　　Number

Secondary school CEEB/ACT code _____ Counselor's e-mail _____

SR-1/**2009-10**

Background Information

Class rank: _____ Class size: _____ Covering a period from _____ to _____ .
(mm/yyyy)   (mm/yyyy)

The rank is ○ weighted ○ unweighted. How many students share this rank? _____

○ We do not rank. Instead, please indicate quartile _____ quintile _____ decile _____

Cumulative GPA: _____ on a _____ scale, covering a period from _____ to _____
(mm/yyyy)   (mm/yyyy)

This GPA is ○ weighted ○ unweighted. The school's passing mark is _____ .

Highest GPA in class _____ Graduation date _____
(mm/dd/yyyy)

Percentage of graduating class immediately attending: _____ four-year _____ two-year institutions

Are classes taken on a block schedule? ○ Yes ○ No
Is the applicant an IB Diploma candidate? ○ Yes ○ No
If you offer AP courses, do you limit the number a student can take? ○ Yes ○ No
How many AP courses does your school offer (in total)? _____
In comparison with other college preparatory students at your school, the applicant's course selection is:
○ most demanding
○ very demanding
○ demanding
○ average
○ below average

How long have you known this student and in what context? _____

What are the first words that come to your mind to describe this student? _____

Ratings Compared to other students in his or her class year, how do you rate this student in terms of:

No basis		Below average	Average	Good (above average)	Very good (well above average)	Excellent (top 10%)	Outstanding (top 5%)	One of the top few I've encountered (top 1%)
	Academic achievement							
	Extracurricular accomplishments							
	Personal qualities and character							
	OVERALL							

Evaluation Please write whatever you think is important about this student, including a description of academic, extracurricular, and personal characteristics. We welcome a broad-based assessment that will help us to differentiate this student from others. (Feel free to attach an additional sheet or another reference you may have prepared on behalf of this student.)

① Has the applicant ever been found responsible for a disciplinary violation at your school from 9th grade (or the international equivalent) forward, whether related to academic misconduct or behavioral misconduct, that resulted in the applicant's probation, suspension, removal, dismissal, or expulsion from your institution? ○ Yes ○ No

② To your knowledge, has the applicant ever been convicted of a misdemeanor, felony, or other crime? ○ Yes ○ No

If you answered yes to either or both questions, please attach a separate sheet of paper or use your written recommendation to give the approximate date of each incident and explain the circumstances.

○ **Check here if you would prefer to discuss this applicant over the phone with each admission office.**

I recommend this student: ○ No basis ○ With reservation ○ Fairly strongly ○ Strongly ○ Enthusiastically

© 2009 The Common Application, Inc.

2009-10 MIDYEAR REPORT
For Spring 2010 or Fall 2010 Enrollment

MR

TO THE APPLICANT

After completing all the relevant questions below, give this form to your secondary school counselor or another school official who knows you better. **If applying via mail**, please also give that school official stamped envelopes addressed to each institution that requires a Midyear Report.

Legal name _____ ○ Female
           Last/Family/Sur (Enter name **exactly** as it appears on official documents.)   First/Given   Middle (complete)   Jr., etc.   ○ Male

Birth date _____ Social Security # _____
        mm/dd/yyyy   (Optional)

Address _____
         Number & Street   Apartment #   City/Town   State/Province   Country   ZIP/Postal Code

School you now attend _____ CEEB/ACT code _____

Current year courses—please indicate title, level (AP, IB, advanced honors, etc.) and credit value of all courses you are taking this year. Indicate quarter classes taken in the same semester on the appropriate semester line.

First Semester/Trimester	Second Semester/Trimester	Third Trimester
		or additional first/second term courses if more space is needed

IMPORTANT PRIVACY NOTICE: Under the terms of the Family Educational Rights and Privacy Act (FERPA), after you matriculate you *will* have access to this form and all other recommendations and supporting documents submitted by you and on your behalf after matriculating, unless at least one of the following is true:

1. The institution does not save recommendations post-matriculation *(see list at www.commonapp.org/FERPA)*.
2. You waive your right to access below, regardless of the institution to which it is sent:
   ○ Yes, I do waive my right to access, and I understand I will never see this form or any other recommendations submitted by me or on my behalf.
   ○ No, I do *not waive* my right to access, and I may someday choose to see this form or any other recommendations or supporting documents submitted by me or on my behalf to the institution at which I'm enrolling, if that institution saves them after I matriculate.

Signature ✎ _____ Date _____

TO THE SECONDARY SCHOOL COUNSELOR

Please submit this form when midyear grades are available (end of first semester or second trimester). Attach applicant's official transcript, including courses in progress, a school profile, and transcript legend. (Please check transcript copies for readability.) Use both pages to complete your evaluation for this student. **Be sure to sign below.**

Counselor's name (Mr./Ms./Dr., etc.) _____
                                  Please print or type

Signature ✎ _____ Date _____
                                                             mm/dd/yyyy

Title _____ School _____

School address _____
                    City/Town   State/Province   Country   ZIP/Postal Code

Counselor's phone (_____) _____ Counselor's fax (_____) _____
         Area Code   Number   Ext.   Area Code   Number

Secondary school CEEB/ACT code _____ Counselor's e-mail _____

MR-1/**2009-10**

Background Information If any of the information on this page has changed for this student since the Secondary School Report was submitted, please enter the new information in the appropriate section below. If your recommendation for this student has changed, please comment in the space below or on a separate sheet. If nothing has changed, you may leave this page blank. *However, your signature is still required.*

Class rank: _____ Class size: _____ Covering a period from _____ to _____ .
(mm/yyyy)   *(mm/yyyy)*

The rank is ○ weighted ○ unweighted. How many students share this rank? _____

○ We do not rank. Instead, please indicate quartile _____ quintile _____ decile _____

Cumulative GPA: _____ on a _____ scale, covering a period from _____ to _____
(mm/yyyy)   *(mm/yyyy)*

This GPA is ○ weighted ○ unweighted. The school's passing mark is _____ .

Highest GPA in class _____ Graduation date _____
(mm/dd/yyyy)

Percentage of graduating class immediately attending: _____four-year _____ two-year institutions

Are classes taken on a block schedule? ○ Yes ○ No

Is the applicant an IB Diploma candidate? ○ Yes ○ No

If you offer AP courses, do you limit the number a student can take? ○ Yes ○ No

How many AP courses does your school offer (in total)? _____

In comparison with other college preparatory students at your school, the applicant's course selection is:
○ most demanding
○ very demanding
○ demanding
○ average
○ below average

How long have you known this student and in what context? _____

What are the first words that come to your mind to describe this student? _____

Ratings Compared to other students in his or her class year, how do you rate this student in terms of:

No basis		Below average	Average	Good (above average)	Very good (well above average)	Excellent (top 10%)	Outstanding (top 5%)	One of the top few I've encountered (top 1%)
	Academic achievement							
	Extracurricular accomplishments							
	Personal qualities and character							
	OVERALL							

Evaluation Please write whatever you think is important about this student, including a description of academic, extracurricular, and personal characteristics. We welcome a broad-based assessment that will help us to differentiate this student from others. (Feel free to attach an additional sheet or another reference you may have prepared on behalf of this student.)

① Has the applicant ever been found responsible for a disciplinary violation at your school from 9th grade (or the international equivalent) forward, whether related to academic misconduct or behavioral misconduct, that resulted in the applicant's probation, suspension, removal, dismissal, or expulsion from your institution? ○ Yes ○ No

② To your knowledge, has the applicant ever been convicted of a misdemeanor, felony, or other crime? ○ Yes ○ No

If you answered yes to either or both questions, please attach a separate sheet of paper or use your written recommendation to give the approximate date of each incident and explain the circumstances.

○ **Check here if you would prefer to discuss this applicant over the phone with each admission office.**

I recommend this student: ○ No basis ○ With reservation ○ Fairly strongly ○ Strongly ○ Enthusiastically

Check specific college information in our Requirements Grid or online to ensure a member institution uses this form.

TO THE APPLICANT

○ Female
○ Male

Legal name _____

Last/Family/Sur *(Enter name **exactly** as it appears on official documents.)* First/Given   Middle (complete)   Jr., etc.

Birth date _____   Social Security # _____

mm/dd/yyyy   *(Optional)*

Address _____

Number & Street   Apartment #   City/Town   State/Province   Country   ZIP/Postal Code

E-mail address _____   Phone (____) _____

Area Code

School you now attend _____   CEEB/ACT code _____

ARTS MEDIUM

Please indicate your area of interest and provide supplementary materials, as required.

○ **Music**   Instrument _____   Voice (part) _____   Composition _____

World Music Tradition _____   Song Writing _____   Other _____

○ **Theater**

○ **Dance**

○ **Visual Arts and Film**

INSTRUCTIONS

If you've made a substantial commitment of time and energy to one or more of the arts and you wish to have that considered as part of your application, please:

❶ Complete this form.

❷ Have an instructor who is familiar with your work send us a letter of recommendation.

❸ Enclose a 10-minute CD or DVD with this form that demonstrates contrasting examples of expression and technique. Please do not submit videotapes. List the contents of the CD or DVD here:

_____

_____

_____

_____

_____

Music

❹ Attach a résumé to this form that summarizes your experience with instrument(s), voice, and/or composition, giving years studied, name(s) of teacher(s) or group(s), repertoire, and awards/honors received.

Theater and Dance

❹ Attach a résumé to this form that summarizes your experience, giving years studied, name(s) of teacher(s) or group(s), repertoire, special programs, and awards/honors received.

Visual Arts and Film

❹ Attach a résumé to this form that summarizes your experience, giving dates, institutions or programs, and awards/honors received. Include a brief description of each course or workshop attended, and describe any related experiences.

No materials will be reviewed until all components of your portfolio arrive. Please send copies only; many schools do not return supplementary materials.

Signature ✎ _____   Date _____

mm/dd/yyyy

AR-1/ **2009-10**

You may leave all school contact information (bottom of page 2) blank *if* you are stapling this Home School Supplement to the Secondary School Report before mailing. Please type or print in black ink. This form should only be used by home school supervisors. Check specific college information in our Requirements Grid or online to ensure a member institution uses this form.

TO THE APPLICANT

○ Female
○ Male

Legal name _____
    Last/Family/Sur (Enter name **exactly** as it appears on official documents.)   First/Given   Middle (complete)   Jr., etc.

Birth date _____ Social Security # _____
    mm/dd/yyyy   (Optional)

Address _____
    Number & Street   Apartment #   City/Town   State/Province   Country   ZIP/Postal Code

TO THE HOME SCHOOL SUPERVISOR

Philosophy

Please tell us why home schooling was chosen for this student, and explain your home schooling philosophy.

Grading Scale

Please explain the grading scale or other methods of evaluation.

Outside Evaluation

If the student has taken courses from a distance learning program, traditional secondary school, or institution of higher education, please detail them here. In addition, if the student has taken any standardized testing other than those listed on page 2 of the Common Application, please also describe below.

© 2009 The Common Application, Inc.

HS-1/**2009-10**

Transcript

Subject	Course Title & Level (AP/College)	Date (To/From)	Grade	Primary Text Used
English				
Math				
Science				
Social Studies				
Foreign Language				
Arts				
Other				

Supervisor's name (Mr./Ms./Dr., etc.) _____
Please print or type

Signature ✎ _____ Date_____
mm/dd/yyyy

Supervisor's address _____
    City/Town   *State/Province*   *Country*   *ZIP/Postal Code*

Supervisor's phone (_____) _____ Supervisor's fax (_____) _____
    Area Code   *Number*   *Ext.*   *Area Code*   *Number*

Supervisor's e-mail _____

Are you a member of a homeschooler's association? ○ Yes ○ No If yes, name of association _____

HS-2/**2009-10**   © 2009 The Common Application, Inc.

2009-10 ATHLETIC SUPPLEMENT AT

For Spring 2010 or Fall 2010 Enrollment

Check specific college information in our Requirements Grid or online to ensure a member institution uses this form.

TO THE APPLICANT

○ Female
○ Male

Legal name _____

Last/Family/Sur (Enter name **exactly** as it appears on official documents.)   First/Given   Middle (complete)   Jr., etc.

Birth date _____   Social Security # _____

mm/dd/yyyy   (Optional)

Address _____

Number & Street   Apartment #   City/Town   State/Province   Country   ZIP/Postal Code

E-mail address _____   Phone (_____)_____

Area Code

School you now attend _____   CEEB/ACT code _____

INSTRUCTIONS

If you anticipate participating in varsity athletics, please complete the grid below. List any team sports played in order of their importance to you. Check year(s) of participation; indicate letters earned and leadership positions. Include the name of your coach(es).

Sport	9	10	11	12	PG	Letters earned JV	Varsity	Event or position	Varsity captain? Check here.	Coach	Coach's phone and e-mail

Please list any times, records, awards, etc.

_____

_____

_____

_____

_____

_____

_____

_____

_____

Optional: Height _____ Weight _____

Signature ✎ _____ Date _____

mm/dd/yyyy

© 2009 The Common Application, Inc.   AT-1/**2009-10**

Appendix C
Sample Student Information Sheet for Letters of Recommendation

To write a recommendation letter for you, counselors and teachers need information that will be used solely and confidentially for that purpose. You benefit when they can provide a comprehensive academic and personal report. Read this entire form before you begin to fill it out to prevent yourself from entering duplicate information. Take your time and answer each question thoughtfully. You'll need to have this same information for your college applications, so it will help you later as well. When you have completed the form, prepare a packet for each person from whom you have requested a letter, which contains the following: the copy of the form and all attachments; the recommendation forms from your colleges; a stamped and pre-addressed envelope for each college; and a listing of due dates. Packets should be submitted to your recommendation writers at least four weeks before the first due date.

Please print neatly or type your responses. You may attach separate sheets as needed.

Student Name _____ Nickname (if any) _____

Phone _____ E-mail _____

1. Test Score Information

ACT

Date _____ Verbal _____ Math _____ Sci _____ Read _____ Writing _____ Comp _____

Date _____ Verbal _____ Math _____ Sci _____ Read _____ Writing _____ Comp _____

Date _____ Verbal _____ Math _____ Sci _____ Read _____ Writing _____ Comp _____

SAT

Date _____ Critical Reading _____ Math _____ Writing _____

Date _____ Critical Reading _____ Math _____ Writing _____

Date _____ Critical Reading _____ Math _____ Writing _____

SAT Subject Test Date _____ Subject _____ Score _____

SAT Subject Test Date _____ Subject _____ Score _____

SAT Subject Test Date _____ Subject _____ Score _____

SAT Subject Test Date _____ Subject _____ Score _____

Future Test Dates for SAT _____ SAT Subject Test _____ ACT _____

AP or IB Test   Date: _____   Subject _____   Score _____

AP or IB Test   Date: _____   Subject _____   Score _____

AP or IB Test   Date: _____   Subject _____   Score _____

AP or IB Test   Date: _____   Subject _____   Score _____

AP or IB Test   Date: _____   Subject _____   Score _____

2. Do your test scores and grades accurately reflect your academic potential? _____
   If not, explain why. _____
   _____
   _____

3. Attach a copy of your transcript (for teacher recommendations only—your counselor already has your transcript). List any college or summer courses taken during high school that are not included on your transcript.

   Course _____ Where taken _____ Year _____

   Course _____ Where taken _____ Year _____

   Course _____ Where taken _____ Year _____

4. Attach a brief résumé (for grades 9–12) listing your extracurricular activities and achievements; academic honors and awards; hobbies, special interests, or talents; community service activities; and work experience. What is most important to you on this list?

5. Attach a copy of your college personal essay if it is completed or, on a separate sheet of paper, answer, "What sets you apart as an individual?"

6. Ask your parent or guardian or a friend to write an anecdote that describes your character and attach it to this form. This should be about one paragraph long.

7. Where were you born? If not in the United States, at what age did you move to the United States? _____

8. Do you speak more than one language? If so, list and indicate fluency.
   _____

9. With whom are you living? Circle: Both parents   Mother   Father   Other

10. Will you be the first person in your immediate family to attend college?

11. Please tell us about your family. List your siblings, providing name, age, current school and grade level, degrees (if any), and occupation. _____

12. Parents' or guardians' occupations and highest level of education completed

    Father/Guardian Occupation _____ Educ. level/degree _____

    Name of undergraduate college, if any _____

    Mother/Guardian Occupation _____ Educ. level/degree _____

    Name of undergraduate college, if any _____

13. Do you have any significant travel experience? Describe, including dates.

    _____

    _____

    _____

14. Have you ever been suspended from school during Grades 9–12? _____

    If yes, when and for what reason? _____

15. Is there any significant, unique, or unusual experience, situation, or involvement that you want to share? _____

    _____

    _____

    _____

16. List three adjectives that you feel best describe you and explain why.

    _____

    _____

    _____

17. List the colleges to which you are applying and the reason why you are interested in attending. If you plan to apply Early Decision (ED) or Early Action (EA) please indicate that next to the name of the college.

    College _____ Reason _____

    College _____ Reason _____

College _____ Reason _____

College _____ Reason _____

College _____ Reason _____

College _____ Reason _____

College _____ Reason _____

College _____ Reason _____

Please feel free to attach any other information that you believe would be helpful to those writing on your behalf.

Before submitting this form, please check that you completed all parts and have attached:

1. A copy of your transcript (see #3 above)

2. A copy of your activity résumé (see #4 above)

3. A copy of a college essay or "What sets you apart?" essay (see #5 above)

Appendix D
Financial Aid Comparison Worksheet

Name of College
_____ _____ _____ _____

Cost of Attendance
_____ _____ _____ _____

Financial Aid Package

Grants/Scholarships
_____ _____ _____ _____

Loans
_____ _____ _____ _____

Work-Study
_____ _____ _____ _____

Total
_____ _____ _____ _____

Expected Family Contribution (EFC)

Student Contribution
_____ _____ _____ _____

Parent Contribution
_____ _____ _____ _____

Total
_____ _____ _____ _____

Unmet Need (If Any)
_____ _____ _____ _____

Appendix E
Cost of Attendance Worksheet

Name of College ⎯⎯⎯⎯ ⎯⎯⎯⎯ ⎯⎯⎯⎯ ⎯⎯⎯⎯

Tuition and Fees ⎯⎯⎯⎯ ⎯⎯⎯⎯ ⎯⎯⎯⎯ ⎯⎯⎯⎯

Room and Board ⎯⎯⎯⎯ ⎯⎯⎯⎯ ⎯⎯⎯⎯ ⎯⎯⎯⎯

Books and Supplies ⎯⎯⎯⎯ ⎯⎯⎯⎯ ⎯⎯⎯⎯ ⎯⎯⎯⎯

Personal Expenses ⎯⎯⎯⎯ ⎯⎯⎯⎯ ⎯⎯⎯⎯ ⎯⎯⎯⎯

Travel ⎯⎯⎯⎯ ⎯⎯⎯⎯ ⎯⎯⎯⎯ ⎯⎯⎯⎯

Total ⎯⎯⎯⎯ ⎯⎯⎯⎯ ⎯⎯⎯⎯ ⎯⎯⎯⎯

College Preparation Time Line

This time line covers key points in the college preparation process. The specifics will vary depending both on you and on the counseling program at your high school. Use this time line as a preview of what is to come and as a general guide, but be sure to supplement and refine it with information provided by your counseling office and the colleges to which you apply.

In preparing the time line, we have assumed that you will begin thinking seriously about college admissions by your junior year. If you are one of the many students who wait until senior year, we have a special Senior Year, Fall Semester time line designed especially for you. You'll find it at the end.

FRESHMAN YEAR

Although no special focus on the college application process is needed during freshman year, the following steps are good preparation for success in general:

- Take challenging courses in "academic solids": English, foreign languages, mathematics, science, social studies.
- Study hard.
- Explore extracurricular activities both inside and outside school to find those that interest and excite you.

- Read as much as you can.
- Plan summer activities that will enrich you in some way: summer school, work experience, family travel, and so forth. Don't be a couch potato.
- At the end of the year, begin a permanent record of your extracurricular and volunteer activities, academic honors and awards, and so on.

SOPHOMORE YEAR

In your sophomore year, you should continue taking challenging courses and developing your extracurricular interests and talents. It is also a time when students take on part-time jobs. Families may begin thinking about college in more concrete terms. Some high schools begin a formal program of college orientation in the sophomore year, but most do not.

ALL YEAR

- Study hard in a challenging curriculum.
- Continue involvement in extracurricular activities; look for opportunities to assume leadership roles.
- Consider volunteer activities.
- If you work part time, be sure to keep on top of your academics.
- Save samples of your best papers and work in the arts (if applicable) for potential later use.

FALL

- Consider taking the PSAT or PLAN (or both) for practice.
- Seek help from your teachers early if you experience academic difficulties.

WINTER

- PSAT and PLAN results arrive in December. After reading the information that comes with your scores, consider meeting with your counselor to discuss steps you might take to address your weaker areas.
- Plan a challenging program of classes for your junior year.

- Begin to make plans for summer activities that will be enriching (paid or volunteer work, classes, or travel, for example).
- Register at school for May Advanced Placement tests, if appropriate.

SPRING

- If your family will be traveling over spring break, consider including a visit or two to colleges that may be of interest to you.
- Consult your counselor and register for SAT Subject Tests, if appropriate.
- Update your record of extracurricular activities, awards, and so on that you began at the end of freshman year.

SUMMER

- Reap the benefits of your earlier planning for a productive summer. Continue to read.

JUNIOR YEAR

Junior year typically marks the start of the college selection process. Junior year grades play an especially important role in college admissions, so a focus on academics is very important. By junior year, most students have identified the extracurricular areas in which they have the greatest talent and passion, although new interests can develop.

ALL YEAR

- Study hard in a challenging curriculum.
- Continue involvement in extracurricular and volunteer activities and seek leadership roles as appropriate.
- If you work part time during the school year, make sure to continue a strong focus on your academics.
- Continue to save samples of your best papers and work in the arts (if appropriate) for potential later use.
- Students interested in athletics at the Division I and Division II level should talk to their coaches and explore eligibility requirements on the NCAA Web site, www.ncaa.org.

FALL

- Buy a copy of a "big book" college guide such as the *Fiske Guide to Colleges*. It will be a useful resource to you over the next eighteen months.

- Take the PSAT in October.

- Study hard in your classes. If you experience academic difficulty, seek help early.

- Complete the "Determining Your Priorities" questionnaire at the end of Chapter Four to help you decide what to look for in a college.

- Many colleges send representatives to high schools in the fall. If your school allows juniors to participate, consider attending those sessions that are of interest to you.

WINTER

- PSAT results arrive. After reading your score report, talk to your counselor about steps you can take to improve your performance on the upcoming SAT or ACT as appropriate.

- Become familiar with the differences between the ACT and SAT and decide whether to take just one or both of them. Register for winter or spring SAT or ACT tests or both. February is a good month to take the ACT for the first time; March is a good month for the SAT.

- Winter is a good time to prepare (via book, software, or coursework) for standardized tests.

- If you have not already met with your counselor to begin discussing college selection, do so now.

- Register at your school for May Advanced Placement tests.

- Choose challenging courses for your senior year.

- Make plans for an enriching summer. Once again, consider travel, coursework, volunteer or paid employment, workshops, or clinics that match your interests.

SPRING

- Continue to develop your college list, ideally in consultation with your counselor.

- Start a filing system to help you keep all your college materials organized.

- Consider using the spring break to visit colleges.

- Register for and take spring SAT Subject Tests, as appropriate, depending on the requirements of the colleges that are of interest to you. Register and take the SAT or ACT (or both) as appropriate.

- Request materials from colleges that interest you.

- Attend a college fair if one is nearby.

- If you want to be a varsity athlete in college, contact the coaches at the schools that interest you if you have not already been contacted by them.

- Consider visiting colleges over the summer and plan these visits early.

- Continue to meet with your counselor as you develop your short list.

- Update your record of extracurricular activities, awards, and so forth.

SUMMER

- Reap the benefits of your planning for an enriching summer experience, whether it involves work, travel, study, or other activity.

- Visit colleges as appropriate to help further refine your college list.

- Consider getting a head start on the college application process by brainstorming about or actually drafting a personal essay.

- If your applications will require a portfolio or audition tape, get started on it now.

SENIOR YEAR

The senior year is the busiest in the college selection process. Some students will choose to apply via processes referred to as "early action" or "early decision," and will need to have a completed application ready to go by November 1 or 15. In general, students should have their college list identified by mid-November so that they can submit their rolling admissions and regular decision applications by the deadlines without being rushed.

ALL YEAR

- Study hard in a challenging curriculum. Colleges will receive your fall grades if you apply in the "regular decision" process.

- Part-time work is often a part of senior year. Again, be sure to maintain appropriate focus on academics.

- Continue involvement in extracurricular and volunteer activities and leadership roles as appropriate.

FALL

- Visit additional colleges if time and circumstances permit. Arrange overnights and on-campus interviews where feasible.

- Meet with college representatives who are visiting your high school.

- Attend a fall college fair and college nights to get more information.

- Finalize your college list in consultation with your counselor. Decide if an early application is right for you.

- Be sure to check and make note of all deadlines for each of the colleges on your list.

- Register for and take fall SAT or ACT tests, if necessary. Be aware of deadlines if you are submitting an early application and want a fall test administration to be part of your application.

- Ask teachers for letters of recommendation at least one month before the first letter is due.

- Finish your essays, having carefully edited them with the benefit of appropriate input from teachers and parents.

- Submit applications by the required deadlines, double-checking that all parts are complete.

- Arrange to have standardized test scores and high school transcripts sent to colleges by their deadlines.

- Participate in alumni interviews as appropriate if applying early.

- If applying early, receive your decision by December 15. If admitted, congratulations! If not, move on. If you haven't yet submitted your regular decision applications, do so right now. Consider an ED II application, if appropriate, to another school that is very high on your list.

- If you will be applying for financial aid, begin the process of learning about the FAFSA and CSS PROFILE, as appropriate, and ask your parents to gather the information needed to complete them. Start your scholarship search.

WINTER

- If deferred when applying early, write to the college and express your continued interest in attending.
- Submit any remaining applications.
- For both deferred and regular applications, send significant new information regarding accomplishments and awards, if any, to colleges.
- Ask your counselor to send midyear reports to colleges.
- Participate in alumni interviews as appropriate.
- Keep focused on your academic work.

SPRING

- Decisions may arrive as early as February or as late as early April.
- Take advantage of "admit weekend" events in April, if possible, to learn more about the colleges that have admitted you.
- Carefully consider and compare your financial aid packages; consider requesting a review if a package is not adequate for your needs.
- Make your final decision about where you want to go and submit your deposit by May 1. Notify the other schools that you will not be attending.
- If you are wait-listed, decide whether to remain on the wait-list. Be sure to make a deposit by May 1 at a school where you have an acceptance. If you decide to remain on a wait-list, write to the admissions office conveying your enthusiasm as well as any new information. Ask your counselor to do the same.
- Enjoy the remainder of your senior year!

WHAT IF YOU ARE BEGINNING YOUR SEARCH IN SENIOR YEAR?

A lot of students put off serious thinking about college until the fall of their senior year. While we don't recommend that approach, don't worry if you are one of them—you can make up for lost time if you use the time you do have wisely and to your best advantage. Once you get to January of your senior year, you'll be in sync with your classmates who started their college search much earlier. The following special fall senior year time line will help you get going.

- Buy the most recent edition of a "big book" such as the *Fiske Guide to Colleges*. You may also want to buy the most recent *College Board College Handbook* or consult it in the library. This book gives detailed information on requirements at thousands of colleges, and contains useful summary tables in the back with information about acceptance rates, student body size, requirements or recommendations for SAT Subject Tests, and so on.

- Make sure you have already taken (or are registered to take) the SAT or ACT and SAT Subject Tests if they are likely to be recommended or required by the colleges to which you may be applying. If you can't complete certain tests in time, you will need to focus on the many colleges that do not require them.

- Read Chapters Four and Five of this book carefully and fill out the "Determining Your Priorities" questionnaire to help you identify your preferences. Meet with your counselor as soon as possible to discuss colleges that will meet your needs.

- Talk to friends, family members, and classmates about colleges they may recommend. Try a couple of online college search Web sites.

- Do careful research on the colleges that emerge from your data-gathering efforts. Read your big book and study college Web sites.

- Watch for visits by college representatives, evening programs, and nearby college fairs. Use them to gather additional information.

- Visit colleges on your list if you have a chance, taking advantage of high school holidays. But don't worry—you'll have another chance to visit in the spring after you are accepted but before you must make a decision.

- Remember that a good application takes time to prepare, especially if it requires a special essay or other custom responses. Keep this in mind as you decide where to apply.

- Make sure that your college list has an appropriate range of colleges: good bet, possible, and long shot. Check back with your counselor before you finish it.

- Ask two teachers whether they would be willing to write letters of recommendation on your behalf. Talk to them as early as you can in the fall quarter once you determine that your probable colleges require such letters. Tell them that you will provide background information about yourself once you have your final college list and application forms. Make sure they have at least three weeks to write their letters.

- Be aware that early action and early decision applications are generally due by November 1 or November 15. You may not have enough time to do a careful job of selecting a college and preparing a strong application by that date. If you would have to rush, don't do it. Some colleges have a second early decision due date in mid-December or early January. This works better for late starters.

- Make sure you know all the deadlines (pre-applications, applications, financial aid, test scores) for the schools you choose. Be sure to release your SAT or ACT scores to colleges on your list.

- Prepare your applications carefully and thoughtfully, and don't forget to proofread everything carefully. Have someone else help you proofread as well.

- Ask your parents to begin gathering necessary information for financial aid applications.

- Use the Common Application whenever possible to save time and effort, even if you also need to complete a supplementary form and essay. Applying online can also make things easier for you.

Glossary

Academic Index
A calculation based on standardized test scores and class rank (or equivalent) that is used by Ivy League colleges to ensure that athletic recruits have academic records that exceed a minimum threshold.

ACT
Short for ACT Assessment. A standardized college admissions test that is an alternative to the SAT.

Advanced Placement (AP)
A program coordinated by the College Board whereby high schools offer college-level courses with specific curricula in a large number of academic fields. Participating students have the option of taking an AP exam at the end of the course to demonstrate knowledge and potentially earn college credit.

Award letter
Financial aid terminology for the document sent to a prospective student that indicates the amount and type of aid to be offered.

Candidate reply date
Postmark date by which students must notify a college about their intention to enroll. May 1 is the standard date for students admitted during the *regular decision* cycle.

Class rank
The student's place based on a rank ordering of students in a class by grade point average (GPA).

Common Application

A standardized application form accepted by more than 350 colleges. Some colleges also require a school-specific supplementary form.

Consortium

Several colleges that join together in a cooperative arrangement that allows students to take courses and use library facilities on each campus.

Core curriculum

A group of specially designed courses in the humanities, arts, social sciences, and sciences designed to give students a strong foundation in general education.

Cost of education

Financial aid terminology for total educational costs, including tuition, fees, books, supplies, room and board, incidentals, and travel home.

CSS PROFILE

Abbreviation for College Scholarship Service PROFILE. A need assessment form administered by the College Board that is used by some schools to determine eligibility for institutionally based financial aid.

Deferral

A decision by a college to delay a final response to an *early action* or *early decision* application until the regular decision cycle.

Deferred admission

A decision by an admitted student to wait until the following academic year to enroll.

Demonstrated need

Financial aid terminology for the difference between the total cost of education and the expected family contribution to the student's education.

Division I, II, and III

National Collegiate Athletic Association (NCAA) groupings of colleges for purposes of athletic competition.

Double deposit
Unethical practice of sending deposits to hold places at two or more colleges while deciding between them.

Early action (EA)
An application option that typically allows a student to apply by November 1 or November 15 and receive a decision by December 15 that *does not bind* the student to attend if admitted.

Early decision (ED)
An application option that typically allows a student to apply by November 1 or November 15 and receive a decision by December 15 that *commits* the student to attend if admitted.

ETS
Abbreviation for Educational Testing Service, the subsidiary of the College Board that administers the PSAT, SAT, and AP tests.

Expected family contribution
Financial aid terminology for the amount of money a family is expected to contribute to a student's education based on methodology that considers income, assets, and other expenses.

FAFSA
Abbreviation for Free Application for Federal Student Aid. Used to determine eligibility for federal financial aid.

Federal methodology
The calculation of expected family contribution to the cost of college using the FAFSA.

Financial aid package
Total amount and types of aid a student receives from federal and nonfederal sources.

Gift aid
Financial aid terminology for the grant portion of the financial aid package that does not have to be repaid or earned through work.

GPA

Abbreviation for grade point average. An overall average of a student's grades.

Hook

A special quality that gives a student an edge in the admissions process over others with similar academic qualifications. Hooks may involve athletic ability, legacy status, exceptional talent, having a parent with the ability to make significant donations, or being part of an underrepresented minority group.

IB

Abbreviation for International Baccalaureate. A special high school diploma awarded to students who complete a rigorous academic curriculum of special courses and who perform satisfactorily on a battery of nationally normed tests corresponding to that curriculum.

Institutional methodology

The formula that calculates the expected family contribution to the total cost of education from the CSS PROFILE or other institution-specific form.

Liberal arts

An academic program that includes the sciences, social sciences, languages, arts, and mathematics, as distinguished from professional or vocational programs that focus on training for specific careers such as engineering, business, and nursing.

Need analysis

Financial aid terminology for the determination of the expected family contribution to college expenses based on the family's financial situation.

Need-aware (or need- sensitive) admissions

Admissions process that considers a student's ability to pay in the final admissions decision.

Need-blind admissions

Practice of reviewing an applicant's file and making an admissions decision without regard to the student's ability to pay.

Pell Grant

Federal grant to students from low-income families.

PLUS loans
Acronym for Parent Loan to Undergraduate Students. A loan taken out by a parent that is not subsidized by the federal government.

PSAT
Abbreviation for Preliminary SAT. A short version of the SAT that is typically taken in the fall by high school juniors (and sometimes by sophomores) as practice for the SAT and as a qualifying test for the National Merit Scholarship Program.

Regular decision
Application process that involves applying by a late fall or early winter deadline in exchange for an admissions decision the following spring.

Restrictive early action
A type of early action plan that places restrictions on the student's ability to apply *early action* or *early decision* to other schools.

Rolling admission
A process by which colleges review and make decisions about applications as they are received. The application cycle usually opens in the early fall and may extend into the spring or until the freshman class is filled.

SAT
The most widely taken standardized test for college admission. SAT is the full name—it is not an acronym. Revised effective March 2005, the test contains three parts: writing, critical reading, and math.

Self-help
In financial aid terminology, the loan and work-study portions of a financial aid package.

Stafford Loans
Low-interest loans to students.

Student Aid Report (SAR)
Official notification from the processing center that gives the results of the need analysis calculated from the FAFSA.

Student search
Mechanism for colleges to receive the names of potential applicants based on interests, grades, and so forth. Students taking the SAT and ACT are invited to participate when they take those tests. Colleges purchase the names and addresses of students meeting certain criteria and use them for targeted mailings.

Subsidized loan
A loan for which the U.S. government pays the interest while the student is enrolled in school.

Transcript
Official record of a student's courses and grades. Colleges usually require an official transcript, sent directly from the high school, as part of the application.

Wait-list
A group of students held in reserve through the late spring after a college makes its admissions decisions. If openings occur, students on the wait-list may be offered admission.

Work-study
A component of need-based financial aid in which the student works part-time in a campus or other job that is supported by government or institutional funding.

Yield
The percentage of students offered admission to a college who subsequently enroll.

Resources

The resources listed here provide additional information on selected topics covered in *Admission Matters*. We've chosen some Web resources and a few books that we think do the job well, although we have not attempted to provide an exhaustive list, since a lot of information is repeated in many sources.

This list is a dynamic one as new materials appear and others become outdated or unavailable. Check our Web site at www.admissionmatters.com for changes.

GENERAL ADMISSIONS INFORMATION

WEB

www.collegeboard.com: College Board site that contains useful information about all aspects of college search and selection. The site has separate sections for students and parents.

www.nacacnet.org: Site of the National Association for College Admission Counseling geared primarily for high school and college counselors but contains a section for students and parents with helpful information.

www.princetonreview.com: Princeton Review site contains a lot of free information about the college admissions process, including test preparation. The site also sells test preparation courses and materials.

BOOK

College Unranked: Ending the College Admissions Frenzy, by Lloyd Thacker. Published in 2005 by Harvard University Press: Edited volume containing excellent advice on keeping the admissions process in perspective.

REFERENCE GUIDES TO COLLEGES

WEB

www.collegeboard.com and www.princetonreview.com: Both sites contain detailed profiles of individual colleges as well as a search feature that identifies colleges meeting criteria entered by the user.

http://nces.ed.gov/collegenavigator/: College Navigator, sponsored by the Department of Education. The site contains a database of thousands of schools that allows search by location, program, and degree offerings.

www.usnews.com: Site provides free limited access to the *U.S. News & World Report* database used to generate college rankings. Although we do not favor the use of these rankings, the data used to generate them can be helpful. The full database can be accessed for an annual fee.

www.utexas.edu/world/univ/state/: Site provides links to the home pages of four-year colleges and universities throughout the United States. The links are arranged by state, but they can also be sorted alphabetically.

BOOKS

Barron's Profile of American Colleges 2009, by Barron's Educational Series. Currently on the 28th edition, published July 2008 by Barron's Educational Series. Updated periodically but not annually: Contains profiles of over 1,650 four-year colleges that are rated according to degree of competitiveness. Includes CD-ROM.

2009 College Handbook, by The College Board. Currently on the 46th edition, published June 2008 by the College Board. Updated annually: Contains profiles of all 3,600 four-year and two-year colleges in the United States. Tables show policies and outcomes for ED, EA, and wait-list applicants.

The College Finder, by Steven Antonoff. Published September 2008 by Wintergreen Orchard House: Helpful lists of recommended programs by major, sport, and other topics.

NARRATIVE GUIDES TO COLLEGES

WEB

www.collegesofdistinction.com: Site that originated with *Colleges That Change Lives* by Loren Pope, but now has expanded to include other institutions as well. This site contains lots of good information about college selection.

BOOKS

Colleges That Change Lives: 40 Schools That Will Change the Way You Think About Colleges, by Loren Pope, published 2006 by Penguin Books: Descriptions of forty lesser-known but excellent liberal arts colleges.

Fiske Guide to Colleges 2009, by Edward Fiske. Currently on the 25th edition, published July 2008 by Sourcebooks. Updated annually: Contains profiles and personal descriptions of more than 330 popular colleges and universities.

Insider's Guide to the Colleges, 2009, by Yale Daily News. Currently on the 35th edition, published June 2008 by St. Martin's Griffin. Updated annually: Contains profiles and narrative descriptions of over 300 schools. The book proclaims itself, "Written and researched by students for students."

Looking Beyond the Ivy League: Finding the College That's Right for You, by Loren Pope, published 2007 by Penguin Books: Contains sound advice about the importance of fit and provides valuable information about some lesser-known colleges that have strong programs.

Best 368 Colleges, by Princeton Review; 2009 edition published August 2008 by Princeton Review. Updated annually: Contains profiles and insights from students on almost 370 colleges.

College Prowler Series: A series of over 250 books, each giving the inside scoop on a specific college. Also available in big books containing information on groups of colleges. Access to all books is available online for a fee at www.collegeprowler.com.

"INSIDER" ACCOUNTS

These are best viewed as windows into the admissions process at highly selective institutions rather than as how-to guides to gain admission to them.

The Gatekeepers: Inside the Admissions Process of a Premier College, by Jacques Steinberg; published 2003 by Penguin: Describes the author's experience observing an admissions cycle at Wesleyan University. As riveting as a novel, it provides valuable insights into the admissions process at a selective liberal arts college.

Creating a Class: College Admissions and the Education of Elites, by Mitchell Stevens; published 2007 by Harvard University Press: Describes the author's experience observing the admissions process at Hamilton College.

SPECIAL INTEREST GUIDES

WEB

www.ajcunet.edu: Site sponsored by Jesuit colleges.

www.hillel.org: Site of Hillel, the Foundation for Jewish Campus Life.

www.womenscolleges.org: Official site of the Women's Colleges Coalition.

www.blackexcel.org: "The College Help Network" for African American students.

http://www.portfolioday.net: Site of the National Portfolio Day Association, a group of accredited arts colleges and university art departments that are members of the National Association of Schools of Art and Design.

BOOKS

K&W Guide to Colleges for Students with Learning Disabilities or Attention Deficit Hyperactivity Disorder, by Marybeth Kravets and Imy Wax. Currently on the 9th edition, published 2007 by Princeton Review: Profiles the services for learning disabled students at more than 300 colleges.

African American Student's Guide, by Isaac Black; published 2000 by Wiley: Advice for African American students.

College Guide to Performing Arts Majors 2009: Real World Admission Guide for All Dance, Music, and Theater Majors, by Peterson's and Fern Oram; published 2008 by Peterson's: Guide to programs in music, arts, theater, and dance.

FINANCIAL AID

WEB

www.collegeboard.com: Click on Paying for College for information on the CSS PROFILE. Many private schools require online submission of the PROFILE for institutional aid. This site also has expected financial contribution calculators for both federal aid and institutional aid, as well as a tool to compare financial aid packages.

www.fafsa.ed.gov: Federal site for Free Application for Federal Student Aid. If you are applying for need-based aid, visit this site. You can complete the FAFSA online.

www.fafsa4caster.ed.gov: Federal site that lets families get estimates of their EFC without actually submitting the FAFSA.

www.fastweb.com: General site with terrific scholarship search as well as expected family contribution calculator.

www.finaid.org: General site with lots of information about all aspects of financial aid.

http://studentaid.ed.gov: Comprehensive government site with information in both English and Spanish.

BOOKS

Scholarship Handbook 2009, by the College Board. Published 2008 by the College Board: Provides information on private, federal, and state funding sources of financial aid.

Guide to Getting Financial Aid 2009, by the College Board. Published 2008 by the College Board: Advice on all aspects of the financial aid process.

ATHLETICS

WEB

www.ncaa.org: Web site of the National Collegiate Athletics Association. A must-read for those interested in varsity athletics at colleges and universities that belong to the NCAA.

BOOKS

Reclaiming the Game: College Sports and Educational Values, by William Bowen and Sarah Levin; published 2003 by Princeton University Press: Analysis of the role of athletics in the admissions processes at Ivy League and selective liberal arts colleges.

The Student Athlete's Guide to Getting Recruited, by Stewart Brown; published 2008 by Supercollege: Guidance on choosing an NCAA division and handling the recruitment process.

Playing the Game: Inside Athletic Recruiting in the Ivy Leagues, by Chris Lincoln; published 2004 by Nomad Press: Critical insight into Ivy League and liberal arts college recruiting.

TEST PREPARATION

WEB

www.collegeboard.com: Information and preparation for the PSAT and SAT. The site can be used for online test registration for the SAT.

www.ACT.org: Information and preparation for the PLAN and ACT. The site can be used for online test registration for the ACT.

BOOKS

The Official SAT Study Guide, by the College Board; published 2004 by the College Board: Official test preparation guide to the SAT, which is published by the College Board.

The Real ACT Prep Guide by the ACT, 2nd edition, published 2007 by Peterson's: "Official" test preparation guide to the ACT prepared by the organization that administers the test.

ESSAY WRITING

On Writing the College Application Essay, by Henry Bauld; published 1987 by Harper-Resource: A former Ivy League admissions officer provides tough and funny advice on coming up with the best essay possible.

The College Application Essay, revised edition, by Sarah Myers McGinty; published 2004 by the College Board: Contains excellent, easy-to-follow advice on writing effective college application essays.

MISCELLANEOUS

www.campustours.com: Site with links to virtual campus tours at hundreds of campuses.

www.collegiatechoice.com: Source to purchase sixty-minute videos of actual student-guided campus tours of more than 300 colleges at $15 each. Tapings are "home movie" quality.

www.nacacnet.org/fairs: Site contains schedules of college fairs nationwide.

www.fairtest.org: Contains a list of more than 775 colleges and universities nationwide that do not require test scores.

www.usafa.af.mil: Site of the U.S. Air Force Academy.

www.usma.edu: Site of the U.S. Military Academy (West Point).

www.usna.edu: Site of the U.S. Naval Academy.

www.usmma.edu: Site of the U.S. Merchant Marine Academy.

www.cga.edu: Site of the U.S. Coast Guard Academy.

Notes

CHAPTER ONE

1. *Chicago Tribune,* April 9, 2008, Tempo, p. 9.
2. *Boston Globe,* March 27, 2008, p. A1.
3. *Philadelphia Inquirer,* December 14, 2008, p. A1.
4. *Christian Science Monitor,* April 23, 2008, p. 1.
5. *New York Times,* April 8, 2007, Sec. 14 WC, p. 1.
6. WBZTV.com, April 21, 2008.
7. *Knocking at the College Door: Projections of High School Graduates by State, Income, and Race/Ethnicity, 1992–2022* (Boulder, CO: Western Interstate Commission for Higher Education, 2008).
8. B. Mayher, *The College Admissions Mystique* (New York: Farrar, Straus and Giroux, 1998), p. 28.
9. G. Casper, letter to James Fallows, editor of *U.S. News & World Report,* September 23, 1996, available online: www.stanford.edu/dept/pres-provost/president/speeches/961206gcfallow.html; access date: February 17, 2009.
10. Casper, 1996.
11. Letter from President William Durden to the Dickinson College community, September 7, 2001. In 2006, Dickinson College announced it would no longer participate in the reputational survey or use the rankings to promote the college. Its current position can be found online at www.dickinson.edu/news/rankings.html; access date: February 17, 2009.
12. Graduation rate performance measures the difference between a school's six-year graduation rate for a given class and the predicted rate for that class based on characteristics of the students as entering freshmen and the school's expenditures on them.

13. L. Bollinger, "Debate over the SAT Masks Trends in College Admissions," *Chronicle of Higher Education,* July 12, 2002, p. B11.

14. R. Toor, *College Confidential: An Insider's Account of the Elite College Selection Process* (New York: St. Martin's Press, 2001), p. 2.

15. G. Goldsmith, cited in D. Golden, "Glass Floor: Colleges Reject Top Applicants Accepting Only Students Likely to Enroll," *Wall Street Journal,* May 29, 2002.

16. S. Dale and A. Krueger, "Estimating the Payoff to Attending a More Selective College: An Application of Selection on Observables and Unobservables." National Bureau of Economic Research, Working Paper 7322, August 1999.

17. Dale and Krueger, 1999.

18. Stacy Dale, personal communication, 2004.

19. D. Davenport, "How Not to Judge a College," Scripps Howard News Service, September 9, 2003.

20. A. Kucsynski, "Best List for Colleges by U.S. News Is Under Fire," *New York Times,* August 20, 2001, p. C1.

CHAPTER TWO

1. G. W. Pierson, "A Yale Book of Numbers: Historical Statistics of the College and University, 1701–1976," 1983; available online: www.yale.edu/oir/pierson_original.htm; access date: February 17, 2009.

2. E. Duffy and I. Goldberg, *Crafting a Class* (Princeton, NJ: Princeton University Press, 1998), p. 35.

3. David Erdmann, personal communication, 2004.

4. R. Shea and D. Marcus, "Make Yourself a Winner," in *America's Best Colleges* (Washington, DC: U.S. News & World Report, 2001).

5. S. McMillen, "In Admission, How Do You Separate the Wheat from the Wheat?" *Chronicle of Higher Education,* June 27, 2003, p. B13.

6. F. Hargadon, "Advice from the Inside." In G. Georges and C. Georges, *100 Successful College Application Essays* (New York: New American Library, 2002), p. 6.

7. S. M. McGinty, "Issues of Access: The College Application Essay," *Journal of College Admission* 177 (Fall 2002), pp. 26–30.

8. P. Marthers, "Admissions Messages vs. Admissions Realities." In L. Thacker (ed.), *College Unranked: Affirming Educational Values in College Admissions* (Portland, OR: Education Conservancy, 2004), p. 79.

9. C. Deacon, cited in E. Craig, "GU Defends Use of Legacy Admissions," *Hoya,* April 16, 2004, p. 1.

10. T. Parker, cited in M. Klein, "Bill Aims to Increase All College Opportunities," *Amherst Student,* November 12, 2003, p. 1.

11. Karl Furstenberg, personal communication, 2004.

12. D. Golden, *The Price of Admission: How America's Ruling Class Buys Its Way into Elite Colleges—And Who Gets Left Outside the Gates* (New York: Three Rivers Press, 2007).

13. W. Bowen and S. Levin, *Reclaiming the Game: College Sports and Educational Values* (Princeton, NJ: Princeton University Press, 2003).

14. L. Summers, address at the American Council on Education's 86th Annual Meeting, Miami, Florida, February 29, 2004; available online: www.president.harvard.edu/speeches/summers_2004/ace.php; access date: February 17, 2009.

CHAPTER THREE

1. The descriptions of the Wesleyan admissions review process are drawn from J. Steinberg, *The Gatekeepers: Inside the Admissions Process of an Elite College* (New York: Penguin, 2003).

2. J. Merrow, transcript of R. Toor, *Inside College Admissions,* broadcast on KVIE, November 15, 2000; available online: www.pbs.org/merrow/tmr_radio/transcr; access date: February 18, 2009.

3. Shawn Abbott, personal communication, 2004.

4. E-mail from Duke President Nannerl Keohane to *Wall Street Journal* reporter Daniel Golden, February 13, 2003.

5. D. Cattau, "Parents Need Not Apply," August 14, 2004.

6. R. Worth, "For $28,000 You'll Get. . . ." *New York Times,* September 24, 2000, Sec. 14 WC, p. 8.

7. M. Jones, "Parents Get Too Aggressive on Admissions," *USA Today,* January 6, 2003, p. 13A.

CHAPTER FOUR

1. Michael Tamada, personal communication, 2004.

2. E. L. Boyer, *The Undergraduate Experience in America* (New York: HarperCollins, 1987); E. L. Boyer and P. Boyer, *Smart Parents Guide to College* (Princeton, NJ: Peterson's, 1996).

CHAPTER FIVE

1. S. Antonoff, *The College Finder* (Westford, MA: Wintergreen Orchard House, 2008).
2. E. Fiske, *Fiske Guide to Colleges* (Naperville, IL: Sourcebooks, 2009).
3. Yale Daily News Staff, *Insider's Guide to the Colleges* (New York: St. Martin's Griffin, 2009).
4. J. Mitchell, *Winning the Heart of the College Admissions Dean,* rev. (Berkeley, CA: Ten Speed Press, 2005).

CHAPTER SIX

1. "What's the difference between the SAT and Subject Tests?" Available online: www.collegeboard.com/student/testing/sat/about/sat/FAQ.htm; access date: February 20, 2009.
2. L. Bollinger, "Debate Over the SAT Masks Perilous Trends in College Admissions." *Chronicle of Higher Education,* July 12, 2002, p. B11.
3. R. Zwick, *Fair Game? The Use of Standardized Tests in Higher Education* (New York: RoutledgeFalmer, 2002), p. viii.
4. C. Jencks and D. Reisman, "Admissions Requirements in the Public and Private Sectors," in *The Academic Revolution* (Garden City, NY: Doubleday, 1968), p. 281.
5. M. Winerip, "SAT Essay Test Rewards Length and Ignores Errors," *New York Times,* May 4, 2005, Sec. B, p. 9.
6. *Chronicle of Higher Education,* June 27, 2008, p. A1.
7. National Association for College Admission Counseling, "Report of the Commission on the Use of Standardized Tests in Undergraduate Admission," September 2008, p. 44.

CHAPTER SEVEN

1. J. Fallows, "The Early Decision Racket," *Atlantic Monthly* 288, no. 2 (2001), p. 372.
2. C. Avery, quoted in J. Young, "Early Applicants Have Strong Advantage at Elite Colleges, Book Argues," *Chronicle of Higher Education,* March 7, 2003, p. 38.
3. C. Avery, A. Fairbanks, and R. Zeckhauser, *The Early Admissions Game* (Cambridge, MA: Harvard University Press, 2003).
4. S. Tilghman, quoted in M. Shapiro and C. McCorkle, "Early Admissions Dropped," *Daily Princetonian,* September 19, 2006; available online: www.dailyprincetonian.com/archives/2006/09/19/news/15838.shtml; access date: February 21, 2009.

5. Avery, Fairbanks, and Zeckhauser, *The Early Admissions Game*, p. 241.
6. T. Parker, cited in D. Chen, "Admissions at Amherst: A Grueling Journey," *Amherst Student*, October 9, 2003, p. 1.

CHAPTER EIGHT

1. Susan Hallenbeck, dean of admission at Hood College, personal communication, 2004. She reported that the student was admitted after giving everyone a good chuckle.
2. D. Phillips, "The Question of the Essay." In G. Georges and C. Georges, *100 Successful College Application Essays* (New York: New American Library, 2002), p. 12.
3. H. Bauld, *On Writing the College Application Essay* (New York: Quill, 1987), p. xvi.
4. S. McGinty, *The College Application Essay*, rev. ed. (New York: College Board, 2004).
5. W. Zinsser, *On Writing Well* (New York: HarperCollins, 2006).

CHAPTER NINE

1. C. Hughes, *What It Really Takes to Get into the Ivy League and Other Highly Selective Colleges* (New York: McGraw Hill, 2003).

CHAPTER TEN

1. The members of the Overlap Group were Amherst College, Barnard College, Bowdoin College, Brown University, Bryn Mawr College, Colby College, Columbia University, Cornell University, Dartmouth College, Harvard University, Massachusetts Institute of Technology, Middlebury College, Mount Holyoke College, Princeton University, Smith College, Trinity College (Connecticut), Tufts University, University of Pennsylvania, Vassar College, Wellesley College, Wesleyan University, Williams College, and Yale University.
2. "Rawlings-Led Group Affirms Commitment to Need-Based Financial Aid," *Cornell Chronicle*, July 12, 2001, p. 1.
3. A. Leider and R. Leider, *Don't Miss Out: The Ambitious Student's Guide to Financial Aid* (Alexandria, VA: Octameron, 2000), p. 42.
4. Carleton College Application for Class of 2008.
5. M. Bombardieri, "Needy Students Miss Out," *Boston Globe*, April 25, 2004, p. A1.

6. D. Teicher, "Not Enough Financial Aid? Seek Counseling," *Christian Science Monitor,* April 26, 2004, p. 13.
7. Teicher, "Not Enough Financial Aid?"
8. J. Russell, "Top Applicants Bargaining for More Aid from Colleges," *Boston Globe,* June 12, 2002, p. A1.

CHAPTER ELEVEN

1. M. Coomes, "Life After the Letter," *Courier-Journal* (Louisville), May 5, 2004, p. D2.
2. J. Lee-St. John, "Getting Off the College Wait List," *Time,* May 5, 2008.

About the Authors

Sally P. Springer, associate chancellor emerita at the University of California, Davis, is a psychologist with more than thirty-five years of experience in higher education as a professor and university administrator. She is the coauthor of *Left Brain, Right Brain* (Freeman, 1998), which was honored by the American Psychological Foundation for contributing to the public's understanding of psychology. It has been translated into seven languages and appeared in five editions. Her second book, *How to Succeed in College* (Crisp, 1992), is a guidebook for college freshmen. Dr. Springer received her bachelor's degree summa cum laude from Brooklyn College and her doctorate in psychology from Stanford University. She has served on the faculty of both SUNY Stony Brook and UC Davis. She has served as a volunteer admissions reader for the Davis campus and is a member of the National Association for College Admission Counseling.

Jon Reider is director of college counseling at San Francisco University High School, an independent 9–12 high school. Before that, he served as an admissions officer at Stanford University for fifteen years, rising to the post of senior associate director of admission. He has two degrees in history, including a Ph.D. from Stanford, and taught there in a freshman humanities program for twenty-five years, for which he won a university-wide teaching award. Previously, he was a Marshall Scholar at the University of Sussex in England and taught sociology at the University of Tennessee at Chattanooga. He has also taught in the College Counseling Certificate Program at the University of California at Berkeley. He is a nationally known speaker and essayist in the admissions profession and is widely cited in the media for his candid opinions and willingness to speak hard truths.

He is a member of the National Association for College Admission Counseling and has served as the chair of its committee on Current Trends and Future Issues.

Marion R. Franck writes about family life and local and national issues in a weekly column in the *Davis Enterprise*. She was the founding writer of the "parents page" of UC Davis's alumni magazine and penned feature articles for the campus's Web-based newsletter for parents from 2002 to 2007. Previously, she worked at UC Davis as an adviser to new college teachers, as a lecturer in rhetoric and English, and as a counselor in the Office of Student Judicial Affairs. Ms. Franck is a magna cum laude graduate of Brown University and has served as an alumna interviewer for more than fifteen years. She holds a master's degree in comparative literature from the University of Wisconsin.

Index

Notification, 212; acceptance, 213–215; deferral, 215–217; denial, 215; wait-lists, 224–229

O

Online search tools, 87–88
Overlap Group, 193–194

P

Parents: advice for, 231–237; and college visits, 98; role of, 59–60; and standardized tests, 128–130
Parker, Thomas, 145
Pell Grants, 195
Pemberton, Stephen, 206
Perkins Loans, 196
Personal qualities, 33–36
Platinum packages, 58–59
PLUS loans, 197
Pocket Guide to Choosing a College, 96
Poirot, William, 158
Possible colleges, 99
Preliminary SAT. *See* PSAT
Prestige, 6
The Price of Admission (Golden), 40
Priorities questionnaire, 82–85
Procrastination, 149–150
PSAT, 114–116. *See also* SAT

Q

Quality of educational experience, 6, 80–81

R

Race-sensitive admissions, 40–41
Rankings, 9–11; concerns about, 13–17; popularity of, 18–20; *U.S. News* formula, 12; what rankings are based on, 11–12
Ratings, of admission files, 50–51
Reach colleges. *See* long-shot colleges
Reclaiming the Game (Bowen), 42
Recommendation. *See* letters of recommendation
Record keeping, and homeschoolers, 185

Recruited athletes, 41–42, 181–182
Rejecting overqualified students, 17
Religious affiliations, 75–76
Reputational ratings, 11. *See also* rankings
Research universities, 67–68
Resources, 297–302
Restrictive choice early action, 132, 138. *See also* early action
Rolling admissions, 145–146

S

Safety colleges. *See* good-bet colleges
Sarah Lawrence College, 126
SAT, 28–30; coachability, 111–112; compared to ACT, 123–124; concerns about, 109–110; history of, 108–110; how much SAT scores influence admission, 112–114; how often to take the SAT, 116–118; midrange, 113; *The Official SAT Study Guide for the New SAT*, 118; preparing for, 118–121; range, 100–101; recent changes, 110–111; SAT-ACT score comparisons, 122; Score Choice, 117–118; score range, 118–119; special accommodations, 126–127; standardized tests overview, 125; subject tests, 127–128; when to take the SAT, 116. *See also* PSAT
Saving for college, 207–208
Scattergrams, 102–105
Scholarship search services, 202–203
Scholarships, 199–203
Scholastic Aptitude Test. *See* SAT
School profile, 28
Search letters, 90–92
Secondary school report (SSR), 170–171
Section 529 College Savings Plans, 208
Selective colleges: admission rates for Class of 2011, 7; defined, 5–6; prestige, 6; quality of educational experience, 6–9
Self-assessments, 62–65, 106
Senioritis, 229–230
Seven Sisters, 22
Shapiro, Morton Owen, 206
Size of the college, 72–73